ERROR AUSTRALIS

THE REALITY RECAP OF AUSTRALIAN HISTORY

BEN POBJIE

Published by Affirm Press in 2016
28 Thistlethwaite Street, South Melbourne, VIC 3205
www.affirmpress.com.au

National Library of Australia Cataloguing-in-Publication entry available for this title at www.nla.gov.au.

Title: Error Australis / Ben Pobjie, author.
ISBN: 9781925344462 (paperback)

Cover design by Josh Durham/Design by Committee
Typeset in 12/18 Garamond Premier Pro by J&M Typesetting
Proudly printed in Australia by Griffin Press

The paper this book is printed on is certified against the Forest Stewardship Council® Standards. Griffin Press holds FSC chain of custody certification SGS-COC-005088. FSC promotes environmentally responsible, socially beneficial and economically viable management of the world's forests.

Praise for *Error Australis*

'This is Australian history like they just don't make it any more. Required reading for history buffs and ignoramuses alike – in fact, everyone. And Henry Ford was wrong, by the way: history is not "bunk". In the hands of Ben Pobjie, one of Australia's funniest writers, it is a great read!' – **PETER FITZSIMONS**

'It's as if Manning Clark had a lobotomy and rewrote his *Short History of Australia* with a crayon. I enjoyed it.' – **SHAUN MICALLEF**

'Savage, provocative, hilarious, deeply depressing and brilliant – should be required reading for secondary students.' – **NONI HAZLEHURST**

'Freaking hilarious, had me gasping with laughter. I recommend all high schools get rid of their current Australian history texts and replace them with this book.' – **JULIE GOODWIN**

Ben Pobjie studied history at the University of Western Sydney before his lust for glamour led him to comedy writing. He is known for his TV columns in *The Age* and *The Sydney Morning Herald*, and political satire for *New Matilda*, *Crikey* and the ABC, among others. He is the author of *SuperChef* and *The Book of Bloke* and has written for the TV shows *Reality Check* and *The Unbelievable Truth*. He lives in Melbourne with his wife, three children and a rising sense of panic.

To the Unknown Emu

CONTENTS

INTRODUCTION

The modern human is obsessed with 'reality'. Like ravenous wolves, we consume the exploits of reality TV stars, dissatisfied with fiction and desperate to be entertained by the lives of 'real people'. Real home cooks, real top models, real singers, real fat people, real whatever the people on *The Bachelor* are – these are what we live for now. And yet, we so often neglect the greatest reality of all: the reality of our nation and how it came to be. If that sentence seems pretty profound, this book is for you.

In history's epic sweep, as in reality TV, we find all the magical elements that make humanity what it is. Drama, suspense, conflict, love, hatred, loyalty, deception, heartbreak, inspiration, violence, joy, sadness, anger, despair, death, alcoholism and horses: history has it all. When we look into the past, we find profound insights into the nature of the human race – only by looking at what has come before can we understand who we are and why we hate one another so much. It is a solemn truth recognised by historians everywhere that there's virtually no problem in the present day that is not, in some way, the fault of someone from the past. And this is something that *My Kitchen Rules* just can't match.

But history is more than a way to absolve oneself of responsibility for the ills of one's own generation. The past also provides a signpost to the future. It is said that those who do not understand history are doomed to repeat it, and even if this is not true, it is certainly pithy, which is even better under most circumstances. And there can be no doubt that to repeat history would be a ghastly fate, given how often people in the past had severe diarrhoea. Far better to understand history – and just as a recap of a reality show seeks to help the reader understand why anyone would want to meet Pete Evans, this book endeavours to promote understanding of what the hell has been going on in what we so carelessly call 'the past'.

Like any good recapper, I've sought to provide an immediate, visceral sense of what it was like to be there *in the moment*. As thrilling as it is to see Delta Goodrem's chair turn around, there is an argument that World War Two was even more exciting, and I hope to make you feel as though you were right there on the Kokoda Track, just as strongly as I might make you feel that you actually watched *The Voice* last night.

In essence, what is recapped herein is nothing less than our country itself, for those who might have missed it or were too busy to pay close attention at the time. As I said, if you don't understand history, you'll have to repeat it. So unless you want to be forced to build the whole bloody thing over from scratch, I strongly advise you to read on.

The Gathering Calm

In which a feisty young continent makes its way in the world

The origins of Australia, much like the popularity of Scott Cam, are shrouded in mystery – very little is known about the continent's earliest days, and what we do know we try not to think about too much. The first inhabitants of Australia were microbial mats made up of billions of bacteria, who kept few formal records and of whose lifestyle we know hardly anything besides their predilection for hydrothermal vents and their deadly fear of heterotrophs[1] – about whom, if anything, we know even less than we do about the bacteria. This is not necessarily surprising, as even today Australians tend to be private people not prone to self-publicity who keep mainly to themselves. Evolutionary biologists believe this national trait began with the microbial mats, whose preference for not making a fuss about things deprived us of valuable historical data, but no doubt allowed them to be fairly relaxed most of the time. Today, little of the microbial mats' culture remains,[2] although Australians everywhere remain deeply suspicious of heterotrophs.[3]

Of course, way back then Australia wasn't an independent landmass, but rather just one part of the supercontinent Pangaea, much

1 From the Greek *heteros*, meaning 'another', and *troph*, meaning 'thing I don't know what it is'.

2 Apart from *A Current Affair*.

3 E.g. Daryl Somers.

like pop supergroup Bardot before Katie left to pursue a solo career. After Pangaea split up due to creative differences, Australia found itself in Gondwana, the more southerly of the two supercontinents of prehistory and, according to geologists, the more emotionally troubled one. This manifested itself most vividly in the early Jurassic period, about 180 million years ago, when Gondwana, after what experts agree was probably a time of tension at home and work, began to break up in what was publicly declared to be 'an amicable manner', but I think we can all read between the lines, can't we?

By this time the microbial mats had ceased to be the dominant Australian lifeform, replaced by dinosaurs, notable for their enormous size and minuscule brains.[4] These included the massive *Muttaburrasaurus* ('lizard from Muttaburra'); the small, armoured *Kunbarrasaurus* ('lizard that looks like a Kunbarra'); the ferocious *Ozraptor* ('stealer of munchkins'); and the swift *Qantassaurus*[5] ('lizard with insufficient leg-room'). These dinosaurs did little, in their several hundred million years, to advance Australian culture or undertake major infrastructure projects, aside from the establishment of Channel Nine.

As the various pieces of Gondwana struck out on their own, seeking fresh challenges and gainful employment, the landmass we now know as Australia began to cut the apron strings around 80 million years ago. This was extremely controversial at the time, as many argued that Gondwana had served us perfectly well for several hundred million years, and if it ain't broke, don't fix it. Yet despite warnings that separation would place too much power in the hands of unelected tectonic plates, the 'Yes' case narrowly passed, and Australia formally became a standalone continent. This demonstrated two things:

4 Now considered to be the forerunners of the modern Senate.

5 This is a real dinosaur. Look it up. It's incredibly embarrassing.

1. You can't fight geology.
2. Dinosaurs are relatively immune to scare campaigns.

So by about 45 million years ago, Australia was more or less independent, geographically speaking if not in psychological terms, and ready to begin what continues to be a long and fruitful association with mammals. While today the country is most closely linked with familiar species such as the koala, the sugar glider and the Young Divas, all those millions of years ago Australian wildlife looked very different indeed: there were, for example, no rugby league players.

One of the most distinguished early Australian mammals was the diprotodon.[6] This was the largest marsupial that ever lived, with a pouch that, it is estimated, could fit an entire volleyball team inside. The diprotodon was a perfect example of Australian 'megafauna' – the enormous animals that roamed this land in the years before smaller, more efficient animals moved in to compete for food and take advantage of the relatively lax regulatory climate of the time. Other megafauna included an echidna the size of a sheep, a metre-long platypus, the giant short-faced kangaroo[7] and the marsupial lion, which was like a normal lion but with more storage space: a forerunner of today's Kia Rios. Sadly, however, all of these animals died out, dooming the continent to an eternity of small, unimpressive-looking animals and Australian wildlife parks that nobody wants to go to.

Theories as to the cause of megafauna extinction include:

1. **The Blitzkrieg Theory:** Despite its name, this isn't a theory suggesting that gigantic marsupials were destroyed by German

---

6 From the Greek *diprotos*, meaning 'two front', and *don*, meaning 'smallgoods'.

7 The subject of the earliest known failed attempt at a 'walked into a bar' joke.

tanks, but rather the hypothesis that the megafauna were eliminated by human hunting. Support for this theory comes from the fact that the earliest human inhabitants of Australia were known to be the sort of guys who really loved hunting – archaeologists have found evidence of rudimentary Facebook photos of them posing next to their kills. The Blitzkrieg Theory is also backed by fossil evidence suggesting that most species of megafauna were extremely vulnerable to being killed.

2. **The Climate Change Theory:** This states that Australia's megafauna were destroyed by climate change, a hypothesis supported by the discovery of fossilised coal-fired power plants in sedimentary rock deposits. Scientists speculate that decreasing rainfall following the split with Gondwanaland, combined with the megafauna's failure to implement a market-based carbon reduction mechanism, may have caused the death of large mammals, who like most Australian lifeforms were known to enjoy drinking. There are those who dispute this theory, however, suggesting it's more likely that the megafauna died out due to economic collapse caused by Green policies.
3. **The Land Management Theory:** This states that humans caused extinction indirectly by destroying the megafauna's ecosystem, and is extremely boring.

Wherever the truth lies, the one fact that historians are almost certain of is that at some point, humans arrived on the continent, a conclusion attested to by archaeological and paleontological records as well as anecdotal evidence indicating that humans continue to inhabit Australia today.[8] This happened when travellers from Southeast Asia, on the lookout for new species that they could drive to extinction, and

8 For a given value of 'human'.

having heard of a land to the south bursting with megafauna, made the trek.

The exact date of the first Australians' arrival is unknown, but thought to have been somewhere between 50,000 and 70,000 years ago. The oldest human yet found in Australia is 'Mungo Man' – not to be confused with well-known political commentator Mungo McCallum, who has not been accurately dated. Mungo Man was discovered in Lake Mungo[9] in 1974, where he had been for some time: it's estimated that Mungo Man is at least 40,000 years old, which puts him a considerable distance ahead of the second-oldest human found in Australia, TV's Sam Newman.

The first Australians developed an extremely special relationship with the land, which to be honest they've been rubbing in everyone's faces ever since. They lived by hunter-gathering and were one of the earliest cultures in the world to adopt the paleo diet, although they failed to fully gain the health benefits due to the lack of modern technologies like the electric blender and tooth bleach. To supply this diet, the men of Aboriginal tribes would go hunting – which is just typical of men, I find – and, if they had a particularly high tolerance for boredom, fishing. The women would dig for roots and vegetables and gather fruits, seeds and berries, which on the one hand was hard, tedious work that lacked the glamour of the men's tasks, but on the other hand carried a much lower risk of being eaten by a marsupial lion or stepped on by a diprotodon. The task of getting food obviously became a lot harder after the extinction of the megafauna: while a diprotodon could feed a family for a month, after they died off the men would have to run outside for a fresh rock wallaby or bag of bilbies every second day. It was perhaps a sobering lesson in the dangers of over-hunting, if the

9 Best known for the hit 'In the Summertime'.

Blitzkrieg Theory is correct, and the origin of the phrase 'killing the megaplatypus that lays the golden eggs'.

Indigenous Australia has a rich and unique belief system centred on the Dreamtime, when the world was new and fantastic creatures roamed the land. These include Bunjil the Eagle, who stopped the sea from rising with his spear, earning him the nickname 'the Tim Flannery of the Dreamtime', and Tiddalik the Frog, who drank all the water everywhere, but spat it up after an eel made him laugh – this is said to be the origin of the common belief that drought in Australia can only be ended by a successful domestic sitcom. Aboriginal beliefs feature many such animal spirits, demonstrating their close affinity with the country they inhabit and the respect for the wildlife that sustains them – although that respect has not always been reciprocated, and some of the animals can be downright rude at times.

Of course, as might be expected, these are fairly naive and primitive beliefs, and it wasn't until the arrival of white settlers that Aboriginal Australians began to adopt proper religions based on more sophisticated concepts such as pregnant virgins and snakes promoting fruit-based diets. So undeveloped were Indigenous religious beliefs that they hadn't even come up with the concept of tax deductibility.

Nevertheless, even without all the benefits and technology and diseases of European settlement, Australia's Indigenous people lived fairly contented lives for many thousands of years, having little contact with the rest of the world and therefore missing out on much of the war, genocide and plague that makes history so much fun. It can fairly be said that Aboriginal Australia had no idea what it was missing. Some of the major events that the first Australians never had the chance to enjoy include:

- The Hundred Years' War
- The Sack of Rome
- The murder of Thomas Becket
- The Black Death
- The world premiere of *Titus Andronicus*
- The time Caligula made his horse a senator
- Braveheart

So it can fairly be said that though the Aboriginal people may have believed themselves to be having a pretty fun time, they were in danger of becoming the wallflowers of the modern world, condemned to miss out on the exciting adventures that the Native Americans had been having since white men arrived to give their humdrum lives a bit of spice. Some Indigenous Australians did worry about this, standing on the shore late at night, gazing out to sea, wondering if they would ever know what it was like to be massacred. 'Somewhere out there,' they would murmur to themselves, 'is a place where dreams come true. A place where anyone can be abducted and forcibly converted to a foreign religion, if they believe in themselves enough. And someday,' they would swear, 'I too will know that feeling.'

But if the first Australians had a major case of FOMO looming, that was all about to end. Australia was ready to enter the modern world, with all its wonders.[10] Life in the great southern land would never be the same.

ESSAY QUESTIONS

1. Was the separation of Australia from Gondwana a good move? How would your life be different if it hadn't happened?
2. Can you wipe your feet on a microbial mat? Show your work.

10 E.g. scurvy.

The Twist That Will Change the Game Forever

In which the great southern land is found to be the perfect place to abandon the scum of the earth, and the seeds of a nation fall upon rocky ground

THE SCENE: THE PRIVY Council, London, 1785. Council members pace the floor, much vexed by affairs of state and the nagging knowledge that their council is named after a toilet. Britain has a problem – too many convicts and not enough foul, disease-ridden holes to drop them into. Overcrowding in prisons has become intolerable, even in the eyes of the British government, which at this time ranks the welfare of convicted criminals some distance below the tasteful ornamentation of snuff boxes in the hierarchy of pressing social problems. Many suggestions have been made to deal with this issue, including the alleviation of poverty, more lenient sentencing for toddlers and the release of myxomatosis among the lower orders – but all has come to naught.

The problem has been exacerbated by the American Revolution, which has seen the new United States government refuse to allow Britain to continue using the country as a dumping ground for convicts, determined as they are to begin what will prove to be an enormously successful programme of producing their own criminals.

All across Britain, gaols bulge at the seams. Prison hulks squat gloomily in the Thames, filled with murderers, rapists, pickpockets, bread thieves, jaywalkers, litterers and other degenerates. Conditions are horrific. Many die, which helps a little, but sadly they die too slowly to keep up with the enormous enthusiasm the 18th-century public had for throwing poor people into dungeons.

The Privy Councillors know that things are getting desperate, and that there's a very real risk of the nation's prisons bursting open and spilling a terrible flood of prisoners across the country, making the streets even more disgusting than they already are. Something must be done. In essence, the government must find a new trash heap on which to hurl its detritus. But where can that heap be found?

The councillors crowd around a map of the world, peering furiously at the various sea monsters and big faces blowing out puffs of wind that were the style at the time.

'What about India?' asks one councillor, stabbing at the map with a chubby, over-privileged finger.

'No, no,' a colleague shakes his flabby patrician jowls, 'we've already got too many people there. We need somewhere more sparsely populated. We should send them to Jamaica.'

'Don't be ridiculous!' snorts a third councillor. 'It's nowhere near big enough – you have to remember how insanely punitive our laws are. We need somewhere wide and spacious.'

'Ireland?' murmurs a councillor who had fallen asleep at the start of the meeting and only half woken up.

'No!' the other councillors cry in unison. 'Ireland is just over there,' the first councillor wheezes, pointing out the window. 'Send them there, and they might come right back and start touching our stuff.'

'So what we need,' ponders the second councillor, stroking his old-timey whiskers and summarising the matter in a most narratively convenient way, 'is a place without a lot of people, with lots of space, a really, really long way away.'

'And that we own,' pipes up the third councillor.

'Oh, that's no problem,' the first councillor waves a dismissive, many-ringed hand. 'We'll just find a spot and stick a flag in it.' There's a general chorus of agreement at this – it is well known that this is the method by which Britain has come to own almost everything.

The councillors stop pacing for a moment and stand, deep in thought. Suddenly one springs forward and points to a neglected corner of the map. 'What about this place?'

'Greenland?'

'Oh, sorry. I mean, *this* place.'

The councillors gather around the table, oohing and aahing and politely not mentioning the overwhelming smell of a room full of men who bathe once a year.

'What *is* that place?'

'They call it ... New South Wales.'

There's an awed silence in the room. Finally it's broken by one councillor's hushed tones. 'That's a pretty stupid name.'

Of course, New South Wales was not unknown to the British at the time. In 1770, the southern continent had been given its name by Captain James Cook, fearless seafarer and noted citrus enthusiast. He was the latest in a series of European explorers who had sailed around the outskirts of what would one day be Australia, without really knowing what the hell they'd stumbled on.

The first documented European landing was made by Willem Janszoon, who in 1606 landed on the western shore of Cape York, which he immediately named 'New Zealand', in line with the 17th-century Dutch craze of calling things 'New Zealand'.[11] The name didn't catch on, of course – in fact, none of the names that Janszoon gave things managed to stick, hence his nickname 'Terrible Ideas Janszoon'. The Dutch didn't explore the continent thoroughly, however, being far too busy trading spices and buying tulips for reasons they did not fully understand.

But as the old saying goes, don't send a Dutchman to do an Englishman's job: an Englishman's job in this case being the acquisition and exploitation of other people's countries. In 1699 the northwest coast of Australia was explored by William Dampier, whose hobbies included navigation, natural history and smacking his crew around. But England didn't get truly interested in Australia until 1770, when Cook arrived, armed only with a small, unattractive ship and a fully stocked lime cellar. Following standard imperial procedure, he made contact with the Indigenous inhabitants and claimed the continent as British territory. The inhabitants took this as one of Cook's harmless and endearing quirks – 'Look at the little fella claiming things,' they cooed affectionately, 'he thinks he's people' – but miscommunication between native peoples and rapacious colonialist marauders was common back in the day.

Having made his momentous discovery, Cook returned to England, where the Royal Society commissioned him to search for the great southern continent, or *Terra Australis*.

'I already found it,' said Cook, showing the Royal Society his maps. 'Look, it's right here.'

But they wouldn't listen. 'If only we could find it!' they cried

---

11 Judging by the fact that Old Zealand apparently looks exactly like both Cape York and Auckland, it must be a hell of a place.

wistfully, ignoring Cook's increasingly agitated map-tapping. 'What a marvellous continent it must be!'

'*LOOK!*' the young captain bellowed, opening up his travel diaries. 'Here's the bit where I claim it for –'

'Who knows if such a magical land exists?' asked the Society members. 'You must go and find out and let us know.'[12]

'FFS,' Cook muttered.

And so Captain James Cook discovered Australia again, leading some to dub him a one-trick pony. 'Sure, he can discover Australia with the best of them,' they opined, 'but is that all there is?' However, his status as a legendary explorer was secure, and to this day no child leaves school in Australia without having gained a vague, poorly informed impression of who James Cook was. Perhaps the greatest indicator of Cook's stature in Australian history is the fact that in 1933 his parents' house was taken apart brick by brick and reassembled in Melbourne, a move that contemporary sources assert 'seemed like a good idea at the time'.[13]

Cook's travels paved the way for the British settlement of the southern land: in particular, the lush surrounds of Botany Bay, which Cook judged the ideal place to build an airport. And so it was that the Privy Council hit on Australia as the preferred warehouse for their morally dubious subjects. Of course Australia was, at that time, not called Australia, but was referred to as New South Wales, New Holland or North Tasmania. Being incredibly remote and extremely spacious, the southern continent was ideal for the purpose. There were also other advantages, which could be divided into two categories: fighting and trees.

---

12 Seriously, the Royal Society was a bunch of morons.

13 Much like Australia itself, really.

1. **Fighting:** In the 1780s, Britain was still in the midst of the period of European history dubbed 'The Age of Everyone Fighting One Another for Reasons That Were at Best Poorly Defined'. France, Holland and Spain, united by the natural human instinct to hate the British, had already assisted in their defeat in the American War of Independence, and the British government, knowing how obnoxious it was, naturally feared them doing it again. A colony in New South Wales, they reasoned, would be an ideal spot from which to launch attacks on Spanish territories in South America, the Philippines and the Dutch East Indies. The British had grand visions of their warships sailing proudly throughout the Pacific, firing convicts stuffed with gunpowder at their enemies and possibly finally answering the question that had vexed humanity: which small European nation should own the entire world?
2. **Trees:** Every government loves trees, and the new continent had a bunch of them. Norfolk Island was particularly well-stocked with flax trees, not to mention hemp – a vital resource for any relaxed colony. The promise of copious quantities of timber and flax excited the Brits, as these were the two main ingredients of ships, which made up a large part of the kill-the-foreigners plan outlined above.

Everything was lining up perfectly. Wide open spaces for criminals to die in, trees to make boats with, a base from which to have wars, all the kangaroos a man could ride – and all completely uninhabited, unless you counted the people who lived there, which in accordance with the *Ignoring Natives Act of 1754*, Britons did not. Indeed, the entire British Empire was founded on the principle of not paying too much attention to anyone who happened to be standing on a spot that a British person wanted. As George III said, 'Nobody ever got anywhere by not assuming he owned everything he found.' (Of course, he also said, 'I am a happy horse, gimme dem oats', but that was later on after he joined the grand tradition of kings going absolutely badger-fiddling nuts.)

The decision to transport convicts to New South Wales sent shockwaves through the convict community, who had always believed they had a firm social contract with the government: they would commit minor insignificant crimes, and the government would imprison them in dank hellholes. The prospect of being sent to the far end of the world, to a strange unknown land, was terrifying. Many convicts began to question why they'd become convicts in the first place. 'This is not what we signed up for,' said the head of the Convict Union in a strident statement. Britain's criminals briefly threatened to go on strike, but sadly their lack of meaningful leverage saw them forced to submit. The powerful emotions generated by the discovery of their fate were eloquently expressed in the classic old song 'Botany Bay':

Farewell to old England forever
Farewell to my rum coes[14] *as well*
Farewell to the well-known Tim Bailey
Who used to teach me how to spell
Singing too-ra-li oo-ra-li addity
Singing bing bong dum doo dad fi-fay
Singing spinkly pom pinkly bom baddity
It's shit down in Botany Bay

---

14 Nobody knows what a 'rum coe' was, except that it was a major wrench to say goodbye to one.

And, just as the song predicted, more than 700 convicts found themselves bound for that mysterious, far-off land: Rio de Janeiro, although after a month in Rio[15] the grizzled old salts of the Royal Navy realised it wasn't in Australia, and the journey continued to Botany Bay.

Of course, not everyone on the First Fleet – named after the fact that it was a fleet – was a convict. In addition to some 775 convicts, there were also around 300 sailors, 250 Royal Marines, 15 officials and passengers[16] and about 50 wives and children of the marines.

During the journey, 48 people died and 28 were born, thus proving that the ocean is more likely to kill you than get you pregnant.[17] Also on board the fleet were six horses, four cows, one bull, 44 sheep, 19 goats, 32 pigs, five rabbits, 18 turkeys, 29 geese, 35 ducks, 122 fowls, 87 chickens, assorted cats and the governor's greyhounds, who found racing on board extremely difficult. How many of these animals were taken as food and how many for companionship, and how many were convicts themselves, is unknown, although it's suspected that a significant proportion of the ducks had committed serious crimes, and several of the pigs were thought to be marines in disguise.

The Governor

Leading the expedition was Captain Arthur Phillip. More than just a greyhound-owner, Phillip had already forged a long and distinguished career at sea. At the age of 16, he had been apprenticed to whalers in Norway, where he learnt to strip whale carcasses and eat reindeer, both skills that were to be of enormous value to him as governor of New South Wales. However, Philip decided early on – possibly under

15 I'm not even making that up. They spent a month in Rio on the way to Australia. Weird, right?

16 Who was stupid enough to buy a ticket on this trip is uncertain.

17 Except during schoolies week.

pressure from Greenpeace – that the life of a whaler was not for him, and instead enlisted in the Royal Navy, where he proved his worth as an Englishman by shooting at as many Frenchmen as he could find.

After the war Phillip embarked on yet another career – marrying rich old women. He married the widow Margaret Denison – he was 24, she was 40. 'I've always had a thing for cougars,' Phillip admitted in an exclusive magazine interview. He and Margaret set themselves up on a farm in Hampshire, where they settled down to a peaceful life of festering hatred. The most apt parallel for the Phillips' marriage would probably be Roald Dahl's classic children's story *The Twits*. Some specifics differ – the Phillips had no pet monkeys, and there is no record of Captain Phillip ever secretly lengthening Margaret's chair to convince her she was shrinking – but the general atmosphere of loathing was similar, and for six years the newlyweds would spend each night, after a day combing the cows or whatever farmers do, sitting in their old-timey rocking chairs staring at each other in tense silence.

In the end, Phillip realised the situation could not persist any longer. He had tried a life of simple domesticity, but had to admit to himself that there had only ever been one woman he loved, and that woman ... was the sea. Or possibly he just missed being able to have men flogged. Either way, he ditched Margaret and returned to the navy.

After fleeing the icy, passive-aggressive embrace of his elderly wife, Phillip worked for a time as a spy in France. Armed only with his native wit and a fountain pen that was also a musket, he carried out surveillance on French naval preparations. This 18th-century Bond did crucial work, sending messages back to England such as 'Frenchmen building some freaking huge boats here' and 'they've got guns on them and everything' – information without which the British may not have been properly prepared for their eventual defeat. He also probably spent quite a bit of time driving flashy carriages and bedding beautiful Frenchwomen, who have always been suckers for a Cockney accent.

So it's no surprise that with his distinguished record as sailor, spy, whale butcher and bad husband, Arthur Phillip was selected by Britain as the man to lead the new colony. Home Secretary Lord Sydney appointed Phillip commodore of the First Fleet, with responsibility for remembering who'd given him the job when it came to naming cities. Phillip immediately began organising the resources needed to establish a colony on the other side of the world, at which point he came into conflict with the British government, who were outraged to learn that their chosen man expected not only to be allowed to found a colony, but also to be given stuff to do it with. The idea of sending poor people to waste away on a distant island lost so much of its romantic appeal when you were asked to pay for it. Phillip had asked for luxuries such as food and shelter, scandalising the upper echelons of British society. 'Did Britain become great,' they asked themselves, 'by handing out bread and canvas to every upstart sea captain who came along claiming we'd asked him to found a colony? Did Henry V need food at Agincourt?' These questions remained unanswered, as the government grudgingly allowed Phillip enough supplies to ensure that everyone on the First Fleet would starve relatively slowly.

The Fleet

On 13 May 1787, the First Fleet set sail from Portsmouth, with a massive crowd gathering at the docks to pay no attention to them whatsoever. The fleet was made up of 11 ships:

- HMS *Sirius*, the fleet's flagship and, according to contemporary reports, definitely the snootiest of the ships. The *Sirius* carried ten guns and was named after Captain John Hunter's attitude to discipline.

- HMS *Supply*, named for its commitment to the trickle-down theory of economics, was an armed tender, a term that refers to a ship that carries guns but remains in touch with its emotions.
- The *Alexander*, a troubled barque on board which more than 30 convicts died from poor bilge management, paving the way for the new colony's TV industry. The *Alexander* was also the site of an attempted mutiny, thwarted when the rebellious convicts and sailors, having armed themselves with iron bars, couldn't find the ship's keys.
- The *Charlotte*, a heavy sailer known to be extremely sensitive about being called a 'heavy sailer'.
- The *Friendship*, a small brig whose name was considered quite sarcastic by the criminals imprisoned on board.
- The *Lady Penrhyn*, a transport ship that carried the first horses to come to Australia and is therefore solely responsible for the huge productivity losses caused each year by the Melbourne Cup public holiday.
- The *Prince of Wales*, an eccentric barque with a difficult marriage.
- The *Scarborough*, a transport made famous by Simon and Garfunkel.
- The *Golden Grove*, *Fishburn* and *Borrowdale*, three store ships carrying supplies and scurvy.

It was a long and dangerous journey, lacking many of the comforts and deck games that we take for granted on ships today. Much of what we know about life on the First Fleet comes from Watkin Tench, a marine officer and keyboardist who wrote two books about his experiences on the way to and during his stay in the new colony. These books were very popular at the time, proving that people in the past had few options for entertainment. Highlights of Tench's account of the journey include:

- Stopping in Tenerife to buy some goats
- A convict drowning
- The fact that the Portuguese use imaginary coins
- The failure of Brazilian women to throw flowers at him[18]
- How disappointing various mountains are
- Bad spelling

What strikes one about Tench's account is the richness of his prose and the vivid picture he paints of ship life. When he writes 'Batavian phlegm', you really get a sense of whatever it is he's talking about. Likewise can anyone read the words, 'Vegetables do not abound, except pumpkins and onions', and not feel, to the depths of their soul, the anguish of a long and arduous sea voyage with only pumpkins and onions to ease the pain?

Tench himself was a gentle, thoughtful man, whom contemporary portraits inform us had an uncomfortable collar and a head too large for his body. He had a kindly disposition towards the convicts under his charge, and wrote glowingly of their good behaviour and of how much he enjoyed being able to release them from their shackles on board the *Charlotte*. This became a bit of a hobby for Tench, releasing men from shackles: sometimes, when he was feeling blue, he'd do it just to cheer himself up, wandering the sleeping quarters at night, unlocking chains and giggling to himself with glee. If all the convicts on board had already been released from their shackles, he'd shackle them again

18 This may be the first recorded instance of friendzoning.

just so he could unshackle them, he loved it so much. A more sinister pursuit among the officer class is hinted at by Tench's words: 'It is hardly necessary for me to say, that the precaution of ironing the convicts at any time reached to the men only' – in today's more enlightened world, ironing a human being, no matter how wrinkly they may be, would be frowned upon.

It wasn't all fun: at the end of the journey, Tench referred to it as 'a service so peculiarly disgusting and troublesome', which goes to show that eight-month voyages with inadequate provisions in severely cramped quarters aren't as much fun as we assume. Many of the convicts were malnourished and emaciated from their long confinement on poor rations, and exhausted from being constantly unshackled by Tench. And yet only 25 people died on the trip, which by the standards of the 18th century, a.k.a. 'The Century of Everyone Dying on Boats', was quite good, although obviously it depends on your perspective: if the First Fleet were a serial killer, it would have been one of the worst of all time. But if all fleets were serial killers, the First Fleet would, again, slide a fair way down the list. So that's a pretty good lesson about the pitfalls of equating ships to murderers.

On 20 January 1788, the Fleet arrived at Botany Bay, where the British immediately came into contact with the Indigenous inhabitants of New South Wales. Many of the Aboriginal community saw their arrival as evidence of their government's lax border protection policies. 'If you'd had the ticker to introduce off-shore processing, these boats would have stopped coming,' they declared, to which their opponents pointed out that the boats had only just started coming, making it difficult to foresee. 'Besides,' they added, 'these poor white idiots need our help, so let us extend the hand of friendship.' But a sentiment grew strongly in the community that the First Fleet had behaved appallingly by attempting to sneak in through the back door rather than going through the proper channels. By coming on unauthorised boats, it was pointed out, the Englishmen had taken places away from those in genuine need. What's more, the journey from England to Australia was long and dangerous, and many Aboriginal people stressed the need to discourage desperate Englishmen from getting on boats and risking their lives.

Also, there was a fear that the new arrivals would introduce a criminal element to the continent, which to be fair was pretty accurate.

Of the meeting between Europeans and Aboriginal people at Botany Bay, Tench poignantly wrote, 'I had at this time a little boy, of not more than seven years of age, in my hand', which is pretty unsettling. He showed the little boy to the natives[19] so they could see his white skin. 'Yes, we get it – you're all white,' the natives replied. 'Leave the little boy alone.' But Tench wouldn't listen. 'I advanced with him towards them, at the same time baring his bosom, and shewing the whiteness of the skin,' he wrote. 'It's spelt "showing", you idiot,' the natives replied, and the misunderstandings only got more problematic from there.

The First Fleeters did not have time to ponder the intricacies of modern race relations just at that moment, however: they were too busy noticing that Botany Bay sucked. Captain Cook had reported that the bay was a rich and fertile spot, but when the settlers arrived, they discovered it was actually a scruffy patch of sand and grass with poor soil, little fresh water and a smell that contemporary accounts report as being 'like your grandma's wardrobe'. Captain Cook had lied to them, and Captain Phillip wondered whether he could ever trust a sailor again. Looking forlornly at the ugly shore, he famously announced,

---

19 They didn't even know they were natives at that point – the British had so much to teach them.

'This is crap', and gave orders to explore other locations to determine their suitability for his hoodlum-zoo.

The answer lay in Port Jackson, to the north of Botany Bay. Cook had discovered this pleasant harbour in 1770 and named it after all the Port Jackson sharks he saw there. In contrast to Botany, Port Jackson had plentiful fresh water in the form of Tank Stream – so named for its ability to manoeuvre over rugged terrain on tracks – fertile soil and a pleasant lemony fragrance. Phillip, overjoyed with the new site, called it Sydney Cove, in honour of Lord Sydney, with whom Phillip had spent many happy days in England planning voyages and Spaniard-massacres. On 26 January, the First Fleet sailed to Sydney Cove, and Phillip declared that from that day on, this date would be celebrated every year by angry and bitter arguments over whether it should be celebrated or not.

Phillip, now governor of the new colony, set to work with all possible speed, issuing directives to all convicts, marines and officials to immediately begin failing to adapt to the new country, then move on to starving to death as soon as they could. Food was a constant issue in the early days, and many of the colonists suffered from eating disorders, inasmuch as they had nothing to eat, which in the 18th century was often fatal. With *The Biggest Loser* still more than two centuries away, the colonists had no way of knowing how to make malnutrition work for them, and many of them found that their own slow deaths were lowering their morale.

The first problem was that the British had no idea how to farm in Australian conditions. The second problem was that most of them had no idea how to farm in any conditions, a result of their government's farsighted 'populate the settlement exclusively with those who have no useful life skills' policy. And so much of the early activity in the colony consisted of hungry men standing around staring at the corncobs they'd stuck in the ground, waiting for them to flower. Governor Phillip's correspondence during this time indicates the scale of the problem:

From the desk of Governor Arthur Phillip,
Sydney Cove, New South Wales 0001

Dear Prime Minister William Pitt the Younger,

How are you, sir? I am fine. I do not wish to trouble you, as I am sure you are extremely busy being Great Britain's youngest ever prime minister and forming the Triple Alliance with Prussia and Holland in order to restrict French influence in Europe, but right now we're having a bit of trouble 'Down Under', to use a term that I just made up. Basically we're all a tad peckish, and we'd love it if you could send us some food and also, if possible, some sunscreen.

Yours,
Arthur Phillip (Governor)

Dear Governor Phillip,

The Prime Minister received your letter of August 5th and has authorised me to tell you that he cannot at this moment send you any of the supplies you have requested as he is extremely preoccupied with the preparations for the French Revolution, which will break out next year and be very troublesome for us all. He suggests you try going fishing or something.

Regards,
Elderfield Humberry-Deccleston the Fourth
Private Secretary to the Prime Minister

Dear King George III,

I hope this missive finds you in good health and that you have not yet gone insane. I write to request some assistance with my little colony here in New South Wales, which is a lovely spot ideal for weekends away and longer summer stays, but suffers the drawback of being hell on earth. I was wondering if you could send us some food rather urgently, as we're having a bit of trouble growing our own. So far the best idea any of us have had is burying a cow and hoping it grows into a cow tree, which may give you some idea of our predicament.

Thank you for your time, sir. Give my regards to your son George IV, and my condolences on the extravagant profligacy and dissolute lifestyle, which he will demonstrate in a couple of decades' time. I imagine that will be a real nuisance.

Yours,

Arthur Phillip (Governor)

Dear Mr Phillip,

Thank you for your letter, which was passed on to me by my chief of staff, a small she-oak. I am afraid I must confess that I have never heard of this 'New South Wales' of which you speak, but I take it that it is some kind of marvellous kingdom in the sky, and so I have taken immediate action, ordering my courtiers to stand in the gardens hurling beef and toast skywards until you are fully provisioned.

Yours,

King George III of Great Britain and Ireland (Mrs)

Dear Lord Sydney,
WTF have you got me into, you bastard?
Yours,
Arthur Phillip (Depressed)

But life in New South Wales wasn't all inappropriate crops and floggings: tensions with the Indigenous population also took up a lot of the settlers' time. Much of this arose from simple misunderstandings: the English didn't understand the Aboriginal peoples' complex society and deep spiritual connection to the land, while the Aboriginal people didn't understand why the English wouldn't just piss off.

Watkin Tench wrote, of the Aboriginal people, that 'our intercourse with them was neither frequent nor cordial', and any fool can tell you how frustrating non-cordial intercourse can be. Tench was put out that the natives seemed to be avoiding the Englishmen, 'either from fear, jealousy or hatred' – he never considered the possibility that maybe their avoidance was due to the fact that last time they'd seen him he'd dragged a seven-year-old boy along and forced them to examine his skin.

Tench assumed that the Aboriginal people hated and feared the white man, which would have been pretty justifiable behaviour on their part. The white man, after all, though arriving with what seemed like a friendly attitude, spent a large percentage of the first few months shooting them, stealing their possessions and giving them fatal diseases. In the white man's defence, he was at the time both near starvation and extremely bored, but it was still behaviour of a sort considered 'dirty pool', and the early settlement at Sydney isn't considered one of the highest points in the history of white people. Although, to emphasise what sort of history that is, it's not all that low on the list, either.

Unmitigated Gaul

As if the difficulties of working the land and getting on with the natives weren't enough, the travellers of the First Fleet also had to deal with the one problem they had been sure sailing around the world would rid them of: the French. Six days after the English arrived in Australia, a French expedition led by Jean-François de Galaup, Comte de Lapérouse[20] sailed up and demanded to know what was going on. '*Ouwat eez zees?*' he asked in his snooty French manner, waving a lacy handkerchief in the air and patting his enormous wig.

Today this French visit is commemorated in the name of the Sydney suburb Rooty Hill, along with the cutting-edge fashions of the Botany Bay area. Lapérouse, however, was a restless soul, and soon decided that the life of an unemployed Frenchman in a penal colony was not for him. He chose instead to leave Sydney and never be seen again – a move that in retrospect may have been misguided.

What with the hostile natives, the non-existent food, and the lingering stench of French perfume, things were certainly desperate, and were not improved by the arrival of the Second Fleet, so named because the organisers took roughly a second to plan it.

The Underwhelming Sequel

The Second Fleet was a fiasco. Like many sequels, they made the fatal mistake of trying to cram in too many new characters: the ships carried over a thousand convicts, which made it difficult to undertake any serious character development. Also, the transporting of convicts was contracted out to a private company, and sadly, for the first and only time in recorded history, leaving an important job to private enterprise went badly.

---

20 Literally, 'Count of the Perouse'.

The firm of Camden, Calvert and King[21] was paid £17 7s. 6d[22] per convict transported, and some might say the operation went awry at the point when the Crown agreed to pay the fee whether the convicts survived the trip or not. Naturally, CCK obeyed the old business maxim 'Don't blow your profit margin on keeping people alive' and, in what experts have called the most predictable outcome of anything to ever have happened, 26 per cent of the convicts on board the fleet died on the way to Australia. This was probably not as bad as it could have been, given a lot of companies would have just dumped all the convicts overboard in the English Channel. Instead, the representatives of Camden, Calvert and King simply withheld food from their charges and kept them chained up below deck, to prevent them interfering with the crew's work or conducting metabolic processes.[23]

Particularly horrific were conditions on board the *Neptune*, a transport ship commanded by Master Donald Traill, described by historian Robert Hughes as a 'demented sadist' and by the convicts on his ship as 'oh God please stop'. The *Neptune* took 499 convicts on board, of whom 158 died without ever reaching Australia. On arrival, Traill set up a market in Port Jackson to sell the leftover supplies, a display of farsighted entrepreneurship that has inspired Australian businessmen for centuries since, and is generally considered to be the forerunner of the modern Liberal Party.

Naturally, news of the nightmarish conditions on the Second Fleet quickly reached England, and an enquiry into the activities of the slave-

21 Hitherto best known for transporting slaves, which everyone agreed was a pretty good omen.

22 In today's currency, approximately 16 billion dollars.

23 One convict wrote that he had stayed shackled to a corpse for a week, pretending he was still alive, so as to get his hands on the dead man's rations – which just goes to show the lengths to which some people will go to receive welfare.

trading, psychopath-employing, prisoner-killing, lice-breeding firm of Camden, Calvert and King led the authorities to the only possible conclusion: they should get them to run the Third Fleet as well. It was indeed a golden age for the dying-on-ships industry.

But back in New South Wales, Arthur Phillip had his own troubles. The new colony was not proceeding according to his plans, inasmuch as his plans had involved a) food; b) friendly relations with the original inhabitants; and c) a military force willing to do its job. This last was particularly vexing, as it was generally agreed that when your country is populated almost entirely by criminals, it's helpful to have some guys willing to keep them in line. Phillip's marines, however, weren't all that interested in convict discipline. Or in marine discipline, for that matter, finding that in the unforgiving southern climate, drinking and fighting were much more enjoyable pastimes.[24] The failure of the marines to enforce discipline meant that Phillip had to put convicts in charge of other convicts, which was a bit like ... well, it was a bit like putting convicts in charge of other convicts.

The implementation of convict overseers to maintain control over their fellow convicts was born of necessity, but it was typical of Phillip's innovative style. He was actually a most progressive leader, although bear in mind that for colonial Britain in 1788, 'progressive' meant giving the brown folk a five-second headstart before you commenced shooting. The governor gave orders to everyone in the new colony that the original inhabitants were to be treated well, which in hindsight probably meant 'don't kill them', but at the time opinion was divided. Some thought that 'treat the Aboriginal people well' implied the avoidance of murder, but others argued that, reading between the lines, killing them was probably what the boss was going for. The governor

24 And let's not pretend they weren't onto something.

had ordered that anyone who killed a native would be hanged, but many of his men considered this to be one of Arthur's little jokes.

The account of Watkin Tench once again gives valuable insight into the relationship between whites and Aboriginal people.[25] Tench describes in vivid detail the early encounters between the British and the local Eora people, which were characterised by distrust on the part of the latter: an unfair attitude to take, since they didn't know yet how awful the British were. 'Give us a chance,' the settlers complained, 'we've barely even started genociding yet.' Phillip was greatly distressed by the fact that the Aboriginal people, despite his best intentions, seemed to resent him filling up their country with convicts and drunken soldiers, and there were several clashes between white and black.

The tensions grew so intolerable that Phillip eventually decided to calm things down by taking the only action possible: abducting and imprisoning an Aboriginal man. 'Once we've shown our willingness to keep them as pets,' the governor confidently proclaimed, 'they will be our friends.' The captured man was taken to the governor's house, and Phillip named him 'Manly', after his favourite rugby league team, although his real name was revealed later to be Arabanoo, an Eora word thought to mean 'let me go, you prick'. Arabanoo got on well with his hosts/captors, and was a source of great wonder and entertainment for them, amazing them with his ability to learn English words, drink tea and be a human being.

Unfortunately Arabanoo's stay with the settlers was to be relatively brief, due to the settlers' next great idea for improving native–colonist relations: smallpox. In just over a year, the locals of Sydney Cove had

25 Or as he called them, 'Indians', which is pretty weird, isn't it? Historians believe Watkin Tench may have been subject to delusional cowboy fantasies.

learnt that British settlement meant getting shot, being robbed and suffering fatal disease, and they were absolutely psyched for what the future would bring.

Phillip, finding that his scheme to achieve racial harmony through kidnapping had fallen short of its goal, decided that the problem was that he hadn't been kidnapping enough. He was sure that if he persevered, eventually he would carry out sufficient abductions to bring about peace in the new country.

One of the men Phillip captured was Bennelong, who became something of a celebrity in later years after travelling to England. Bennelong was a smart and spirited young man, who learnt English quickly and developed a great enthusiasm for his captors' liquor – indeed, he drank so much that he almost qualified for an officer's rank in the Marine Corps. According to Watkin Tench, 'love and war seemed his favourite pursuits': like most red-blooded Australian males, Bennelong enjoyed sticking his spear into people, and when he wasn't doing that, he liked fighting.

After some time living among the British, Bennelong escaped, but maintained friendly relations with Phillip, much like Batman and Commissioner Jim Gordon, and set up a meeting between Phillip and the Aboriginal community at Manly. Delighted to meet the man who had brought such interesting new murderers and diseases to their home, the natives welcomed the governor with a traditional assassination attempt. Tench's report suggests that the man who speared Phillip did so out of fear, though why an Aboriginal person would have any reason to fear a white man remains a mystery to this day. In Tench's words:

> *The Indian, stepping back with one foot, aimed his lance with such force and dexterity, that striking the governor's*

> *right shoulder, just above the collar-bone, the point glancing downward, came out at his back, having made a wound of many inches long.*

This account has led most historians to agree that 'this must have hurt like an absolute bastard'. Yet Phillip survived: it would take more than a little spear through the shoulder to bring down the James Bond of the 18th century, and he was soon back at work, busily failing to control his troops or feed the convicts. Phillip ordered that there should be no reprisals against the natives for the attack, and so rather than killing and maiming Aboriginal people in revenge, the settlers were forced to kill and maim Aboriginal people just because they felt like it.

The haphazard village of Sydney, meanwhile, struggled on. As more convicts arrived, many too sick and weak to work, it found itself with more mouths to feed and not a hell of a lot to feed them with. Military officers harangued Phillip, demanding he give them plots of land to mismanage for themselves. This was a request the governor was not empowered to accede to, although he could have just gone ahead and handed out whatever land he wanted, since nobody back in England gave a pair of rabbit pellets what was happening in New South Wales. The southern continent was Britain's own Pacific oubliette: a hole to put people in order to forget about them. It could easily have descended into chaos and anarchy, and it may be that Arthur Phillip's greatest achievement lies in the fact that *Mad Max* wasn't a documentary.

Instead, the one-time sea captain, whaler and spy laid the foundations for a nation that would one day grow beyond its penal origins to bestride the world as a moderately independent middle power with several Winter Olympic medals and multiple tourist attractions featuring gigantic fruit.

Because by 1792, the little colony at the unfashionable end of the world was, if not thriving, at least still existent, and in the opinion of many now bore favourable comparison with many of England's most popular slums.

Governor Phillip, in poor health and heartily sick of the heat and the flies and the lack of political will for meaningful financial services reform, decided it was time to head home. The decision was made easier for him by the fact that his awful wife had died, so the main reason he left England in the first place was gone. He set sail in late 1792 on the *Atlantic*, taking with him his good friend Bennelong, in order to show the Establishment the benefits of kidnapping in the cause of cross-cultural understanding.

Back in old Blighty, Phillip married again, but a couple of years later went back to sea, thus continuing a pattern of marrying and then abandoning women that presumably caused a lot of snide comments at the time. He fought the French a few years more, just to keep his hand in, and eventually retired as an admiral in 1805. In retirement he fought for the interests of New South Wales with the British government, to the point where people would avoid him at parties. 'Look out, here's Arthur,' they'd say, rolling their eyes, 'coming to bang on about kangaroos again.' He died in 1814 at the age of 75, in Bath.[26]

Phillip was succeeded as governor by John Hunter, a Royal Navy officer who had captained HMS *Sirius* in the First Fleet and who stands out as one of Australian history's most boring people. He took office a couple of years after Phillip left, a miscalculation that turned out to be the harbinger of great troubles ahead for the plucky young colony.

---

26 Or possibly in *the* bath. Not sure.

ESSAY QUESTIONS

1. Was sending people to Australia an effective deterrent to crime? Do you think a similar programme could work today? Would it be more or less effective if applied to criminals already in Australia?
2. Imagine being speared in the shoulder. Do you think it would hurt? Give examples.

Project Rum Way

In which the demon drink gains mastery of a young colony, and an able seaman finds marines less trouble than merinos

At the turn of the 19th century, the young colony of New South Wales was experiencing a certain number of growing pains.[27] The problems had begun in 1792 when Governor Arthur Phillip left the colony, and the authorities, in a truly epic feat of procrastination, didn't get around to hiring his replacement until 1795. In most lists of Best Governors of New South Wales, 'nobody' ranks fairly low, and with good reason: things got somewhat out of control during that period.

Without a governor, the colony was effectively under control of the NSW Corps, the colonial military. These were men of such powerful work ethic and skilled professionalism that guarding convicts in a desolate hellhole on the other side of the world seemed like their best shot at a lasting career; or, in other words, they were the worst soldiers on earth. This may have been the reason why, for the first and last time in recorded history, a group of military personnel abused its power.

The Corps of the Matter

The NSW Corps was commanded by Major Grose, and not for nothing was he referred to as 'Grose by name, and also a complete bastard'.

27 Although some claimed this was actually gout.

Upon taking command of the governorless colony, Grose issued an order to his troops that it was now every man's duty to get as rich as possible as soon as he could. Slaves to duty, they obeyed. The Corps was particularly keen on the 'rum' trade – at that time rum referred to any kind of alcoholic drink, because the fledgling colony was too poor to afford other words. NSW Corps officers cornered the market in alcohol and started producing their own. Rum became the de facto currency of the colony, which on one hand seriously exacerbated the problem of alcoholism, but on the other hand was a step up from using koala dung, as they had been.

When Governor John Hunter rode into Sydney, fixin' to clean up this stinkin' town, it caused much distress among the Corps officers, who were suddenly faced with the possibility of their criminal cartel being broken up. Their distress didn't last long, however, as they quickly realised one pertinent fact: Hunter couldn't actually do anything to stop them. Every time the new governor caught an officer doing something illegal and tried to have him arrested, the other officers would instead turn around and beat Hunter up in a classic switcheroo.

The sad fact was, the more Hunter tried to crack down on the rogue troops, the more the troops sassed him, leaving tacks on his chair and pinning insulting signs to his back and so on. In the end, the officers sent letters to the government in Britain accusing Hunter himself of corruption, and the hapless man was removed from office.

His replacement, Philip Gidley King, worked hard to improve the colony's situation, but like Hunter faced insurmountable odds, and despite triumphs (such as the publication of Australia's first book and the founding of Australia's first newspaper), his failures (such as the invention of Tasmania) were too great to overcome. He left office with the iron grip of the Rum Corps entirely intact.

And so the Empire, at its wits' end, turned to William Bligh, notorious martinet and reigning world champion in the long-distance involuntary ocean-paddle, based on the principle that when you're fighting jerks, the only way to win is with a bigger jerk. For Bligh, it was another chapter in a strange and irritating life.

A Man of Mutiny

On James Cook's final, ill-fated voyage, which for the captain ended with the Hawaiian natives' massive overreaction to the Brits' good-natured 'stealing the king' prank, the ship *Resolution* was guided back to England by its sailing master, the 24-year-old William Bligh. It was the breakthrough moment of a brilliant career that had begun when Bligh signed up with the Royal Navy at the age of seven, his parents apparently unable to stand him one day longer. The young man earned an impressive reputation as a navigator and cartographer, and was elected a Fellow of the Royal Society, who commended him on his excellent surveying skills, but were less complimentary of his natural ability to be mutinied against.

Rising through the ranks, Bligh fought the Dutch at Dogger Bank and the Spanish and the French at Gibraltar as part of the American War of Independence, in a series of geographically confusing battles that instilled in him the strong desire for order that was to prove his downfall so often that it almost got boring by the end.

In 1787, Bligh was placed in command of the *Bounty*, a small cutter commissioned to sail to Tahiti to get breadfruit, a fictional plant invented by Pacific pranksters competing with each other to come up with the stupidest possible story that the English would believe. Bligh was tasked with transporting the breadfruit plants to the West Indies, where they were in urgent need of a crop that could provide cheap food for slaves and cut down on the need for bakeries.

Once in Tahiti, Bligh found his task slightly more difficult than he had anticipated, as his crew found that in order to collect breadfruit plants, it was first necessary to go through a long and painstaking process of having sex with Tahitian women over and over and over again. 'Bloody red tape,' the *Bounty*'s crew muttered in exasperation, eager to get on with their appointed task, if it weren't for all these beautiful island girls clogging up the works. For five months this went on, until finally the *Bounty* left Tahiti, laden with its imaginary fruit and a lot of extremely reluctant sailors.[28]

Was it Bligh's forcible removal of the crew from a tropical paradise filled with bracingly open-minded young women that earned his men's ire? Or was it his iron discipline, his short temper and increasing taste for floggings? Whatever it was, at some point the men of the *Bounty* decided that the switch from a lifestyle of drink, sex and lying on beaches to one of being screamed at, physically assaulted and accused of stealing coconuts by a uniformed maniac was not a positive one. And so the seeds of mutiny were sown.

Fletcher Christian, master's mate and an old friend of Bligh's, led the mutiny on 28 April 1789. With his co-conspirators he seized the ship's muskets, grabbed Bligh from his bed and cast him adrift in the ship's launch, along with those who remained loyal to him. These men may have regretted their loyalty later, as they spent the next 48 days in the company of Bligh and his personality disorders, sailing almost 6000 kilometres to Coupang in Timor, in what would be more widely recognised as one of the greatest feats of navigation and endurance in maritime history if it weren't for the fact that Bligh is generally agreed to have been kind of a jerk.

---

28 Who had, inadvertently, invented the end-of-season football trip.

But even if William Bligh was the sort of maniac who would break up the monotony of an arduous sea voyage by challenging his colleagues to sword fights at awkward moments, in making that astonishing voyage in an open boat with scarce provisions, he had proven himself a masterful sailor and a man who knew how to get things done – even if the things he got done were often, by any reasonable measure, terrible.

For their part, Christian and the mutineers reached Pitcairn Island, where they settled down to a life of domestic bliss punctuated by regular murders that is now seen as the basis for the TV show *Dating Naked*. Their descendants still live on the tiny island, some of them carrying on their ancestors' traditions of proud self-reliance and sexual assault.

Many men would have been ruined by the events that transpired on the *Bounty*, but William Bligh was not many men: in fact, most experts agree that he was, at most, one. Far from disgraced, Bligh was acquitted of responsibility for losing his ship and then promoted, the Admiralty reasoning that since the average sailor was a dissolute scumbag, anyone who pissed them off so much that they threw him overboard must be a decent chap. A year later, he returned to Tahiti and was this time successful in bringing breadfruit to the West Indies, though unsuccessful in finding out what breadfruit even is.

With his record of navigational skill, courage in adversity and driving men to acts of violence, it's no wonder that the government considered Bligh the perfect man to take control of the colony of New South Wales. But possibly, the Empire underestimated just how big the jerks they were fighting were. Because for all Bligh's reputation as the hard man of the waves, down in Old Sydney Town there was a bête noire waiting for him, and as bêtes go, he was one of the noirest.

The Farmer Wants a Fight

John Macarthur is known as the Father of Australian Sheep, although not literally as far as we know. Most primary sources indicate that he imported his first sheep from England as opposed to spawning them from his own loins, which would have been cheaper but far more physically taxing.

The original importation of merinos came as the infant colony was then desperately searching for an industry upon which it could build its fortune. Sheep may have seemed an unlikely candidate for that industry, being among the stupidest and least personable of animals in the civilised world. Many alternatives were proposed for the role of primary livestock of the young country, including the highly intelligent pig, the cheap and plentiful chicken, and the majestic lion, king of the jungle. And yet in the end it was the humble sheep that became the iconic beast of European settlement in Australia.

For this we can thank the farsighted business acumen of John Macarthur, who realised very early on that at some point in New South Wales's development there would be schools; and those schools would be attended by children; and those schoolchildren would at some point have to do Social Studies projects; and when they did those projects, they would need small pieces of material to glue onto the cardboard. Wool, Macarthur surmised, was the ideal substance to fill the children's needs, being soft, divisible into small portions and possessing a slightly unsettling smell.

Macarthur didn't actually come to Australia to raise sheep: he arrived on the notorious Second Fleet as a lieutenant in the British Army, having already gained a reputation for starting fights with anyone who looked at him funny.[29] Appointed a commandant at Parramatta

29 Sadly, after he started hanging around sheep all the time, people looked at him funny a lot more often.

– the thriving settlement west of Sydney that had already gained a reputation as one of the Empire's most eel-infested communities – he quickly realised that although military service was all very well, the real money was in agriculture and corruption. At the former he proved most skilled – or at least his wife did, which was the same thing back then – and at the latter he was almost without peer in the new world.

Major Grose granted Macarthur 100 acres at Rose Hill in 1793 as part of the acting governor's aforementioned 'Give Stuff to All My Friends' scheme, and in 1794 gave him another 100, because Macarthur seemed to really enjoy owning large amounts of property, and Grose just couldn't resist those big brown eyes. That same year, Macarthur began his experiments in sheep breeding, pre-empting Mary Shelley's *Frankenstein* by some 24 years. Macarthur crossed Indian ewes with Irish rams, producing fleeces of mixed hair and wool, and a catastrophic outbreak of terrible jokes about potato curries. The idea of producing fine wool in New South Wales was thus suggested to Macarthur, and he set about acquiring a flock of sheep, using the money he had earned as a member of the criminal cabal controlling the colony. It remains one of the most inspirational tales of determined entrepreneurship in Australian history, right up there with those of Dick Smith, Sir Frank Packer and Tony Mokbel.

Having gained possession of some high-quality Spanish merinos from the Dutch government, via one of the geographically convoluted chains of events that seemed to go on all the time in the olden days, Macarthur rapidly became the number one sheep farmer in New South Wales, with the size of his flock and the quality of his wool spoken of far and wide by incredibly dull conversationalists.

By then Macarthur was spending little time on military duties, preferring to concentrate on business interests and his twin hobbies of fighting duels and destroying the careers of governors. Governor Hunter's arrival threatened to curtail his activities, because Hunter had radical ideas about law and order, i.e. he thought there should be some. Casting around for a way to get Hunter out of the way, Macarthur's eye lit upon a big pile of rum that he was currently trafficking in, and he had a brainwave. One allegation that Hunter trafficked in rum later, and it was Macarthur 1, Governors with Some Sense of the Rule of Law 0.

The scoreline worsened with King, who got into a tussle with Macarthur over an assault case in which the governor overturned the sentence of a man convicted of attacking the sheep tycoon. Macarthur responded by trying to get everyone in Sydney to give King the silent treatment: any time King spoke, he told his fellow officers, they were to look idly around and say loudly, 'Did you hear something? I didn't hear anything.' Macarthur's boss Colonel Paterson refused to engage in such childish behaviour, believing it'd be much better if Macarthur and King sorted out their differences in the gym after class. Macarthur responded to this by trying to blackmail Paterson, to which Paterson responded by challenging Macarthur to a duel, to which Macarthur responded by shooting Paterson in the shoulder, to which King responded by having Macarthur arrested and sending him to England for trial, to which Macarthur responded by stealing the evidence against him on the way, to which King responded by saying, 'Screw this, let him have the frigging colony to himself then.' This is why today's historians refer to the early 1800s as 'The Age of Responses'.

And so John Macarthur, no longer a soldier but still holding considerable sway over the Rum Corps, found himself the most powerful man in New South Wales. When Governor Bligh rode into town, under the distinct impression that *he* was the most powerful man in New South Wales and with the fancy jacket to prove it, there was bound to be an explosive confrontation.

Two Men Enter ... One Man Leaves Eventually

In August 1806, William Bligh landed at Sydney, looked around, emitted a happy sigh and muttered to himself, 'Yes, this will make a fine spot for inspiring my next mutiny.' Excited to be provoking subordinates to rebellion in an exotic new location, he got to work straight away, pausing only to send the commander of the convoy he'd arrived with back to England for a court martial, on the grounds that 'he got right on my wick'.

Bligh's first order of business was to put a stop to the illegal rum trade. He prohibited the use of alcohol as payment for goods, demanding that all residents of the colony use the officially approved currency: breadfruit.[30] 'What's that?' asked the colonists. 'Shut up,' Bligh explained.

He also stopped giving big bits of land to the colony's richest men, which infuriated them. 'Where's the incentive to become fabulously wealthy,' they asked indignantly, 'if the government won't make us even wealthier?' Shocked and saddened by Bligh's refusal to reward hard work and effort by giving massive gifts to people who had expended no hard work or effort for them, many settlers threw up their hands and stormed off to found the Australian mining industry. But many stayed to fight, believing that having seen off two governors already, ridding themselves of a third couldn't be that hard. Little did they know just how committed Bligh was to unpopularity.

Standing in the way of honest hard-working kleptocrats wasn't Bligh's only attempt at reform. He also introduced innovative new

30 WARNING: Do not refer to this fact when answering exam questions.

techniques of governance, such as holding men under arrest after they had been acquitted of the charges against them, putting others in prison for writing rude letters, and sacking New South Wales's assistant surgeon for no reason whatsoever. Bligh also sacked the surgeon-general as a magistrate, raising serious questions about why surgeons were going around being magistrates, but then it was a new colony and people needed to multi-task – the archbishop of Sydney was also chief sewage engineer.

That surgeon-general, Thomas Jamison, was miffed by this turn of events, considering it disgraceful that an upstanding medical professional should be denied the chance to also be an upstanding legal professional for no other reason than his involvement in illegal trading activities. Bligh's interference forced Jamison to depend almost entirely on his actual job, and the surgeon-general did not care for this at all. In fact, he went crying to his friend John Macarthur, who probably challenged Bligh to a duel – his response to most problems he encountered. Bligh, however, was not the sort to engage in vulgar shootouts, preferring to settle his problems by getting into a lifeboat and sailing several thousand miles away from them, and so tensions continued to simmer.

In a way, the real problem between Bligh and Macarthur was a simple personality clash: Macarthur had the kind of personality that enjoyed progressively getting richer, while Bligh had the sort of personality that liked arresting people. It was a love–hate relationship, inasmuch as they both hated each other, but at the same time they both loved hating each other. Like two mighty sperm whales preparing to mate, these huge colonial characters were on a collision course, and just like the whales, they were about to make a very big splash.

Bligh embarked on an anti-Macarthur campaign so ferocious,

a rumour started that he had been mauled by a sheep as a baby. He prevented Macarthur distributing rum to the Corps. He stopped him importing stills into the colony. The pair clashed over differing plans for land in Sydney. Macarthur borrowed Bligh's pencil and refused to return it. Bligh spread a tale that Macarthur wet his bed. Things became extremely nasty in short order.

Matters reached boiling point when a convict escaped Sydney by stowing away on Macarthur's ship the *Parramatta*, causing the bond lodged by the ship's owners as security against such an eventuality to be forfeited and the ship to be impounded. Macarthur refused to pay in order to get the ship back, leading to the crew violating landing regulations by coming ashore to buy food. Based on the allegation that the owners were refusing to feed the crew, Macarthur was ordered to appear in court.

Enraged at being disrespected over such a boring and forgettable story, Macarthur refused. Enraged at being disrespected by Macarthur, Judge Advocate Richard Atkins had him arrested. Enraged at being arrested, Macarthur demanded that Atkins pay him the money he had owed him for years, probably for some mutton or a woolly hat or something. Enraged at being expected to pay his debts, Atkins told Macarthur to shove it. Enraged at this being exactly what he wanted Atkins to do, Macarthur demanded he be barred from presiding over the upcoming trial, due to the likelihood of bias. As levels of enragement in New South Wales reached near-dangerous levels, Atkins resisted this claim, pointing out that despite being a drunkard with no legal training whatsoever, he had risen to the position of judge advocate, so he must have something going for him.

On 25 January 1808, the trial of John Macarthur on charges of unlawful importation, sedition and general dickishness began, with the colony's wealthiest man and most prominent sheep-tamperer to be judged by a panel consisting of the festively unschooled Atkins and six of Macarthur's best friends, in one of the most shining examples of the absurdist avant-garde comedy that was the early NSW legal system. Atkins was, at the time, the only man in the colony empowered to act as a judge. To say that Britain's new imperial outpost was lagging in its development of sophisticated jurisprudential systems would be both an understatement and slightly pretentious. Still, the Unqualified Judge Plus Six Random Military Officers was the best system available at the time. Unfortunately for Atkins, it was not conducive to the successful prosecution of irritating wool moguls, as demonstrated by the opening morning of the trial, when Macarthur disrupted proceedings by loudly eating chips throughout, officially entered a plea of 'you're a dick', and repeatedly referred to the judge as 'Judge Fatkins'.

Justice was not seen to be served. Without a judge, the trial was unable to proceed, and Macarthur was free to strut about the town making obscene hand gestures to his heart's content.

Here the infant nation that would one day become Australia stood on a knife's edge. What kind of future was being constructed in this far-flung outpost of the British Empire? Was it a future where arrogant soldiers and sheep-worriers would be free to toss rum about willy-nilly and thumb their nose at authority, because authority was them? Or was it a future where the rule of law would be supreme and every home would have its own breadfruit tree?[31] It is not the best-remembered slice of Australian history, but in the crisis that confronted Bligh in January 1808, there was a real danger that future generations would be forced to buy their groceries with Jim Beam. Bligh knew he had to take action to prevent this, but more importantly, he knew he had to

31 If breadfruit grows on trees. I have no idea. Seriously, I think it's made up.

take action to make sure Macarthur knew what a gigantic tool he was. He would one day elaborate on this in his autobiography *Bligh: A Full and Thorough Account of All the Gigantic Tools I've Known*, a long and somewhat angry book; but for now, Bligh was forced to use his powers as governor in an attempt to slap the sheep-man down.

On 26 January 1808, Bligh put a real dampener on Australia Day celebrations, not only by cancelling the scheduled Twenty20 international, but by issuing orders for Macarthur's arrest. Major George Johnston interpreted this to mean that Macarthur, after being arrested, should immediately be released, in accordance with the colony's strict 'Help a Brother Out' laws. Johnston was, to be fair, already in a fairly irritable mood after crashing his gig[32] a couple of nights earlier, in the very first incidence of the proud Australian tradition of powerful government officials drink-driving.

Upon being released, to show that there were no hard feelings, Macarthur drafted a petition to have Bligh arrested. The other Corps officers signed the petition, sealing Bligh's fate and inventing GetUp! in one motion.

And thus New South Wales entered the Age of Two Guys Trying to Arrest Each Other. Traditionally, in a situation where a governor is trying to arrest someone, and that someone is simultaneously trying to arrest the governor, the governor holds the whip hand. But New South Wales in 1808 was not a place beholden to tradition. It was the land of opportunity, where any man, had he the drive and the determination, could arrest anyone he liked. Especially if the entire army was on his side, but that too was testament to Macarthur's drive and determination, not to mention his general lack of morals.

32 The Easybeats, Annandale Hotel.

Bedtime

At 6pm on Australia Day, normally a time when people would be getting prepared for the fireworks and a concert starring several *X Factor* runners-up, the NSW Corps arrived at Bligh's house, bent on some harsh frontier justice.

The first obstacle they encountered was Bligh's daughter Mary, who stymied them through the cunning tactic of shutting the garden gate. The Corps stopped, uncertain of how to deal with this unforeseen circumstance: nothing in Corps training manuals specified the procedure to follow in the event of a young woman closing a gate. Mary shouted at them, calling them 'traitors' and 'rebels', and demanding, 'Kill me if you will, but spare my father!' Some of the Corps thought this was quite a good idea, but others argued that killing the governor's daughter and leaving the governor alone wouldn't achieve much. The arguments raged on, with some suggesting they fire on the gate with a cannon. The stalemate lasted until one particularly enterprising officer thought to open the gate, and so the siege of Government House came to a dramatic end. Mary responded by hitting the leading officers with her umbrella,[33] but her resistance had been broken, and the Corps stormed the house in search of the unhappy governor.

Here is where the history gets a bit contentious. The rebels claimed that Bligh was found hiding under his bed, from where he had to be dragged by soldiers. This may have been the Corps' public relations strategy, to discredit the governor by painting him as a coward, though in reality it makes him more relatable: if armed men are invading your house, hiding under the bed seems, frankly, like the most sensible course of action you can take. This was, though, an unedifying image to imprint on the public consciousness: the supreme executive officer of

33 Actual History.

the colony curled up among the dust bunnies, hoping like hell his little girl could keep him safe. The allegation that this was how it went down was reinforced by a popular painting exhibited not long afterwards, although why anyone trusted the word of a painting is beyond me. It wasn't even a very good painting: if the artist didn't know what human legs look like, how were they supposed to know what happened in Bligh's bedroom? In any case, it severely damaged Bligh's reputation and earned him the nickname 'Bedsprings Bligh', which was arguably even worse than his previous nickname, 'Breadfruit'.

The counter-claim, from Bligh supporters, is that the governor was hiding behind the bed in order to destroy certain sensitive documents and prevent them falling into dastardly Corps hands. This theory aligns with Bligh's long record of courageous acts at sea, and with his well-known love of ripping up pieces of paper. But sadly nobody ever painted a picture of him shredding documents, so this narrative never gained popularity.

After the extraction from the bed of the cowardly and/or heroic Bligh, Major Johnston wrote him a letter – which was completely unnecessary, because he was right there outside the house – informing him that he was no longer the governor. 'Uh, yeah, I got that,' retorted Bligh, sarcastic to the last. Bligh was placed under house arrest, and the Corps began a wild celebration, drinking all night, lighting a bonfire and drawing unflattering pictures of Governor Bligh, which I guess counted as debauchery in the 19th century.

The aftermath of Bligh's second mutiny was messy and contentious. Macarthur was made colonial secretary in recognition of his services to the development of organised crime in the new world. Lieutenant-Colonel Joseph Foveaux arrived in July and assumed the post of acting lieutenant-governor, which bugged Macarthur something chronic.

'How many governors do I have to knock off before they stop sending new ones?' he whined.

Bligh remained under house arrest. He could have left for England at any time, but refused to until he had served his term as governor, which just goes to show that he wasn't the sort of guy you want to go on a camping holiday with. 'When I am finished being arrested,' he would warn, 'I am going to arrest you all *so hard*.'

Sick of managing the frankly irritating colony, Foveaux asked Colonel William Paterson, one of several spare colonels that Britain had knocking about the place at the time, to come sort it all out. Paterson, though having no idea what he had to do with anything, complied, and sent Johnston and Macarthur to England to be court-martialled. Johnston was dismissed from the service, while Macarthur was never tried at all, due to the Teflon tuxedo he apparently wore at all times.

Bligh was given a ship and told to return to England, and so naturally he sailed to Tasmania and tried to get the governor there to help him get New South Wales back, because this dude just would not let anything go. His ship stayed in Tasmania for a year, with him on board, because the entire world was fed up with him and couldn't think of a good place to stick him.

In the end, Bligh did find his way back to England, where he and Macarthur engaged in some more bitching at each other, to which the government replied, 'Oh my *GOD*, we are *SO* sick of you both, please go away.'

By that time, New South Wales had gained a new governor in the eminent Lachlan Macquarie, who hit upon the novel idea of running an actual government, as opposed to the alcohol-soaked series of toddler slapfights by which the colony had been run up till then.

Bligh went on to be acquitted in two more courts martial, get promoted to admiral and for some reason design a wall in Dublin,[34] before his death in 1817. He was buried at St Mary's, Lambeth, although there are reports that shortly afterwards several corpses in surrounding graves banded together to overthrow him and take over his plot.

Macarthur returned to Australia and lived a long and happy life, committed to his passions of selling wool, dictating government policy and taking credit for his wife's work. He was, for a time, a member of the NSW Legislative Council, before being suspended due to mental illness, which was pretty unfair considering that you'd be hard-pressed to find a 19th-century politician who wasn't out of his mind.

Macarthur can be considered the victor of the Rum Rebellion, ending up rich and powerful, and with his face on the two-dollar note, while William Bligh ended up being played by Hannibal Lecter in the movies. Macarthur is known, to this day, as the father of the Australian wool industry, while Bligh is known as the guy who pissed off everyone he ever met and then hid under his bed. In the public relations battle, there's no doubt who came out on top.

But what is the judgement of serious historical recappers, such as Geoffrey Blainey and myself? Things are not so simple. Debate still rages over whether Bligh was an irrational tyrant, unfit for command, standing in the way of the fledgling colony's economic growth and progress towards nationhood, or whether he was a man of steadfast ideals and unimpeachable integrity, dedicated to duty and the stamping out of corruption, brought low by amoral profiteers with no sense of duty. Or, indeed, whether Macarthur was an innovator and pioneer who kickstarted the transformation of Australia from a backwater

34 Mid-life crises were a lot less interesting in the 1800s.

penal colony to a thriving new country, or whether he was a grasping spiv ready to ride roughshod over the government, the law and basic human decency in order to enrich himself.

These aren't easy questions to answer, and it is up to the reader of these recaps to decide where the truth of the Rum Rebellion lies. But whether your sympathies are with Macarthur or with Bligh, one lesson of the era stands undeniably: practically everyone in Sydney in the early 1800s was a massive dick. And argue all you want about whether the period was the forerunner of Australia's tradition of anti-authoritarianism, or the forerunner of Australia's tradition of entrepreneurship, or the forerunner of Australia's tradition of men hiding under beds – it's beyond a shadow of a doubt that it was the forerunner of Australia's tradition of wealthy powerful men being immature wankers.

It was this country's first and, to date, only armed overthrow of government, and it remains a salutary reminder of the historical principle that in high-level conflicts, the safest judgement is to hate everyone on both sides.

ESSAY QUESTIONS

1. Is rum really that good?
2. What is breadfruit? Do you know? Admit that you do not.
3. Have you ever ridden on a sheep's back? Is this a viable mode of transport for a modern economy?

Sail of the Century

In which two men in a boat discover the shape of things to come, and an infant nation finally gets a name

New South Wales was established, and Britain was well-pleased. The convicts were tucked away neatly, the rum was flowing and the sheep were happily growing their fleeces, blissfully unaware of their pivotal role in colonial power plays. Life in Sydney Cove was peaceful and pleasant, unless you were most of its inhabitants, in which case it was an unremitting nightmare, but those guys were mostly your disreputable types.

Yes, the little colony was proving a success, but that famed Anglo-Saxon wanderlust was creating an itch that had to be scratched. The more adventurous among the colonists were asking, 'Is that all there is?' Having settled the little patch of land around Port Jackson, they began to cast their eyes to the horizon, wondering what the hell else was out there. So while the soldiers profiteered and the convicts sweated, these hardy souls resolved to get up off their chaise longues and find out. Thus began the Age of Exploration in Australia, one of history's most fertile epochs of adventure, discovery and ignoring Indigenous populations. Explorers dashed in every direction a la *It's A Mad, Mad, Mad, Mad World*, keen to earn the title of 'Discoverer of (insert location that had been discovered about 40,000 years earlier here)', and therefore win fame and fortune and some serious petticoat action.

It is thanks to the brave explorers of colonial Australia that today several of us live outside Sydney, so assign credit and blame accordingly. The task of figuring out exactly what kind of lump of rock the First Fleet had landed on began early, because paintball hadn't been invented yet and there was nothing else to do.

Early on it was decided that proper Australian explorers, like girls going to the bathroom, came in pairs, and that has a lot to do with Messrs George Bass and Matthew Flinders, two visionaries who believed that a better world could be created, if only men of good heart would spend more time on boats. Some call the partnership of Bass and Flinders Australia's first great love story, but others say that's a pretty stupid way of looking at it.[35]

In many ways, the partnership of Bass and Flinders was a case of 'opposites attract'. Bass, a surgeon from Aswarby in Lincolnshire; Flinders, a surgeon's son from Donington in Lincolnshire – was there ever a more wackily mismatched pair? Bass with his white wig, Flinders with his black crewcut; Bass looking to the right in his portrait, Flinders to the left; the differences keep mounting up. Yet somehow these two peas in completely separate pods became friends while journeying to Australia, and upon discovering a mutual love of making maps, took the logical next step and decided to write an epic fantasy trilogy. Discovering that epic fantasy trilogies didn't exist yet, they concentrated instead on settling the vexed question of what shape Australia was.

Of course Australia wasn't yet called Australia, because young Flinders hadn't got around to telling everyone that this was what it was called. He was far too busy for that, as soon after his arrival he and

---

35 Australia's *real* first great love story, of course, was Des and Daphne.

Bass set out on their first expedition. It began on 26 October 1795, when the two men climbed into an eight-foot-long boat named the *Tom Thumb*, due to Bass's love of the music of Bob Dylan, and sailed it down to Botany Bay. From there they proceeded up the Georges River, and shook the world by proving beyond a shadow of a doubt that this river was slightly longer than some people had thought before. Their journey allowed them to ascertain the suitability of a settlement on the Georges' banks upstream. Two years later, this led to the foundation of Bankstown, which most scholars now believe to have been a mistake.

Flushed with success, Bass and Flinders realised with some excitement that the key to effective navigation was to have a boat called *Tom Thumb*, and so in March 1796 they set out again in the *Tom Thumb*, but not the same *Tom Thumb* as before. They had started a craze, and for a while people all over the world were calling their boats *Tom Thumb* with reckless abandon.

The voyage of the second *Tom Thumb* was a troubled one, as the policy of making journeys only in tiny, poorly equipped boats proved less a stroke of genius than Bass and Flinders had hoped. Still, they achieved their aim: to find out if Port Hacking existed. Upon arriving at Port Hacking, they discovered that it did – and, in honour of the discovery, named it Port Hacking after itself.

At this point, a rift appeared between the two bosom companions. They'd had an enormous amount of fun zipping up and down rivers and almost drowning, but Bass, who was three years older than Flinders and already had his driver's licence, felt the need to spread his wings. 'I think we should explore with other people,' he told Flinders.

'What?' Flinders replied, shocked. He'd thought everything was going so well.

'I'm just feeling really suffocated right now – I need some space.'

'We can get a bigger *Tom Thumb*. How about 12 feet this time?'

'No, Matthew, I … I need to find myself.'

'Can't you find yourself after we do another expedition?'

'There's no time, Matthew – I'm going to die at the age of 32, I really need to get a move on.'

'But why can't we go *together*?' Flinders whined. 'You know I get scared alone at night.'

'You don't understand,' Bass said sadly. 'I need to do this. I won't be away long, only a couple of years, sailing around, discovering some islands, maybe getting a strait named after me …'

'A-*ha*!' Flinders exploded, pointing an accusing finger. 'I knew it. This is all about the strait!'

'It's not like that,' stammered Bass. 'I want to have some time to myself.'

'*LIAR!* You want the strait all to yourself. You never did like my idea for the Matty and George Friends Forever Strait.'

'It's too long, Matthew.'

'What about the M&G Channel?'

'No.'

And so it was that George Bass hopped aboard a whaleboat and began his career as a single explorer, with six other men. He sailed all the way down the east coast to Western Port Bay, which he named in honour of his own lack of imagination. When in 1800, Port Phillip Bay was discovered just west of Western Port Bay, thus rendering the name kind of dumb, Bass was red with embarrassment; but they kept the name because it was already on the letterhead.

Bass's trip also backed up his belief that Van Diemen's Land was an island separated from the mainland by a strait. He reported this back to his superiors, with a note reading, 'So we better find a name for that strait, right? Hmm, dunno what we could name it? What's a good name for a strait discovered by Bass? Let me know if you guys have any ideas.'

But perhaps Bass's most important discovery on this expedition was that of the Kiama Blowhole, which vastly increased the contemporary scientific understanding of big wet holes. Without Bass, 600,000 tourists would not be getting drenched by freezing seawater every year, and that alone is testament to his greatness.

Of course, you couldn't keep Bass and Flinders apart for long: they went together like fish and chips, like a horse and carriage, like Bligh and breadfruit. Before long they were up to their old shenanigans again: Bass apologised to Flinders for breaking up with him, and Flinders confessed that he couldn't stay mad at that face. And so they were reunited, on board the *Norfolk*, a 25-ton sloop constructed on Norfolk Island, from Norfolk Island Pine – sadly, no record remains of how the ship got its name.

The *Norfolk*'s task was to make sure, once and for all, just in case, that Tasmania was an island. Sure, Bass had said it was, but Governor Hunter never really trusted Bass, because he'd caught him taking stationery home from the office, and he wanted the assurance that only a confirmation from Flinders would bring. Had they thought to open a book, they would have seen that Tasmania is *called* 'The Island State', which is a bit of a giveaway, but nobody thought to check, and hence much money was wasted on this pointless expedition.

During the voyage of the *Norfolk*, Bass and Flinders encountered many Indigenous inhabitants of Van Diemen's Land, but never bothered to stop and ask, 'So, is this an island or what?' because to be honest, they were grateful for the opportunity to get some quality time together and wanted the trip to last. Instead they approached an

Aboriginal man and gave him a swan, which he seemed to like.[36] They then stood around in the kind of awkward silence that is to be expected when men exchange swans with strangers. Today the incident of Bass and Flinders' swan-giving is almost forgotten, but modern students of history would do well to bear in mind this momentous event in the exploration of our island continent. Until that day, no explorer had ever given a swan to a Tasmanian Aboriginal person,[37] and the gesture changed the way we think about waterfowl as gifts forever, and may have led directly to the infamous incident of Strzelecki's Pelican.

The rest of the journey was fairly uneventful: spoiler alert, Tasmania turned out to totally be an island, and Bass and Flinders high-fived each other and bumped chests and exchanged boxes of Cadbury's Favourites. Flinders named the waters between the mainland and the island 'Bass Strait', because by that time he would have done anything to stop Bass dropping his clumsy hints.

Then, sadly, the rift reopened. Flinders was of the belief that there was still life in the partnership, with new lands to explore, new coastlines to map, new moonlit nights at sea to gaze into each other's eyes on. Bass, however, had different ambitions. 'Ever since I was a boy,' he wrote in a letter to his wife Elizabeth,[38] 'I have dreamed of one day sailing to Chile and never being seen again. I feel that in my mysterious disappearance lies the key to my restless search for destiny.' Sadly, Elizabeth never read this letter, as she found reading tedious and threw out all her mail unopened. But Bass proceeded nevertheless to set sail

36 The Detour required them to either give a swan to a stranger, or construct a tandem bicycle and deliver a bag of apples to a candlemaker, and the swan seemed less time-consuming.

37 And relatively few since.

38 Between 1750 and 1850, British law stated that at least 80 per cent of subjects of the Crown must be married to a woman called Elizabeth.

for South America, and then proceeded to vanish. He is remembered in the myriad places named for him: Bass Strait, the Bass Highway, Bass Point, Bass Hill, the Bass River, the Bass Guitar, Billy the Big-Mouthed Bass, and so on.

Flinders was sorry to see his old comrade go – but, let's be honest, not all that sorry. He was consumed more by that old passion: the shape of the continent. At the time, a variety of theories swirled as to what New Holland would look like from space. Some believed it was a perfect circle, while others were sure it was a circle with a small bump at the top. There were those who claimed the continent was the shape of a dog barking at a chicken, while a competing hypothesis declared it was 'the same exact shape as Italy, only longer'. And, of course, there was the famous Breadfruit Theory.[39] Flinders set out to prove all these armchair cartographers wrong, in the only way he knew how because there was no Google Maps in 1801: sailing around the edge and drawing pictures of everything he saw.

Flinders circumnavigated Australia in a ship called *The Investigator*, because he felt he had to spell everything out all the time: geez, Matty, give us some credit, will you? It was a vital mission, because at the same time that he was tracking the coastline, so was Captain Nicolas Baudin, sent by France to likewise find out the shape of New Holland. Flinders' superiors were extremely keen that he stay ahead of Baudin, whose scientific expedition they believed to be a covert attempt to claim new territory for the French. And if there was one thing that the British government loathed, despised and abominated, it was someone stealing *their* land before they could steal it from someone else.

The rivalries of state, however, were of no interest to men of science

39 Which convinced few people, given nobody knew what shape a breadfruit was either.

like Flinders and Baudin. They concerned themselves not with petty political pointscoring or diplomatic intrigues or a basic knowledge of current events. They were a couple of total ignoramuses, too lazy to educate themselves about the world around them, so they just paddled around in their stupid boats like idiots. God, I hate them.

Um, anyway, the point is, Flinders and Baudin met each other while sailing along the southern coast. Their meeting was cordial, and they exchanged information about their discoveries thus far – fairly similar information given they'd been discovering the same place, but it passed the time. The two men expressed mutual respect, which, in light of the fact that their nations were currently at war with each other, was quite remarkable and technically meant they were both traitors. In honour of the meeting, Flinders named the spot Encounter Bay, ignoring the Admiralty's suggestion of Port Slimy French Weasel.

Heading back to Sydney, Flinders then began his circumnavigation, sailing north to Queensland, west along the north coast and around the Gulf of Carpentaria.[40] Proceeding down the west coast, then back east along the south before sailing back up to Sydney Town, Flinders was finally able to assert, without fear of contradiction, that New Holland was shaped like a poorly made pikelet, ending the bitter debate for good. His survey of the coastline was not as exact as he'd hoped, however, as for much of the trip his ship was slowly disintegrating and his crew slowly dying. Six men died on the expedition, but their grieving families at least had the consolation of knowing they gave their lives in service of a goal that could have easily been achieved a bit later, if the ship had returned home so sick crew members could get medical aid, with no particular negative consequences for the cause of the science of navigation. Flinders' decision to press on with the circumnavigation

40 Named because of all the explorers who had longed to be close to it.

despite the ship's hull rotting away beneath him and men dropping like flies around him is one of the most gallant and inconsiderate actions in Australian naval history. Not that it was any picnic for the explorer himself: the crew's affliction was dysentery, which meant the healthy men on board spent all their time mopping the decks and spraying Glen 20 about the place.

Flinders did future Australians an enormous service, of course – without his efforts, nobody would know what the coastline of Australia looks like. Unless someone else charted it, which definitely would've happened in a very short amount of time. But then you could say that about every explorer, really. That's why all explorers ever wasted their lives.

That was not the end of Flinders' career. He wasn't like Bass, with his mad dreams of unsolved disappearances. Flinders had more humble ambitions: he wished only to be imprisoned by the French. And would a man of his work ethic and initiative ever stop until he'd achieved his aim? Of course not! With a fierce inner drive that we would do well to learn from, young Matthew set out for England in 1803 and cannily put in at Mauritius (or as it was known then, Dodo Adventure Park) for repairs. Unfortunately, Mauritius was at the time controlled by France, and because 1803 was a year with a '1' in it, France and England were at war. The governor of Mauritius, suspicious of this cocky, bad haircut-wearing Englishman, had his suspicions confirmed when Flinders refused to have dinner with him and his wife:[41] in what could qualify as the worst episode of *Come Dine With Me* ever, Flinders was detained for being a possible British spy and forced to remain on Mauritius for more than six years, with nothing but the antics of

41 Real history: this actually happened. Amazing how many significant historical events happened because most people are petty little douchebags.

the crab-eating macaques to amuse him. It was a difficult period for Flinders, but he was finally paroled in 1810, a few months before the British took Mauritius from the French, leading to Flinders' legendary bon mot: 'Suck a fat one, Napoleon!'

After his time in prison, which was still probably more fun than living in Sydney in the 19th century, Flinders returned to England and worked on his book, titled *A Voyage to Terra Australis, undertaken for the purpose of completing the discovery of that vast country, and prosecuted in the years 1801, 1802, and 1803, in His Majesty's ship The* Investigator, *and subsequently in the armed vessel* Porpoise *and* Cumberland Schooner. *With an account of the shipwreck of the* Porpoise, *arrival of the* Cumberland *at Mauritius, and imprisonment of the commander during six and a half years in that island*. Four years later, he finished writing the title, but sadly the effort was too much, and he died the day after it was published, a tragedy that led directly to laws limiting the titles of books to 50 words or less.

What is the legacy of Matthew Flinders? He was probably the most influential explorer in Australian history. Certainly heaps more influential than George Bass, who in comparison was kind of a loser, you know? I mean no judgement, but you feel like he could've made a bit more of himself. Flinders and Bass were basically the Simon and Garfunkel of colonial exploration: one guy with a sweet voice and memorable hair, and one guy who, if we're honest, did all the work.

Flinders' influence, like Bass's less impressive influence, is seen in the number of landmarks named after him: the Flinders Ranges, Flinders University, Flinders Street Station, the street that Flinders Street Station is on, Flinders Peak, Flinders Chase, Flinders Fish Fingers, and so forth. Also there is a genus of citrus trees called *Flindersia*, in recognition of Flinders' renowned resemblance to a tree, and a 'Flinders bar' is the iron bar used to compensate for the effect of a ship's magnetism on a compass – that's an actual history and science fact that you can use to amaze people at parties.

Also, the cafe at the State Library of New South Wales is named after Matthew Flinders' cat, and not even Christopher Columbus can claim that.[42]

But, of course, the biggest legacy that Flinders left Australia is the name of the country itself. The term *Terra Australis*, meaning 'southern land' and derived from the popular Icehouse song, had been used for centuries to refer to the mysterious 'southern continent' that had long been speculated about and that would eventually cause such enormous disappointment when it was found. The name 'Australia' had also been used, but it was Flinders who campaigned for it to be made the official name of the continent, and for formal recognition of the fact that 'New Holland' is a stupid name. If it hadn't been for Flinders, Australia might still be called New Holland today, or something even worse, like, I don't know, Bassland or Macarthuria.

Sadly, Flinders didn't live to see the official adoption of the name, but that only increases his street cred: nobody cool ever lives to see things they'd like to.[43]

ESSAY QUESTIONS

1. What shape do you think Australia is? How could it be improved?
2. Would you prefer to have a) a strait named after you; b) an island named after you; or c) dysentery?

---

42 Although the disabled toilets at Frankston TAFE are named after Columbus's pet turtle.

43 E.g. Van Gogh only became famous after he died, Heath Ledger won a posthumous Oscar, Vlad the Impaler never saw Francis Ford Coppola's *Dracula*, etc.

Opening the Mystery Box

In which varied and diverse adventurers resolve to unlock the secrets of the wide brown land, but find it full of horrors and rivers

Of course, Bass and Flinders did some nice stuff around the edges of Australia, but even in the early days of European settlement, people had noticed that the continent had a middle bit, and thought it might be a good idea to see what was in it. These brave men[44] opened up the heart of the continent to future generations, who weren't exactly impressed, but grudgingly appreciated the effort.

The Blue Mountains

The early settlers of New South Wales, huddling around Sydney Cove and Parramatta, couldn't help but notice one interesting fact about their new home: there were some big frigging mountains over there.

Of course, time would tell that in fact they weren't big mountains at all. They were actually quite small, unimpressive mountains, so measly and pathetic that when Australia got together with other continents and the conversation turned to mountains, it would always try to change the subject to prevent the other continents making fun

44 Women rarely felt the need to go exploring, due to their lack of toxic masculine insecurity.

of it. In comparison with other landmasses, Australia barely even has mountains: we're still wearing training bras.

But the point is, the people who'd recently arrived in the great flat southern land were puny little English folk, and to them those mountains looked pretty damn big and not at all the sort of thing you'd want to try to go up without stretching your quads out thoroughly beforehand. They also looked blue, which was weird because they totally weren't.[45] More importantly, the Great Dividing Range had the annoying habit of, you know, dividing – it separated the restless denizens of New South Wales from whatever was on the other side.

And that was the rub: nobody really knew what was on the other side. They asked the Aboriginal people if they knew, but the Aboriginal people refused to tell, because things had been very tense between them lately, what with the attempted genocide and all.

It was an important question to be resolved, because on the other side of those mountains could be *anything*. Maybe there was a vast desert in which men could heroically die. Maybe there were lush jungles in which men could heroically fight lions and tigers and then die. Maybe there was a frozen tundra on which men could heroically freeze until they died. Or perhaps there were more profitable lands. Fertile country to farm? Mighty forests to log? Rich seams of precious metal or gemstones to mine? Magical lands full of fabulous beasts, noble elves and dashing pirates? The settlers just didn't know.

Of course, there's an argument to be made for maintaining a sense of mystery, and many reasonable people believe the settlers should have stayed where they were and enjoyed the wonderful uncertainty of what

---

45 Scientists believe the blue appearance of the mountains is caused by something called 'mie scattering': the scattering of ultraviolet radiation by atmospheric particles. But frankly this sounds made up – more likely the people looking at them were high.

was over the mountains. It would certainly make modern life a lot more exciting, and it would have brought Adelaide a lot closer. If nobody ever crossed the Blue Mountains, Adelaide would probably now be somewhere in Parramatta, which would make it much more convenient when you want to visit the pandas in the zoo.

But they were a mercenary lot in Old Sydney Town,[46] and there was much interest in whether the land to the west of the mountains could provide lucrative business opportunities. Also, the colony was rapidly filling up with sheep and cows and various other disgusting animals, and the smell was becoming intolerable. So it was decided that somebody had better pop over the mountains and check it out.

Back then, this wasn't as simple a matter as it is now. Folks in the 18th and 19th centuries didn't have the jetpacks and magnetic boots and electronic automatic grappling hooks that I assume present-day mountaineers have. In the 19th century, scaling mountains involved three basic steps:

1. Walk.
2. Keep walking until you notice you're higher than you were before.
3. Die, probably.

So it was no task for the fainthearted. But then, neither was settling a big, dry, horrible place like Australia, so there were plenty of hardy souls willing to take the task on. The first to try was Lieutenant William Dawes, who took a bunch of fairly unmotivated men on a 24-kilometre trek before turning back because their feet were sore. Dawes was so traumatised by the experience that he went straight out and became the governor of Sierra Leone, an incredibly reckless act.

46 The actual one, not the theme park. Which is now also, ironically enough, history.

Next came William Paterson, one of Major Francis Grose's First Mounted Insufferable Gits Regiment, who would later gain fame as acting governor following Bligh's removal in the War of the Two Jerks. Paterson led an expedition up the Grose River[47] in 1793, hoping that it ran through the mountains. When he discovered that it did not, he became quite dispirited, vowing that he would never again involve himself in the deceptive behaviour of mountains. He did, however, go on to explore quite a few more rivers. 'At least with rivers you know where you are,' he peevishly said.

Despite Paterson's failure, Henry Hacking tried again the following year, and claimed he got 30 kilometres further inland than any other white man. But we've only got his word for it, and if you want to trust the word of a man who was convicted of stealing from Matthew Flinders' ship, go ahead. (Yeah. There's a twist. Didn't see that coming, did you? Now who looks stupid, Hacking fans?)

Matthew Everingham got further than his predecessors in 1795, when he took the novel approach of looking for a way through the Blue Mountains, rather than what had been the preferred method up till then of walking in a straight line until you hit a big bit of rock, turning around and going home. Everingham's party tried a variety of different routes, but found that no matter where they went, there were more mountains. This raised the possibility that maybe there was nothing on the other side of the mountains – maybe the entire continent was mountains all the way to the west coast. This would have been very cool and interesting, but still explorers insisted on finding a way over.

Ex-convict John Wilson set off in 1798 and found a way to the other side, ending up near Goulburn sometime after the rest of his party had given up and turned back. This appeared to be a breakthrough, but

47 Named for Major Grose, who like the river was famously wet.

Wilson had actually not crossed the mountains, but found another way around, like tunnelling or hang-gliding or something.[48]

Frenchman Francis Barrallier had another stab at it in 1802, but achieved nothing except an extremely whiny travel diary in which he just would not stop bitching about the food and his feet and all the waterfalls that kept getting in his way.

Finally there was George Caley, who declared – because he was quite up himself – that the mountains were not impassable and set out to prove himself right in 1804. In attempting to cross the Blue Mountains, Caley formed certain forthright opinions of the area, reflected in the names he gave to places he discovered, including Devils Wilderness, Dismal Dingle, Pincushion Hill, Skeleton Rocks, Pain in the Arse Ridge, Sonuvabitch Valley, the Kill Me Now Cliffs and What's the Deal With All These Fucking Mountains National Park. Caley gave up when, after scaling Mount Banks,[49] he looked upon the vista before him and, seeing only a bunch more mountains, decided that mountaineering was literally the stupidest thing in the whole world.

The Blue Mountains-crossing business went into a lull at this point: nobody tried the trip for another ten years, and fortunately this time they weren't such a bunch of do-nothing wusses.

Blaxland, Wentworth and Lawson

Gregory Blaxland, after whom the Blaxploitation genre of films was named, was born into wealth in Kent, England. His family were friends of Sir Joseph Banks, because there was a rule that every single person who did anything in Australia before 1850 had to be a friend of Sir

48 Nobody ever pointed out that if it was so easy to get around the mountains, there wasn't much need to find a way over them at all. Not big thinkers, the early colonists.

49 Named after George Banks, hero of Mary Poppins.

Joseph Banks.[50] Young Gregory emigrated to New South Wales after being promised free land and convict servants, which was a pretty cynical reason if you ask me.

Blaxland became a prosperous businessman in the colony, achieving particular success in the meat trade, but by 1813 was facing the problem of cattle overcrowding. In need of more grazing land, he asked Governor Macquarie if he could please duck over to the other side of the Blue Mountains and grab a bit of space to become even more fabulously rich on. Macquarie said sure, because he was quite keen on making contact with the fairy folk himself, so Blaxland made preparation to become a famous explorer as well as a prominent cow-pimp.

The first obstacle Greg ran up against was the fact that he had no idea what he was doing. He had never climbed a mountain in his life, and he had to be shown some detailed diagrams before he fully grasped what a mountain was. His first idea was to cross the Blue Mountains on cow-back, but some kind friends dissuaded him from the notion. What he needed, Blaxland realised, was a right-hand man, a loyal second to provide assistance and support and advice as to what these big rocky things they were walking on were. He turned to Lieutenant William Lawson. Lawson had studied to be a surveyor, but went into the military after discovering that nobody actually knew what a surveyor does. He joined the NSW Corps and was sent to Norfolk Island to help keep Colleen McCullough under control. Blaxland recruited Lawson to help with the crossing due to the latter's experience with walking long distances and not falling into gorges, and Lawson served him well, providing invaluable advice on matters such as which way was up and whether kangaroos are poisonous.

With Lawson's rugged military bearing and Blaxland's fat well-

50 Voted 'World's Most Popular Botanist' by *WHO Magazine* 40 years running.

fed wallet, all the expedition needed was the energising kick of young blood. Enter William Charles Wentworth, the son of a highwayman and a teenage convict who'd met on the Second Fleet and somehow managed not only to not die, but also to engage in acts of horizontal Greco-Romanism on board ship. Like many career criminals, Wentworth's father became a rich landowner in the new colony[51] and sent his son to England for an education, because the teachers in New South Wales were too beholden to the unions. Returning to Sydney, Wentworth won Australia's first official horserace, or at least sat on the winner of Australia's first official horserace while it won.

So it was no wonder that when Blaxland and Lawson were seeking a well-educated jockey to join their mountaineering party, they looked to W.C. Wentworth as the motivated young self-starter they needed.

While crossing the Blue Mountains, Blaxland, Wentworth and Lawson all kept journals of their journey, which means that we have an excellent record of the day-to-day proceedings of the expedition, and also that all three of these men were giant nerds. Wentworth's journal is mostly about soil and rocks, so I guess you could Google it if that's what you're into. Blaxland's is the most interesting of the three journals, containing inflammatory passages such as this:

> *On Tuesday, May 11, 1813, Mr. Gregory Blaxland, Mr. William Wentworth, and Lieutenant Lawson, attended by four servants, with five dogs, and four horses laden with provisions, ammunition, and other necessities, left Mr. Blaxland's farm at South Creek, for the purpose of endeavouring to effect a passage over the Blue Mountains, between the Western River, and the River Grose.*

51 Not a trend that has slowed in the years since.

You can imagine how that got under some people's skin! There were also downright racy sequences, like:

> *On Monday, the 17th, having laden the horses with as much grass as could be put on them, in addition to their other burdens, they moved forward along the path which they had cleared and marked, about six miles and a half.*

Now, if *that* doesn't get you feeling frisky …

As noted above, the trip began on 11 May 1813, with the three pioneers and their servants, horses and dogs – who were of roughly equal social status at the time – looking westward with vast tracts of prime grazing land swimming in their heads. Their first major hurdle came on the second day, when they unexpectedly encountered some bushes, an eventuality none of them were trained for. Already the expedition was proving more difficult than anticipated: not only because of the bushes, but also because the horses kept falling over and the dogs were killing kangaroos, souring relations between the explorers and the local marsupial community.

Despite the early vegetational setbacks, Blaxland, Lawson and Wentworth proved an unstoppable team – or, at least, unstoppable by mountains, which was more than the losers previously mentioned could say. They succeeded by travelling on the ridges, rather than through the valleys, and since then almost everyone trying to go over mountains has done so by going over the mountains, thanks to the trio's revolutionary approach.

Not that their mission was an easy one: there were many hardships to endure. At one point, the men were forced to consider eating their horses, but decided to eat the food they'd brought with them instead. At other times they ate the kangaroos that the dogs kept killing, which may account for the expedition's low fat content and minimal contribution to greenhouse emissions. Other highlights of the expedition included:

- The time they heard an emu
- The time they heard some dingos
- The time they saw a wombat's footprints
- The time they took Sunday off and got really depressed about the whole thing
- The time they got annoyed by prickles

It was, in a nutshell, non-stop action. The journal entries of these three brave men provide a vivid first-hand portrait of what it's like to walk up hills, then down hills, then up hills again, and repeat the process for several weeks.

On 22 May, the party seemed on the brink of a breakthrough when they reached the summit, or 'top', of a mountain from which they could see open country to the west. They found it impossible to go that way, however, due to a great wall of rock that stood in their way. Upon surveying the barrier, Blaxland gave utterance to what has become his trademark phrase: 'Bugger.' But Gregory Blaxland had not become obscenely rich by running to his mother every time he saw a big rock, and after several attempts they managed to get past the stone wall. By 31 May, their spirits had revived so much that Blaxland nearly got lost chasing a kangaroo, leading to the local Indigenous tribes granting him the honorific 'Great White Toddler'.

He can be excused his joie de vivre, though, given that 31 May was the day the expedition reached a distinctive sugarloaf-shaped mountain, and after a brief delay while Wentworth tried to eat it, looked westward and saw the country spread out before them.

'We've found the way across the mountains!' exclaimed Blaxland in delight.

'God be praised!' Lawson expectorated.

'Tastes like rocks,' Wentworth exulted.

All that remained was to name this now-famous peak, on which the mission came to fruition. 'Maybe we could call it Mount Lawson,' said Lawson.

'Shut your neck,' Blaxland explained.

And so the three men – and their servants, whose identities, as working-class people, aren't very important – made their return from Mount Blaxland to announce to an eager public that the path through the range had been discovered, and all in the colony would now be free to have their beef industry monopolised by Blaxland to an even greater degree.

Blaxland, Wentworth and Lawson were three of Australian history's most significant pioneers. If it hadn't been for them, to be honest, someone else would've done it instead. But in the immortal words of Manning Clark, just because honey is easy to make doesn't mean we can't admire a bee. (What did he mean by this? It's a mystery.) The point is, after the intrepid trio found their way across the Blue Mountains, myriad possibilities opened up for the young colony. No longer did the New South Welsh have to cling to the coast like a baby lizard riding its mother: now they could really stretch their legs and get a bit of breathing space. Cows and sheep and wheat and feral rabbits spread across the countryside like wildfire – as, frequently, did wildfire.

Today, each of the three mountain-crossers are remembered in the names of numerous places: Blaxland lives on in Blaxland Creek, Blaxland Waterfall and the town of Blaxland, and by his honorific of 'The Father of the Big Merino'. Wentworth is commemorated at Mount Wentworth, Lake Wentworth, Wentworth Falls and Wentworth Women's Correctional Centre. And, of course, Lawson was honoured in the naming of one of Australia's hardest-working fast bowlers.

We salute Blaxland, Wentworth and Lawson as three of the noblest sculptors who carved a nation out of this raw slab of rock, and whenever we go into the Blue Mountains and see how little they are, their achievement looks a bit less impressive, so we don't salute them that much if we're honest.

Hume and Hovell

Many explorers who are lauded in the history books have one thing in common: a good sense of direction. So it's a nice change of pace to look at Hume and Hovell, one of Australia's greatest and most frequently wrong partnerships.

In 1824, Hamilton Hume met William Hovell, and the two men instantly formed a deep and abiding mutual dislike. Like Bass and Flinders, they were two very different men: Hovell, a rugged, experienced seaman who enjoyed sailing and incorrect navigation; and Hume, a cocky young explorer prodigy whose hobbies included bushwalking and taking credit for the work of others. There were bound to be fireworks. And yet, they agreed to work with each other in the cause of furthering knowledge of the unknown regions of the continent, until such time as they couldn't stand each other any longer.[52]

Governor Brisbane, who was, confusingly, the governor in Sydney, ordered Hume and Hovell to find new grazing land in the south and to find out where New South Wales's western rivers flowed. 'Do they

52 Just like the *MasterChef* judges.

flow to the sea? To the sky? Into a giant's enormous saucepan? I need to *KNOW*!' Brisbane shouted angrily at Hume and Hovell, who eyed each other awkwardly.

Shaking hands, the two men agreed to bitch and snipe at each other all the way to Western Port, and set out from Hume's house to discover just how much scope there was in New South Wales for the destruction of the natural environment. They were accompanied by six convicts: six desperate men who for their crimes had been sentenced to listening to Hume and Hovell for several months.

They struck their first obstacle in the shape of the Murrumbidgee River, which they assessed as extremely dangerous – being, as it was, full of water. Hume suggested building a raft. 'You're an idiot,' said Hovell, who wanted instead to construct a giant slingshot to carry them across the raging rapids. In the end Hume built his raft, and Hovell went into a sulk.

Their next trial came when the party found their way blocked by mountains, and Hume and Hovell argued bitterly over which way to take to get past them: Hume thought they should follow an arc around to the east, whereas Hovell suggested the invention of the helicopter.

The disagreement grew so intense that the explorers resolved to split up, and this immediately turned the expedition into an episode of *I Love Lucy*. They divided their equipment and supplies and, after consulting their bibles, decided to cut their tent in half. Hume and Hovell then fought over the party's one frying pan till it fell apart. One man took the pan, the other took the handle, which seemed like a fair compromise because by this stage everyone involved had clearly lost their minds.

I mean, I didn't even make that up. That actually happened: two of the most significant explorers in Australian history had a fight over a frying pan. Can you believe that? It goes to show that just because someone's in a history book, it doesn't mean he wasn't the biggest moron you've ever heard of. History, sadly, doesn't record whether the two men also painted a big line down the middle of their tent and had to stay on their own sides of it, or agreed to do each other's jobs for a week to see who really had it tougher. Many historians believe that at one point Hume copied off Hovell's maths test, and there is some anecdotal evidence that at least one of them inadvertently ended up taking two different girls to the big dance.[53]

Eventually Hovell returned to the party, possibly after realising that a frying pan handle by itself is completely useless. The journey continued to be unbearably tense, with Hume accusing Hovell of using his toothbrush, and Hovell claiming that Hume kept touching him. Things came to a head when the party again came across a river, something that by now was becoming a theme of the journey. 'What is this, freaking River Month?' Hovell complained in a letter home, before going on to detail how loudly Hume breathed through his nose whenever Hovell was trying to read at night.

The river they had reached was the widest yet, and Hume named it 'Hume's River', which was a terrible mistake given that it was really called 'the Murray River'. He decided to, again, make a boat to cross the water, and again Hovell objected. Hume understood his partner's concerns and engaged him in sensitive and constructive dialogue, telling him, 'If you don't do what I tell you, I'll throw you in!' Hovell saw Hume's point and agreed that he may not have considered all sides of the issue. Also, he knew he'd never survive in the wilderness with just a frying-pan handle.

---

53 Legend has it that the *Hume and Hovell Christmas Special* was especially entertaining.

And so they crossed the mighty Murray and entered Victoria. Obviously, at that time, the explorers didn't know that this was Victoria, but Hume's journal does record that after the crossing the coffee seemed to get much better.

They travelled through the Victorian Alps, traversing terrain that would be covered in a much less passive-aggressive way years later by Pawel Strzelecki, the Polish nobleman who became Australia's most difficult-to-pronounce explorer. Hume and Hovell were responsible for naming many of the features in this part of the countryside: the Goulburn River, after the almost completely uninteresting Major Frederick Goulburn; Mount Buffalo, after their favourite species of cattle; the Ovens River, after the mysteriously well-stocked commercial kitchens they found on its banks; and Mount Disappointment, after Hovell's children.

It was at this point that Hume and Hovell made the classic blunder of people travelling to Western Port: not travelling to Western Port. Exactly why the mistake was made has long been a matter of conjecture: Was it damaged instruments? Was it damaged explorers? Were they too busy fighting over kitchen utensils to notice where they were? Some say the mistake was made by Hovell when calculating longitude, while others say it was made by Hume when deciding to bring Hovell on the trip.

To be fair to Hovell, the coastline of Australia is extremely long, and it's fairly hard to hit one specific part of it without being, like, a professional explorer or someone who knows how to use a compass or something. And he did get within a couple of hundred kilometres, which is probably better than you or I could do unless we were trying. If you were looking at a map, the distance might only be about a centimetre, so if you didn't understand how maps work, it was a very easy mistake to make. Did renowned explorer and experienced sailor William Hovell understand how maps work? History does not record.

Wherever the blame lies,[54] the party ended up at Corio Bay, on the far side of Port Phillip Bay. Overjoyed with the lush and fertile territory they found, they reported back that Western Port was an ideal place to settle and farm. This news was received rapturously by the authorities, who established a settlement there in 1826, and then abandoned it several months later upon finding out that Western Port was a terrible place to settle and farm. Confused, Hovell went back to Western Port for a reappraisal and found it hauntingly unfamiliar.

Some people consider Hume and Hovell's expedition to be a bit of a stuff-up, and even go so far as to suggest that explorers should be able to go in the right direction. But the pair's accidental Corio Bay detour eventually led to the foundation of the city of Geelong, so the mistake, though embarrassing at the time, ended up being a huge boon for the decorative bollard industry.

As for Hume and Hovell themselves, they both went on to live long and productive lives of hating each other. In 1853, almost 30 years after the frying-pan incident, Hovell gave some speeches in Geelong in his capacity as Accidental Idiot Father of the City. Hume heard reports that in those speeches, Hovell had claimed credit for the expedition. Many would have thought that, considering how the expedition went, you'd be happy to let someone else take the credit for it – but Hume was incandescent with rage. So angry was he that he proceeded to carry out the most extreme act of malice that a 19th-century man could undertake: he published a pamphlet.

Hume's *A Brief Statement of Facts in Connection with an Overland Expedition from Lake George to Port Phillip in 1824*, published in 1855,

54 With Hovell.

caused quite a sensation, pamphlets being bizarrely popular at the time. It went into three editions, a huge achievement even for the Golden Age of Pamphletry.

In response, Hovell brought out the big guns, publishing not one but two pamphlets. *Reply to A Brief Statement of Facts in Connection with an Overland Expedition from Lake George to Port Phillip in 1824* and the slightly more creatively titled *Answer to the Preface to the Second Edition of Mr Hamilton Hume's 'A Brief Statement of Facts'* were as incendiary and shocking as the pamphlet to which they were replying, and today stand as testament to these two proud explorers' passionate refusal to move on from anything.

They also stand as testament to the weird obsession people in the past had with pamphlets. Look at pretty much any historical period before 1900 and you'll find it infested with irritable men throwing pamphlets at one another. Sometimes they fought duels, but if they couldn't find pistols at short notice, they'd write a pamphlet. Sometimes they fought duels *over* the pamphlets.[55] Modern-day people, whose experience with pamphlets is mainly restricted to retirement home advertisements and STI awareness, can often find it difficult to understand just how dull and annoying historical figures were. A glance at *A Brief Statement of Facts in Connection with an Overland Expedition from Lake George to Port Phillip in 1824* may enlighten them, both to the nature of life in the colonial era, and to Hamilton Hume's flexible definition of the word 'brief'.

In the end, the story of Hume and Hovell is one of adventure and discovery that helped to expand possibilities for future generations, but

55 American Founding Father Alexander Hamilton famously wrote a pamphlet about how he cheated on his wife, and he was then shot in a duel by the vice-president in a very good demonstration of how mental the past was.

it is also a tragedy about the failure of two proud men to work together and agree on an effective roster system for the sharing of frying pans. In their exploration and bickering, though, they helped build a nation and, at the same time, created the template for the casting of *X Factor* judges, so we owe them a hell of a lot.

John Batman

John Batman's greatest achievement is the foundation of Melbourne. Born to English parents at Rosehill near Parramatta, he dreamt from an early age of establishing a place where people of sensitivity could meet and paint on walls and reassure each other that things definitely weren't better in Sydney.

As a young man, Batman travelled to Van Diemen's Land, where he became a grazier, which in modern times means a person engaged in pastoral farming, but in the 19th century apparently referred to someone who spent most of his time shooting and capturing Indigenous people.[56] Batman quickly gained a proud reputation as one of that colony's foremost massacrers of Aboriginal people, and thus contributed to the rich Tasmanian culture developing at the time. He was a prominent fighter in the Black War of 1830, which arose from a dispute between British settlers, who wanted more land to farm on, and the original Tasmanians, who wanted not to be murdered all the time. For Batman, who was passionately committed to his people's traditional cultural practices – which included murder, as well as wrongful imprisonment and grand larceny – the refusal to allow themselves to be wiped out in an orderly fashion was an outrage, and he fought bravely for his beliefs. There are those who believe there was something unethical about Batman's career as a hired killer, but to be

56 Another word for a person who did this in the 19th century was 'Englishman'.

fair, records indicate that he didn't only kill Indigenous people: he also believed that he owned them. So there's nuance there.

Following the Black War, Batman continued ticking off his Historical Horrors Bucket List by contracting syphilis. Many historians now consider him to have been one of the most influential venereal disease-ridden mass murderers in Australian history.[57] Having thus established his credentials as an authentic frontier psychopath, Batman headed back to the mainland, eager to find more spacious acres on which to graze livestock and gun down people of different races.

Exploring Port Phillip in 1835, he came upon the site of current-day Melbourne and, noticing the fertile soil and tram tracks, wrote in his diary, 'This will be the place for a Village', which was extremely farsighted of him given the cinema industry hadn't even got off the ground yet. He never wrote, 'This will be the place for a city', which suggests that after Batman's arrival things got really out of hand.

The land was already occupied by the Kulin people, so obviously Batman was determined to pay a fair price for it. Ha-ha, just kidding! But he did at least negotiate a treaty with the Kulin, which for a man who up till then had separated Aboriginal people into two categories – possessions and clay pigeons – represented a kind of progress.

The treaty was negotiated in present-day Northcote, probably after a poetry slam. Batman proposed to rent[58] the land in return for an annual fee of 40 blankets, 30 axes, 100 knives, 50 scissors, 30 mirrors, 200 handkerchiefs, 100 pounds of flour and six shirts (interestingly, economists estimate that this remains the total value of Melbourne today). The Kulin, possibly thinking it was a reasonable price for whatever the white guy was babbling on about, agreed to receive the

57 At least until the premiere of *Big Brother*.

58 Steal.

goods in exchange for Batman not bothering them anymore. When they came back the next day and found the whites building convenience stores and installing public art, they started to get a very bad feeling about things.

But at least they had their payment for the land. Or at least they *did*, until Governor Richard Bourke ruled the treaty invalid. Under English law, there was basis for the claim that the land belonged to its owners, and so it was decided that instead of Batman's Treaty, Melbourne would be settled on the usual British terms: under which the British got the land and some of the natives got to live. Although many settlers arrived soon afterwards to develop the city, it is Batman who holds the honour of the city's original establishment. The man himself settled at Batman's Hill at the end of Collins Street,[59] and in 1839 he died of the syphilis that had crippled and disfigured him in his final years. Thus ended the romantic and noble tale of the foundation of Melbourne.

Batman was responsible for sowing the seeds of what became one of the world's great cities, sort of. And if he was a flawed individual,[60] he deserves credit for the vision that allowed him to make such an indelible mark on the nation.

Also, and let's not beat around the bush here: his name was 'Batman'. Can you believe that? It's to this nation's great and lasting shame that we do not make a bigger deal about the fact that one of our country's early pioneers was literally called 'Batman'. When he first founded Melbourne, he called it 'Batmania'. It was renamed 'Melbourne' after the British prime minister, which is, without a skerrick of doubt, the most idiotic thing that has ever been done in the history of the world: like changing 'Castle Grayskull' to 'East Burwood'. Imagine having a

59 Not the good end. The other end.

60 And apparently most of the people he killed thought he was, a bit.

city called Batmania and deciding to *change its name* – what kind of halfwit would do that? Governor Richard Bourke, probably, the silly Irish git.

If you live in Melbourne, I want you to think about the fact that you could be living in Batmania, and I want you to weep for the tragedies that history's unfathomable chaos inflict upon us all.[61] I mean, really. What might have been. The tourism opportunities alone from having the city of Batmania in our country could've ensured a federal budget surplus in perpetuity.

That's the story of Australia's explorers in a nutshell: missed opportunities and failures of imagination all over the shop. And yet, it may also be said that to these brave adventurers, we owe a great debt. At least I think it may be said. I read it somewhere, once.

ESSAY QUESTIONS

1. How do you pronounce 'Strzelecki'? Use only one side of the paper.
2. If you were in charge, would you rename Melbourne 'Batmania'? If not, why do you suck?

61 The new town was also briefly called 'Batville', which isn't quite as great as Batmania, but would still have been *AWESOME*.

I'm an Incompetent Explorer, Get Me Out of Here!

In which courage and ineptitude join forces to tell a story of heroism and tragedy, and two unlucky men discover that camels are no substitute for commonsense when you're in the desert

'Burke,' croaked William John Wills, his dry cracked throat barely able to get the words out.

'Yes, Wills?' Robert O'Hara Burke, weak and exhausted himself, clutched his friend's hand, eager to hear what he had to say at this time of utmost crisis.

'Come closer, Burke.'

'I don't want to, Wills. You don't smell very good.'

'Burke ... I want you to leave me behind.'

'Okay.' Burke nodded and tried to stand, but Wills kept holding on to his hand.

'Burke, I don't want you to feel bad. It's alright. For your own sake, go on without me.'

'Yes, I will,' Burke replied, tugging feebly to break the grip.

'No arguments, Burke!' Wills insisted. 'I don't want to hear your noble objections. I know you don't want to leave me, but you must.'

'Yep, you're right. Bye.'

Wills's eyes filled with tears. 'You are too good to me, old friend. If you cannot bear to tear yourself away, I suppose I cannot make you go.'

Burke didn't hear him say that: he'd already left.

Nobody could have foreseen this catastrophic conclusion ten months ago when the Burke and Wills expedition set out from Melbourne. Or to put it another way, pretty much anyone could have foreseen it, but they were all very positive people who didn't like to dwell on the gloomy side of exploration.

The object of the expedition was to travel from Melbourne north all the way to the Gulf of Carpentaria, crossing the entire continent and finding out what the hell was in the big scary middle bit of Australia. Whether it was an inland sea, a huge glittering city or a string of violently erupting volcanoes, one thing was for sure: it wasn't any of those things. But still, it seemed important at the time to find out more about it, because the maps looked untidy with blank spaces all over the place. Another motivation was Victoria's desire to be the first colony to explore the interior, and show those snobbish New South Welsh just who had the most liveable colony. In New South Wales they found this kind of cute.

Planning for the expedition fell to the Exploration Committee of the Royal Society of Victoria. Calling for offers of interest for the position of expedition leader, the committee received numerous applications from experienced explorers, but found their experience and qualifications show-offy and gauche.[62] 'Wouldn't it be better,' said the committee, 'if we chose someone who was less boastful and arrogant about his exploring abilities, because he had none?' And with

62 An approach that survives today in the preselection process of the Australian Labor Party.

this principle of the humble incompetent in mind, they selected Robert O'Hara Burke.

It wasn't that Burke was a man of no talents: it was just that none of his talents involved exploring. Born in Ireland, he had served in the Austrian Army, the Irish Constabulary and the colonial police force, but in his heart he had always harboured a secret desire to one day get a job doing something he had no idea how to do. The committee thought him eminently suitable to lead the inland exploration, not being deterred even when Burke referred to the expedition's camels as 'the ugliest dogs I have ever seen'. (These camels, incidentally, had been purchased from India and were stabled at Parliament House in Melbourne before the expedition set out. To this day, Victoria has maintained the tradition of keeping camels in Parliament, occasionally even elevating them to premier.)

George Landells was made second-in-command of the expedition in recognition of the fact that he was the man who'd brought the camels, and in the position of third-in-command, astronomer and surveyor, was placed William John Wills, a doctor's son from Devon with a thirst for knowledge and an insatiable desire to be subordinated to those less qualified than himself.

On 20 August 1860, the Victorian Exploring Expedition (VEE) set off, with 19 men, 23 horses, six wagons, 26 camels and an all-embracing atmosphere of doom. They left Royal Park around 4pm, and several minutes later one of the wagons broke down. By midnight they had reached Essendon, where two more wagons broke down. Based on his prior experience of exploration, Burke considered that everything was going pretty well.

As they kept slogging their way north through heavy rains, poor roads and terrain completely unsuitable for camels, God became frustrated at the party's failure to realise that He really, really didn't want the expedition to happen. 'What do I have to do,' the Supreme Being asked in exasperation, 'drop some freaking locusts on them?' He refrained from doing so, although most historians are agreed that a plague of locusts would probably have improved the trip: it certainly couldn't have made it any worse, and maybe they could have asked the locusts for directions.

The expedition's progress wasn't made any speedier by Burke's firm commitment to a hyperactive Human Resources Department. Espousing the principle that workers are more efficient when under constant threat of unemployment, he kept up a regular schedule of firing and hiring. This ensured that Burke rarely became bored with any of his colleagues' company, but whether it made for a more harmonious group experience is up for debate.

Burke was also worried about the expense of the hired wagons, so he offset this cost by sacking more men, which resulted in one of them challenging him to a fight. Things were certainly going swimmingly. Those men whom he hadn't fired yet were ordered to restrict themselves to only 30 pounds of luggage each and told they would have to walk the whole way so the animals could be saved for carrying stores. The men were unhappy, claiming that none of this was in the brochure. Upon discovering that their deposits were non-refundable, they stayed on, but there was a definite feeling that at any moment Burke might be made into the new Bligh.

It wasn't that Burke didn't have the best interests of the expedition at heart – he just didn't have much idea what the best interests of the expedition were. Like a marathon runner who has misguidedly started the race wearing a suit of armour, he was frantically trying to rid the VEE of excess weight as he went along. At Balranald he dumped the sugar and the lime juice, leaving the entire expedition without a reliable source of cordial for the rest of the trip. At Bilbarka he ordered the disposal of the 60 gallons of rum that the party had brought along. This not only lightened the load, but also prevented the men from getting drunk on duty – which was probably for the best, all in all.

This move, however, did not please Burke's vice-captain, Landells, who had brought the rum along not for recreational use, but for the camels: he claimed it was necessary to keep them from contracting scurvy. Burke was unsure of how to respond to this claim. Should he slap Landells' face? Have him committed to an institution? In the end he didn't need to make a decision: Landells resigned, declaring that he could not be held responsible for the welfare of any expedition reckless enough to deny its camels regular shots of rum. It is from this famous incident that we get the traditional Australian expression 'as dumb as George Frigging Landells'.

Wills was promoted to second-in-command, and the VEE found itself in Menindee in New South Wales on 12 October. It had taken them 53 days to get there from Melbourne, a trip the mail coach could do in a week or so. But nobody ever said crossing a continent from north to south would be easy or fast or advisable or done by competent professionals.

Burke was panicking. The VEE's pace while travelling during the day was almost the same as their pace while sleeping at night. The Royal Society was running out of money, and the men didn't know if they were going to be paid. The explorer John Stuart had set out from Adelaide to claim a prize offered by the South Australian government to the first man to cross from the south coast to the north coast, west of the 143rd meridian, and Burke was terrified of being beaten to the punch. Everything was going wrong, and yet with the natural daring and lack of intelligence that had brought him this far, he pressed on.

On 11 November, Burke and Wills reached Cooper's Creek, the outer limit of European exploration to that point. They made camp there, then made camp again a short distance away, after a plague of rats arrived at the first camp. This was further proof of God's deep hatred of everyone involved with the expedition, but again Burke and Wills ignored the obvious signs that they should go the hell back.

This was an important juncture in the journey. Having successfully reached Cooper's Creek, the VEE could camp until autumn, avoiding the heat of the brutal Queensland summer, which would have made travel exceedingly difficult. This was a reasonable and obvious course of action that any half-sensible explorer would take in the circumstances, so it was hardly surprising when Burke decided to set off north again on 16 December, right in the middle of summer. By this time God had stopped worrying, realising that nothing he could do to the expedition would be as destructive as what Burke was doing to it.

Burke, Wills, John King and Charles Gray started the last leg to the Gulf of Carpentaria, while the rest of the VEE stayed at Cooper's Creek. 'Wait for us three months, then head home,' said Burke, before striding into the unknown.

'Actually, make that four,' said Wills, quietly so Burke wouldn't hear him: he knew that Burke was a proud and yet pathetically ignorant man.

And so, the intrepid four staggered northward, guided by Wills's survivalist skills and Burke's indomitable pigheadedness, battling the merciless heat. The temperature in the region could reach up to 50°C in the shade – more when you take into account the impractical underpants people wore in the 1860s – and, if anything, their travels were conclusive proof of the fact that people living in Australia was a terrible idea in the first place.

Yet somehow the expedition endured. They trekked through desert, mountains and scrubland, much to the chagrin of the camels, who were recorded in Burke's journal as 'bleeding, sweating and groaning' as they pushed through the Selwyn Ranges: though this may have been seen as an improvement on the average camel's normal practice of spitting, vomiting and biting people.

When you're walking through north Queensland, the January sun beating down upon your backs, the arrival of cool, refreshing rain must come as a blessed relief, although the continuation of cool refreshing rain quickly starts to get right on your wick, as Burke and Wills discovered when the Gulf's wet season arrived and they found themselves knee-deep in water watching their camels sink into the mud in much the same fashion as the faithful horse Artax in beloved fantasy film *The Neverending Story*: a movie that has many similarities with the Burke and Wills saga, including the fact that it's about a mission undertaken by a dangerously unqualified individual, as well as its extremely disappointing ending.

Say what you like about Burke and Wills, but one thing you can't deny is that they were stupid to ever even try this dumb expedition. But another thing you can't deny is that they had guts. After being fried in the desert and then nearly drowned in the floods over the course of a few months, they finally reached their destination. Sort of.

On 9 February,[63] they came up just short of the actual coast. They recorded that they could taste the salt water of the sea, which seems like a pretty inadvisable thing to do, but could not make it to the open ocean due to the mangrove swamps in their way. You'd think they

63 My birthday, by the way, so there are two reasons to celebrate the date.

could've tried a bit harder though, to be honest. I mean they were only swamps, how hard could it be? The ocean was right over there, and they turned back because things got a bit swampy. Yes, Burke and Wills certainly were born quitters.

Having reached the northern shore (but not really [but they were all like 'let's not and say we did' about it {but they got closer than anyone else, and it's more than you ever did}]), the men turned back. From Cooper's Creek to the Gulf had taken them two months, and they had only 27 days' worth of food left. 'I told you we shouldn't be having seconds,' Wills berated Burke.

Of course, when I say they had 27 days' worth of food left, I'm not counting the camels and horses, which provided a series of delicious and nutritious meals for the four men. They ate three camels in all, which is a hell of a lot of camel jerky.

They also ate Burke's favourite horse, Billy, causing Burke to suffer a haunting flashback to the day he first got his steed. 'Don't give him a name,' his mum said. 'You'll just get attached, and then it'll be all the more heart-rending when you have to eat him.' How he wished he'd heeded his mother's advice! Once again, the Burke and Wills expedition was infused by the spirit of Artax, as Burke wept over Billy's lifeless body in between taking bites out of it.

Still, the four men struggled on towards Cooper's Creek, where their comrades awaited, and despite the camel sandwiches, food ran short again. If they'd ever seen *I'm A Celebrity ...* they would've known you can make simple but nutritious meals out of spiders, worms and buffalo testicles, but it wasn't on air yet, and they foolishly restricted themselves to things that vaguely resembled food. Charles Gray killed a python, which was a bit of a treat, but as the Bible says, man cannot live on snake alone, especially when man has dysentery, which Burke and Gray got shortly after eating the python. Did the snake-based diet contribute to the illness? It's hard to say. But not that hard.

During the dysentery period, which was naturally a time of great tension and copious mopping among the group, Wills caught Gray stealing flour. Had he been stealing from them all along? We may never know, although certainly Gray was the oldest member of the party, and old people are notoriously untrustworthy. To be fair, though, he was also starving and dying of dysentery, and maybe they could've cut him some slack.

Slack-cutting, though, was no more in Burke's vocabulary than were intelligent planning or realistic goals. He subjected Gray to 'explorer's justice', i.e. he beat the living crap out of him. Burke believed that Gray was not only a thief, but also a malingerer. He thought he was faking the whole dysentery thing, and also possibly the starvation thing and the 'being old' thing, and aimed to punish him thoroughly.

Two weeks later, Gray was unable to walk. 'Oh, give the man an Oscar,' said Burke, applauding sarcastically. A week after that, the others woke up one morning to find Gray dead in his swag. 'Nice one, Gary Oldman,' sneered Burke, 'amazing performance.' For the rest of the day, King and Wills dug Gray's grave, while Burke continued to clap and make snide remarks about Stanislavsky.

Five days after Gray's death, Burke, Wills and King staggered back into the camp at Cooper's Creek, grateful and relieved to be reunited with their companions.

The camp was deserted.

'Those guys,' said Burke, eyes welling with joyous tears. 'Imagine throwing a surprise party for us! What great friends I've made on this trip. I hope we all keep in touch.'

'I think they're gone,' said the ever-pragmatic Wills.

'No, no,' Burke insisted, 'any minute now they'll jump out with a cake. Just wait.'

'I don't –'

'*JUST WAIT!*' Burke screamed.

So they waited through the night, for the shout of '*Surprise!*', but it did not come. Slowly, two indisputable facts began to dawn on Robert O'Hara Burke:

1. It wasn't his birthday.
2. The other members of the VEE had left Cooper's Creek and weren't coming back.

In fact, in probably the most heartbreaking Australian historical tragedy of the pre-Daryl Somers era, the others had left Cooper's only a few hours before, on the morning of 21 April, having waited a full 18 weeks for their colleagues' return. Burke, Wills and King had entered camp that evening. After the horrific journey south, they and their two remaining camels had no chance of catching up with them.

Upon a tree at Cooper's Creek was carved the word 'DIG'. Obeying this, they found a box of provisions and a note from William Brahe, who had been charged with command of the Cooper's Creek Depot:

> *Dear Burke and Wills,*
>
> *I hope this letter finds you well. We decided to go home, as we were getting bored and we are sick of cleaning up camel vomit. See you in Melbourne – it's your round!*
>
> *Yours,*
>
> *William Brahe*

The tree under which the provisions were found is known today as the 'Dig Tree' and is one of Australia's more famous trees, along with the tree Blinky Bill lives in, and the one who did the stunts for the Ents in *Lord of the Rings*. Thousands of enthusiasts travel to Cooper's Creek each year to look at the tree and say, 'Huh. It's a tree.'

After a couple of days' rest and recuperation, they set out again. Wills and King wanted to go back the way they had come, but after all he'd been through, Burke saw no reason to start being good at his job now. He decided instead to head for the cattle station at Mount Hopeless, a mountain that surprisingly had been named before the Burke and Wills expedition set out. 'It'll be more poetic,' he told the others.

While Burke, Wills and King headed towards Mount Hopeless, Brahe met up with another member of the original VEE, William Wright, travelling north from Menindee to bring supplies to Cooper's Creek. Together they returned to the camp to see if Burke and Wills had returned. 'No sign of them,' said Brahe. 'Back we go.'

'Hmm,' said Wright. 'Why don't we see if those provisions you left here have been taken? Maybe they did make it back here, dug up the provisions, decided to move on, wrote a letter explaining what they were doing and buried it in the same spot for anyone who came back here to find.'

'Nah,' Brahe replied. 'That doesn't sound much like something that'd happen in real life. Taking five minutes to dig under a tree would be a total waste of our time.'

'You're probably right,' nodded Wright. 'Let's go.'

And so they did.

Which is how Burke, Wills and King found themselves stranded, weak and starving, beyond help, on the banks of Cooper's Creek, far from Mount Hopeless and near to death. The nights were freezing. The only food was what the local Aboriginal people were willing to give them: mostly fish or flatbread made from the seeds of the nardoo plant.[64] At Breerily Waterhole, all seemed lost.

'This is Brahe's fault,' raged Burke. 'He could've left us some of his camels or a bike or something.'

'I'm sure he did what he could,' said Wills wearily.

'He always was a selfish bastard,' Burke muttered. He sighed. 'This wind goes right through me. If only we still had that blanket.'

'The one you burnt.'

'I did not!' Burke protested. 'It happened to *get* burnt, after an unfortunate accident while I was cooking dinner.'

'Everything else got burnt too,' Wills noted.

'The fish didn't. It was done beautifully.' He sighed again. 'I wish we had some of it now. I wonder why the natives ran away like that.'

'Maybe it was because you shot at them.'[65]

'Maybe, maybe.' Burke nodded philosophically. 'The Aboriginal psyche is such a mystery. Who knows what causes him to flee thus?'

'I bet getting shot at would do it, though.'

'Let's not play the blame game, Wills.'

'Sorry, Burke.'

And that's where this chapter came in. Wills, suffering from malnutrition, exposure and Burke's company, asked to be left at Breerily while Burke and King made a last-ditch effort to find the Yandruwandha tribe who had been so helpful previously until Burke's playful gunplay caused them to keep their distance. Wills's last testament was his journal, in which he wrote on 20 June that the

64 A four-leafed clover created by George Lucas.

65 He did, too. He really was a tool.

nardoo was causing 'enormous stools': words that are as true today as when they were written.

As for Burke and King, they continued upstream for two days before Burke became too weak to continue and asked King to leave him unburied with his pistol in his hand, in case he became a zombie and had to fight off zombie hunters. Burke died at eight in the morning. King stayed with his body for two days before returning to Breerily, where he found that Wills had also expired.

King went on to find some of the Yandruwandha, who gave him food and shelter. On 15 September 1861, he was found by the Victorian Relief Expedition, one of several search parties sent out to find Burke and Wills, and returned to Melbourne.

What was the legacy of Burke and Wills? They represent perhaps the most romantic episode in the history of Australian exploration, if by 'romantic' you mean 'depressing'. Modern readers can only marvel at the sheer courage, resilience and refusal to accept reality of these noble men. Burke and Wills proved once and for all, beyond a shadow of a doubt, that with enough will and determination, a man *can* die alone in the desert, and that is no small thing.

It's worth noting that the expedition did, in fact, achieve its goal of crossing the continent from south to north, covering more than 3000 kilometres before running afoul of the iron-clad law of adventurers: once you've got somewhere, you've got to go back. The exploits of Burke and Wills provided many valuable insights into the nature of this land, mostly revolving around how awful it is. They also supplied future explorers with crucial data regarding how to go about further explorations. But, despite this, people kept doing it for some reason.

ESSAY QUESTIONS

1. What is better for carrying supplies on a doomed desert expedition: a) camels; b) horses; or c) a tree?
2. Rank the members of the Burke and Wills expedition in order of intelligence. Then rank them in order of enormous stools.

The Great Australian Dig-Off

In which the promise of fortune brings the world to Australia's doorstep, and the colonies discover how true it is that mo' money mo' problems

Now, I Ain't Sayin' He's a Gold-Digger

Edward Hargraves looked with grim despondency upon the barren, rocky ground before him. He was down to his last penny, and down on his luck. After years of struggling to make his fortune, he'd almost run out of chances. In one day he'd lost his job and his girlfriend had walked out on him. In desperation, he enlisted with the US Army ...

Wait, no, that's not right – that's Bill Murray from *Stripes*. Sorry, I'll start again.

Hargraves was, in fact, down on his luck. Born in England, son of Lieutenant John Hargraves and Elizabeth Whitcombe,[66] he had come to New South Wales at the age of 16 in search of a quick buck, only to find the whole place depressingly fixated on sheep. He scraped a living as a farm worker at Bathurst, and for a while gathered sea cucumbers in the Torres Strait, before realising what strange behaviour this was. He then moved on to the respectable profession of failed farmer,

66 In accordance with the aforementioned law.

before marrying merchant's daughter Elizabeth Mackay[67] and using her money to buy a hotel north of Sydney. Later he took land on the Manning River, but found this as resistant to his unique combination of ignorance and laziness as all his other endeavours had been, and in 1849 he sold up and set out across the seas.

Hargraves was 32 years old and realised that he'd reached a crucial juncture in his life. He knew he had to face up to his responsibilities and make some changes. He had a wife and several children, and he saw that it was time to knuckle down, put his nose to the grindstone and abandon them. He found himself on a ship to California, where the gold rush had just begun, and the air was thick with the promise of riches and luxury and not having to think about your wife and kids.

In California, Hargraves learnt much about gold prospecting, like for example how to sit around watching other people do it. He hatched a brilliant plan: What if he could go back to New South Wales and find gold there? Even better, what if he could go back to New South Wales and tell other people he'd found gold there and get them to give him massive amounts of money basically for doing nothing? This last bit particularly appealed to Hargraves, whose burning ambition had always been for a life of lucrative sloth. In 1851, he returned to Australia with a plan.

And so here we see Hargraves, soon to become one of colonial Australia's foremost layabouts, at Lewis Ponds Creek near Bathurst with his friend John Lister.

'Okay, let's get some gold!' enthused Hargraves.

'Yes!' replied Lister effusively.

'Yes!' Hargraves affirmed.

There was an awkward silence as the two men looked at each other.

---

67 And likewise.

'How exactly do we get the gold?' asked Lister hesitantly.

'Well, in California they just sort of ... picked it up off the ground, I think,' said Hargraves, trying to remember exactly how it was done. He was afraid he might have missed a vital step in the process: they always seemed to start prospecting before he got up.

Lister looked at the ground on the banks of the creek. There were many pebbles, but none of them were yellow. 'I don't see any gold to pick up here, though. Are you sure this is the right spot?'

'Positive,' Hargraves said firmly. 'This is definitely where the gold is to be found. There's a place in California that looks exactly like this.'

'Ah. And they found gold there? They just picked it up?'

'Yeah, they – wait!' Hargraves had a brainwave. 'I think they got it out of the water.'

'Out of the water like a fish? So I should get my rod?' Lister was, by this stage, hopelessly confused, but remained eager to help in any way he could.

'No.' Hargraves was thinking as hard as he possibly could. 'They sort of ... had these saucepans, and they kind of ... dipped them in, and when they pulled them out there was gold in them.'

Lister glanced around nervously. They were a long way from town, and if Hargraves went insane in this moment, he wasn't at all sure anyone would hear his screams for help. 'They dipped their saucepans?' he asked cautiously.

'Yes. I mean not actual *saucepans*,' Hargraves clarified loftily. 'They were special professional prospecting saucepans.'

'So you wouldn't make a stew in them.'

'No. I mean, not right after prospecting anyway. You'd wash them out first.'

'Ah. Yes.'

There was another lengthy silence as both men contemplated the vast acres of knowledge about prospecting that they did not possess. After some minutes of this contemplation, it was agreed that the best thing to do would be to 'just sort of poke around' until something turned up. And so a period of splashing in the creek and aimless digging in the bank ensued, until finally Hargraves' cry of triumph rent the warm Bathurst air.

'I found some!' he crowed, capering with excitement. 'Look!'

Lister looked. 'You found some dirt?'

'No, *in* the dirt! Look closer, man!'

Lister looked closer. And it was true: in the handful of soil that Hargraves was holding out, there were five minute specks of gold. 'Are we rich?' he asked.

'Not yet, John, not yet,' said Hargraves. 'Stay calm. But these specks are just the beginning. Soon we will find *more* specks, and before long we'll have enough gold to put in a little vial of water and sell to children on school excursions.'

'Wow.'

It was true: those five specks eventually grew to 16 specks, and Hargraves put his master plan into action. Rushing back to Sydney, he met with Edward Deas Thomson, colonial secretary of New South Wales.

'Check *this* out, Thomson!' he said with a grin.

'What?' Thomson squinted at the handkerchief Hargraves was holding out.

'You see that?'

'It's a hankie.'

'But *in* the hankie ...'

'What?'

'Gold! It's gold, man! I have discovered a huge, magnificent goldfield.'

'Oh,' said Thomson. 'Well. Good on you.'

'So, I was thinking you'd maybe give me 500 pounds.'

Thomson eyed Hargraves uncertainly. He wasn't sure that his staff were near enough to come to his aid if Hargraves had gone insane.

On 7 April, while Hargraves was still in Sydney, John Lister and his neighbours James and William Tom found two nuggets of gold in Lewis Ponds Creek, the colony's first recorded discovery of a quantity of gold that couldn't comfortably fit under a baby's fingernail. They wrote to Hargraves to tell him of their discovery and asked him to keep quiet about it. 'Ha, ha, ha,' Hargraves replied, and immediately wrote to the *Sydney Morning Herald* to tell everyone about it. He then gave a lecture in Bathurst to inform the public about where the gold was and how to look for more. He then named the spot where gold had been found 'Ophir', after the gold mines of King Solomon, because Hargraves was nothing if not an incredibly obnoxious show-off. Although history doesn't record that he wore an all-gold suit and a hat with a flashing sign reading 'EDWARD HARGRAVES, THE FATHER OF GOLD', it would fit pretty well with his overall personality.

By 15 May there were over 300 prospectors at Ophir, sticking their saucepans in the water and digging up dirt in hopes of getting rich. Stupidly, they sought their fortune by actually finding gold and then selling it, in contrast to Hargraves' much less labour-intensive method of telling everyone about the gold he'd found and asking for cash from the government.

It was a remarkably effective method, too. NSW Governor Charles FitzRoy[68] gave him the £500 he'd been looking for, as a reward for

68 Known as Australia's first hipster governor.

being the first to find gold in Australia, and an additional fee to find more gold, which he promptly did not do. Two years later, the NSW government paid him £10,000 and appointed him Commissioner of Crown Lands, and the Victorian government gave him £5000. Later in his life, New South Wales awarded him a pension for life for his service to the colony, service that was generally agreed to have been so invaluable that it almost existed.

Just before Hargraves died, an official enquiry found that Lister and the Tom brothers were the rightful discoverers of gold in Australia, and that Hargraves' honours were erroneously given, a finding to which Hargraves responded with a coquettish giggle and the immortal words, 'Up yours, dummies, I already got paid.'

The life of Edward Hargraves has many lessons to teach us about the nature of fame, the realities of entrepreneurship and publicity, the historical spirit of fortune-hunting and the unexpected paths that the histories of emerging nations may take. But perhaps the greatest lesson it can teach us all is 'Don't ever make friends with Edward Hargraves.' This colonial proto-Donald Trump was in many ways a con man and a hustler, but his contribution to Australia's prosperity is extremely deniable.

Rush Hour

The discovery had been made, gold had been found, and so it was time for mass idiocy to take hold of the colonies. America had had its gold rush, and in what was already becoming an Australian trademark, the people couldn't wait to copy the Americans.

The goldfield at Ophir was a source of much vexation for the NSW government, which like any government had hoped to keep its citizens as poor as possible forever. Reports from California told them that besides prosperity, the discovery of gold had resulted in violence, crime, murder and popular miniseries. The colonial government was naturally eager to avoid that kind of malarkey, so they sent officials to Ophir to tell them that any gold they found belonged to the government, not the finder.

'You are not allowed to look for gold here,' the officials said. 'All your gold is belong to us.'

'Cool story, bro,' replied the diggers.

So the officials returned to Sydney to work on a new plan. It was apparent that unlike drugs, the problem of gold digging could not be easily solved by prohibition. Instead, they decided to regulate and again copied the yanks: licences were issued at 30 shillings[69] a month, which permitted the licence-holder to work a claim, keep any gold he found and sell souvenirs and canned drinks to any tourists who might pass by.

The miners went along with the licence system, realising it was only fair that as they were doing all the work and assuming all the risk, the government receive more money than the gold they found was actually worth. This was mostly what happened, particularly at Ophir, which didn't have that much gold in it – some historians speculate that this gold was just residue from a watch shop that exploded upriver, which would also explain John Lister's famous collection of second-hand leather straps.

The failure of many prospectors to find fabulous riches at Ophir worried the governor, who by this stage was just starting to look paranoid. 'You're not happy if they find gold, you're not happy if they *don't* find gold,' complained his wife. 'Make up your freaking mind.' (Mrs FitzRoy was herself a fairly dissatisfied woman, due to having

69 In today's money, $800,000.

died four years earlier, just more evidence of the ineffable mysteries of history.)

Anyway, the point is that, with the possibility of disgruntled miners everywhere with expensive licences and no gold, it was in the interests of the government to find more goldfields as soon as possible. Of course they first asked Hargraves to do it, which in hindsight is rather touching – but really they had been underestimating the innate human knack for deluded greed.

The fortune hunters of Australia needed no help finding gold: they flocked to the region around Bathurst and began scooping up the stuff in large amounts; this was not all that difficult as most of the gold was 'alluvial', meaning 'at the back of the throat'. Suddenly New South Wales had found a new commodity to drive prosperity, replacing its previous economic staple: breadfruit.[70]

On 16 July 1851, the *Bathurst Free Press* reported that 'Bathurst is mad again', a remarkably prescient foreshadowing of the invention of touring car racing. The paper was reporting on 'golden fever', a dreadful disease that people got from eating too much gold. The specific story was that of Jemmy Irving, an Aboriginal shepherd who had discovered a 35-kilo chunk of gold at Meroo Creek. For his discovery, Irving was handsomely rewarded by his employer, Dr William Kerr, which was incredibly generous of Kerr and also pretty risky, taking into account the strict laws in force at the time that forbade any white man from giving Aboriginal people what they deserved.

The discovery of Jemmy's rock inflamed the public in Sydney, and even in England, where gold was quite popular. Suddenly Australia was no longer just a place to send criminals and inept military personnel: it was also a place to pull stuff out of the ground, a process that remains

70 Hope you're enjoying these callbacks. I am.

ongoing. Accordingly, gold-diggers began to flood in from overseas, to join the multitudes fleeing their homes in Australian towns for the promise of a better life scrabbling around in the mud.

The Rush Goes South

There was a particular exodus from Melbourne, capital of the brand-new colony of Victoria, which had been separated from New South Wales in July 1851 and named after a popular local beer. Melbourne had only just recovered from the devastating blow of not being called 'Batmania', when suddenly everyone started quitting their jobs, buying shovels and buggering off up Bathurst way. A group of Melbourne businessmen, attempting to keep the labour force closer to home, offered a £200 reward for the discovery of a goldfield within 200 miles of Melbourne. Victorian Governor Charles LaTrobe increased the reward to £10,000, having received advice from expert economists that gold was a good thing to have.

Soon after the reward was offered, gold was found near Melbourne. That seems a bit suspicious, doesn't it? Gold being found right after a reward was offered for gold being found? It's a bit convenient, is what I'm saying. But apparently nobody asked any questions about the shady characters who came prancing into Melbourne, waggling their nuggets, and so they got clean away with it.

The Victorian gold rush got started in earnest after gold was discovered on a sheep property northwest of Melbourne called 'Ballarat', a name derived from the local Wathaurong peoples' name for the area, *balla arat*, which may mean 'souvenir shop'. The first man to stumble on gold at Ballarat was James Regan, who had walked 50 miles from Geelong in the company of his 75-year-old friend John Dunlop, mainly out of a desire to see an old man die from exhaustion. At Buninyong, near Ballarat, they found nothing but mud, so Dunlop persuaded Regan to walk another 50 miles to the goldfield at Clunes, probably planning to carry out his revenge murder once they got out of earshot.

But instead, they walked across Ballarat station and came upon a vein of gold at a spot subsequently named Golden Point in honour of Regan's lack of imagination. News spread quickly, and Ballarat suddenly became, for the first and hitherto only time, a popular place to go. Fortune hunters thronged there in greater numbers than they had to any goldfield by that point, and Ballarat soon became synonymous with filthy homeless men crying in tents.

As more and more people flocked to Ballarat, the Victorian government worried about the effect on the colony. Melbourne was being drained of its population, and businessmen suddenly realised that even if your employees run away to Ballarat instead of Bathurst, they're still, you know, gone. It was pretty obvious, right? I mean, when you read about their plan to find gold near Melbourne above, you probably thought to yourself, *Hmm, they didn't really think this through*, and you were right. Melbourne's government and business community were comprised mainly of congenital idiots – pretty much what you'd expect from people who could've been living in Batmania but decided not to.

The government was also worried that gold would attract ex-convicts, who would bring crime to Victoria. Which is pretty funny when you think about it.

With a thousand people at Ballarat within a month of Regan's find at Golden Point, Governor LaTrobe acted to rein in the hysteria as New South Wales had, with a licence system. For 30 shillings,[71] you got a small square of land to dig in until you went insane.

Soldiers were sent to Ballarat to enforce the licence laws, to which

71 In today's money, $18.50.

the miners objected strongly. 'Piss off and die,' they shouted, to which the soldiers replied, 'Ooh, that's a bit cheeky.' Fearing violence, LaTrobe recruited more goldfield police, knowing that increased repression always soothes agitated spirits.

Within two months of the Ballarat discovery, more than 5000 people were camped there, sure that fabulous wealth was just one lucky strike away. Most of them didn't actually find gold, but at least they had the consolation of knowing that they'd wasted their lives. It was pretty hard work digging at Ballarat: most of the gold was deep beneath the surface, and many miners who showed up armed only with a shopping trolley to carry all the gold they'd be picking up off the ground ended up hugely disappointed, while others who showed up willing to put in the hard work of digging deep ended up with hernias. When news came of a new goldfield where the gold was near the surface, requiring only a small trowel to fill a trolley, Ballarat almost emptied.

This was the beginning of the Mount Alexander gold rush, which was fairly uninteresting, but it did lead to the foundation of the town of Castlemaine, which is the birthplace of Frank McEncroe, inventor of the Chiko Roll, so God only knows where the culinary heritage of this country would've been without it.

Bendigoing, Going, Bendigone

More interesting was the rush at Bendigo, the greatest of all the Victorian fields. Bendigo was named after Bendigo's Creek, which itself got its name from the fact that it was a creek belonging to Bendigo.

The identity of the first discoverer of gold at Bendigo is disputed: some say it was stationmaster's wife Margaret Kennedy; some say it was shepherd Ben Hall; some say it was a roaming band of mischievous leprechauns. Whatever the truth of the matter, the fact is that in December 1851, the *Argus* newspaper reported that folks were prospecting at Bendigo, and immediately crowds began to flood to Bendigo from the city and from the incredibly tedious fields at Castlemaine.

An early description of the goldfields at Bendigo was a poem written by digger William Sandbach:

O, lift your eyes, ye sighing sons of men;
The long-fled golden age returns again.
See! youthful riches, with his yellow wand,
Touching the hills and valleys through the land
'Cause tramps like us, baby we were born to run

This is known as the earliest poem written about the Bendigo goldfields, which implies there has been more than one poem written about the Bendigo goldfields, which is a frankly bewildering fact. You can't help thinking that poets should go and get real jobs.

Bendigo proved to be the sort of place that one would normally metaphorically refer to as a goldmine, but you can't in this instance because it's literally a goldmine, so you'd have to find some other metaphor to describe it. Perhaps you might say that Bendigo turned out to be a real superannuation fund.

Over the next few decades, tales of lives changed and fortunes made abounded, like that of George Lansell. Lansell was an English grocer who made millions of pounds in Bendigo following one simple philosophy: dig often, and dig deep. In the 1870s it was a common sight to see Lansell striding about the Bendigo fields, bellowing at his employees. 'Deeper, deeper!' After a while it became disturbing, especially when Lansell was standing next to an open shaft screaming,

'Push it deeper! Pound that quartz!' and thrusting his hips wildly. But the method worked, and Lansell became one of the richest men in Victoria.

It was near Bendigo, at Moliagul, that the legendary Welcome Stranger nugget was found. This is the largest nugget ever discovered in Australia, and was found when John Deason and Richard Oates stubbed their toes on it in 1869. A salutary lesson to us all that the best way to get rich is to just wander around aimlessly until you see some gold sticking out of the ground, the nugget was named 'Welcome Stranger' in recognition of the fact that nobody had ever met this particular nugget before. It weighed 3.523.5 troy ounces, a 'troy ounce' being defined as being 1/128th of a man called Troy. In normal-people weight, the Welcome Stranger was 78 kilos.

Of course, stories like those of George Lansell and the Welcome Stranger often prevent us from remembering the stories of the many thousands of people who flocked to the goldfields and found nothing but heartache, which is a good thing because those stories are depressing. Let's move on.

The Golden Age of Golden Gold

The colonies were held in gold's iron grip, which was a confusing alloy to be held in. Fortune hunters were flocking to Australia like bad magicians to an *Australia's Got Talent* audition. Bendigo was booming. The miners had flooded back to Ballarat after realising that digging deep for gold was preferable to digging shallow for dirt.

Although there had been a lot of hand-wringing about the exodus from Melbourne, with workers leaving their jobs, policemen and soldiers abandoning their posts, and ships left unmanned in Port Phillip Bay, the gold rush ended up to the city's advantage: migrants from overseas and interstate thronged to Melbourne as the colony's shipping and supply centre. They were also attracted by a Lonely Planet poll naming Melbourne as the goldfields' Most Liveable City. By 1865, Melbourne was also the most populous city in Australia, a title it would hold until Sydney took it back after the opening of Featherdale Wildlife Park.

The boom in Melbourne led to the establishment of Parliament House, the Treasury Building, Victoria Barracks, the State Library, Melbourne Town Hall, St Patrick's Cathedral and Old Melbourne Gaol (the name of the last being a complete mystery for many years). This flurry of construction was a real shot in the arm for the Melbourne community: up till then, the idea of having buildings in the city hadn't really occurred to them. Of course, the authorities realised that the gold rush couldn't last forever, so in 1859 Australian Rules football was codified, and in 1861 the first Melbourne Cup was run, twin initiatives designed to ensure that Victorians would remain in the grip of irrational hysteria after the gold ran out.

The rush also resulted in the foundation of Melbourne's Chinatown, just one of the developments flowing from the deluge of migrants to the goldfields. Naturally, given the fact that the Australian colonies were themselves the result of an influx of foreigners encroaching on a new land, the residents of Australia welcomed the migrants with open arms, as indeed have Australians down the ages to the present day, infused as we are with a spirit of openness and a commitment to the grand Australian tradition of multiculturalism.

Ha-ha! Did you spot the clever joke in the previous paragraph? Of course what actually happened was that all the Australians hated the migrants and immediately began starting fights with them, infused as they were with a spirit of suspicion and a commitment to the grand

Australian tradition of xenophobia.

The fortune hunters' journey to Australia was not an easy one. The ships were terrible and riddled with disease, much like the goldfields themselves. Five per cent of travellers to Australia in 1852 died before they got there, which put a major crimp in their mining plans. The *Ticonderoga* lost 165 passengers to typhoid fever, a terrible and agonising disease caused by living in history.

There were other risks too. One ship from California only reached Australia because its passengers had spent most of the trip pumping water out of it. They objected, but the captain told them they had a choice: either pump out the hold or swim the rest of the way. This caused even more outrage. 'Why didn't you tell us we could swim from the start?' they asked angrily. 'That option wasn't even mentioned on the ticket.'

But these dangerous trips were positively luxurious compared to the hardships suffered by Chinese migrants, who were condemned to inhuman conditions after it was discovered that they were not, technically, white people. Most of them spent the trip to Australia below decks in quarters that in the 21st century would be the subject of a devastating exposé on *Four Corners* on livestock abuse, but that in the 19th century were considered a Super Saver Family Fun Deck Vacation. The Chinese diggers were mostly peasants who had their passage to Australia paid by businessmen in return for a share of any gold found, the rest to go towards rescuing them from their life of grinding poverty, which of course didn't happen because of how much they had to pay the businessmen who'd outlaid the cost of their weevil-infested pleasure cruise. But if the trip was a nightmare, and life on the diggings exhausting and painful, there was the consolation that most nights all the other diggers would pass out drunk and the racial abuse would stop for a bit. In those moments it was almost worth working yourself to death in a hostile alien hellscape.

Those arriving in Melbourne found the city itself strange and disturbing. For a start, men would row out to the incoming ships and charge massive fees to bring passengers ashore. It was a lot like an Italian airport. Once they got to shore, they would find cashed-up diggers, splurging their gold earnings on fancy carriages and racing their horses in the streets. In these respects Melbourne hasn't changed all that much, though the races in the street nowadays are much noisier and cause far more offensive fumes.

One eyewitness said that Melbourne was 'a most frightful place for drinking', but it's hard to see why. All the evidence indicates that it was a fantastic place for drinking – why else would everyone be doing it there? Drinking was one of the number one hobbies of gold rush-era Melburnians, alongside vomiting, passing out and roller derby. Pubs grew like mushrooms all over the city, affirming the iron law of economics: if people have money, other people will sell them beer.

Many boring tight-lipped moralistic types got themselves into a froth over the decadence of old Melbourne town, seeing in its free spirits, heavy drinking and festive punch-ups a resemblance to the lawlessness of the San Francisco gold rush. All the hallmarks of Frisco were there: violence, debauchery, wacky car chases. Were the Australian colonies, hitherto the most sober and respectable bastions of morality that brutal open-air prisons could ever aspire to be, going down the road of tasteless American-style Wild Westery?

Yes, they were – and a damn good thing too, because if there was a duller city than Melbourne before 1851, I haven't heard of it.

Did Gold Matter?

The massive injection of wealth into the colonies changed Australian society and taught the continent's inhabitants how to be more grasping and obsessed with status. It also introduced many different cultures to Australia, allowing the previously staunchly British monoculture to be enlivened by a wide range of racist attitudes that live on today as part of the great antipodean mosaic. Gold, found as far west as the Pilbara and as far north as Cooktown, caused population booms all over the country and fast-tracked Australia's transition from a society based on the internment of convicted criminals to one based on the ambitions of unconvicted ones.

It also, of course, began the Australian tradition of getting rich by yanking rocks out of the ground, and without that early example of the gold rush, who knows whether the coal rush or the iron-ore rush would ever have happened? We might never have met Clive Palmer, Gina Rinehart or that other guy. We might have far fewer massive holes in this land, were it not for the brave pioneers of the gold rush.

This isn't to say that without gold, Australia would never have evolved into an advanced, prosperous 21st-century nation: we still would have had sheep and *Neighbours*. But the gold rush definitely helped push the process along. In the same way that a kitten will grow into a cat even if you don't force-feed it steroids, just not as quickly or as impressively, the gold rush acted like the steroids in the bloodstream of the kitten that was Australia, supercharging the country's development until we see the country we live in today: strong and muscular, and prone to sudden fits of irrational rage.

Yes, Edward Hargraves may not have known what he was starting back in '51, and he may have cared even less, and if we're honest it wasn't even really him who started it, but ... the gold rush was definitely something, and you can't say that about everything.

As the saying goes, 'Where there's wealth, there are dudes trying to bash one another's brains in', and it's as true of the gold rush as any other time in history. The next chapter will show you just how dangerous life on the diggings could get.

ESSAY QUESTIONS

1. What is 'gold', exactly?
2. When was the last time you had a Chiko Roll? You never see them around anymore, do you?

Whose Mine Is It Anyway?

In which tensions bubble over, and the powers that be find the humble prospector to be absolutely revolting

Of course, no historical tome would be complete without the bit where people are beset by troubles and things, and so it was in the middle of the gold rush, when those troubles came along to become the defining feature of the period we know today as the Period of Troubles.[72] It's hard to believe, but the discovery of gold somehow attracted a certain criminal element. These included your average straightforward robber: the bluff, manly type who doesn't mess about but gets straight to it, sticking a pistol in your ribs and taking all your money. There was to this lifestyle a rugged nobility, and it's no wonder that Australians have always loved armed robbers.

If robberies of people travelling to and from the goldfields had been the only issue, nobody would've worried that much – in fact, it added to the local colour. Sadly, the violence spilled onto the fields themselves, where miners fell into angry disputes frequently and often came to blows. High-pressure situations often produce frayed tempers, and in an era before scented candles and rainforest sound CDs, there was nothing to calm tensions. The diggers even resorted to lynchings: a miner at Mount Alexander was hanged by his fellow miners after being

72 Not to be confused with popular educational film *The Trouble with Periods*.

accused of murder, while when another was caught stealing at Ballarat, he was held over a fire.

Yes, justice could be rough and improvisational on the goldfields, and the authorities, being primarily concerned with collecting licence fees, had little to no interest in maintaining the rule of law. This was a lethal combination of circumstances in places where pretty much everyone was armed. As the old American saying goes, the only thing that can stop a bad guy with a gun is a good guy with a gun, but inhabitants of the goldfields soon discovered that bad guys with guns were also often stopped by other bad guys with guns. It was a Bad Guys with Gunsathon out on the fields. Ellen Clacy, a young Englishwoman who travelled to the diggings after deciding that her life didn't have enough filth and squalor in it, wrote of a typical night on the goldfields:

> *Imagine hundreds of revolvers almost simultaneously fired ... murder here – murder there – revolvers cracking – blunderbusses bombing – rifles going off – balls whistling ...*

It certainly sounds like a fearful place to be; although why she put in the bit about the whistling balls is unknown. Perhaps some clue may be found in the introductory remarks to her book, *A Lady's Visit to the Gold Diggings*, in which she wrote:

> *Although the time of my residence in the colonies was short, I had the advantage (not only in Melbourne, but whilst in the bush) of constant intercourse with many experienced diggers and old colonists.*

Wow. Not just intercourse, but 'constant'! The girl knew how to party – it's no wonder that when Ellen was in town, there were whistling balls aplenty. It's even more impressive she got it done in the midst of all that shooting. So the only real question left is the obvious one: what exactly is a 'blunderbuss'?[73] I'm not sure, but it sounds utterly obscene: Ellen would've loved it.

Why did men fight so often on the goldfields, leading to fisticuffs, gunplay and mayhem? There were many reasons: brawls might break out over disputed claims, envy of another's good luck at the diggings could trigger violence, and accusations of theft flew thick and fast, usually with good reason. In addition, sometimes a fight would break out for the very simple reason that everyone was sick to bloody death of these bloody diggings. To illustrate this point, do an experiment: go out to a big empty field somewhere, put up a tent and live there for a month, making sure to spend 14 hours a day digging holes and finding nothing in them. Also, send all your money to the government. If you can last more than three days before you feel an irresistible urge to shoot someone, you're a better man than I.

Plus, of course, there were the old racial tensions to deal with. A glorious patchwork of nationalities lived on the goldfields. Although most of the prospectors were Australian or British-born, the possibility of a better class of jewellery had enticed aspiring millionaires from places as varied as Russia, Spain, Holland, France, Belgium and Switzerland. But the biggest impression was made by the aforementioned Chinese.

When it comes to the clashes between whites and Chinese on the Australian goldfields, it's hard to say exactly where the blame lies. On the one hand, the European diggers exhibited savage hostility to

73 Insert your own joke about the public transport system in your city of residence here.

their Chinese neighbours, launching numerous violent attacks upon them. At one point in New South Wales, the Europeans petitioned the colonial government to kick the Chinese out of the country due to their 'filthy habits' and 'heathen' practices, which were 'repulsive to the feeling of the Christian population'.

In the Europeans' defence, the Chinese were wearing some *very* unusual clothes. There were other provocations, of course: besides their loose pants and weird hats, the Chinese miners insisted on looking Chinese despite all reasonable requests for them to desist. Some of them wore pigtails, which was deeply offensive to the devoutly idiotic Europeans. They also spoke Chinese, which anthropologists have since learnt is a typically Chinese way of pissing white people off. And they ate Chinese food, which was unfair because the other miners couldn't afford nice restaurants. Plus they burnt incense in their temples, and they smoked opium – an obvious cause for suspicion among the salt-of-the-earth working men of the diggings, who believed that God intended that if a man is to take mind-altering substances, those substances should be in liquid form and should make him want to punch everyone in the face. All the opium did was make people want to lie around and not fight anyone, which was deeply un-Christian.

But perhaps the most offensive thing the Chinese did on the goldfields was this: they worked. *Hard*. Like, *all* the time.[74] White miners would always be asking them to take Sunday off and have a hit down the oval, but the Chinese would shake their heads and say they had to keep digging. Or, at least, the Europeans thought that's what they were saying – nobody spoke Chinese. Maybe they were saying that they didn't have the proper shoes. (Which was true: their shoes were weird too, that was another reason everyone hated them.) Whatever the

---

74 Can you even imagine?

truth, the Chinese were industrious and conscientious to what seemed an aggressive extent. Indeed, no sooner had a ruggedly handsome white man thrown down his pick in disgust and abandoned a useless trench that had yielded no gold, than a busy Chinese interloper would leap in, dig deeper and pull out a bunch of shiny nuggets. It was utterly infuriating, and there were only two ways for the Europeans to solve the problem:

1. Develop an atmosphere of mutual respect and shared cultural understanding, and realise that all people are deserving of dignity and the right to life, liberty and the pursuit of happiness, while also absorbing the lessons that their Chinese brothers had to teach them and putting them into practice by working even harder on their own claims, thus coming to a higher level of enlightenment about humanity's place in the world; or
2. Beat them all up.

After much discussion and vigorous debate, it was decided to go with option two. White diggers bored with bashing and shooting one another reinvigorated themselves by bashing and shooting Chinese diggers. It was a refreshing feeling for them: it made them remember why they got into this business in the first place.

Fortunately, the colonies weren't totally lawless, and the Victorian government was there to facilitate a satisfactory resolution to the racial problems on the goldfields, which would be fair and equitable for all. They did this, naturally, by imposing a £10 tax on every Chinese person arriving in Victoria: an early example of Australian authorities' tireless efforts over more than a century to promote racial tolerance and harmony by keeping other races out of the country.

The imposition of the Chinese tax might have seemed like a good idea, as long as you started from the premise that you were a massive racist – which described basically every European at the time – but it failed to take into account one of the reasons the tax was needed in the first place: the Chinese miners' infinite resourcefulness and unquenchable work ethic. Unable to afford the tax that would be charged if they rocked up in Port Phillip Bay, they sailed instead to South Australia or New South Wales and walked overland to Victoria. Unsurprisingly, a fair number expired on the trek, but as even many of their European miner enemies would have agreed, death was a small price to pay for the chance to deny the government their cash.

Two years after the arrival tax, Victoria added a £1 tax on every Chinese person in the colony – one can say what one likes about colonial governments, but you can't deny their never-say-die attitude to bigotry.

Anti-Chinese sentiment eventually boiled over into full-blown riots. In May 1857, a band of Chinese tax-dodgers were walking from South Australia to Bendigo when they happened to find gold at Ararat.[75] Outraged that people who didn't even have the decency to wear close-fitting trousers had stolen the best bit of their honest Australian earth, a furious gang of local miners attacked, bashing the Chinese men, destroying their belongings and chasing them out of Ararat.

Later that year, the Californian diggers on the Buckland River celebrated Independence Day by burning and looting Chinese tents and driving them from the goldfield, just as George Washington would have done. Several Chinese miners were killed, and three white miners

75 Named, of course, after the biblical mountain where Noah and his family beat up some Chinese immigrants.

were wounded by retaliatory Chinese bullets: if the Chinese refused to assimilate to Australian culture in any other way, they'd at least learnt the advisability of gun ownership. Some of the Americans were arrested for starting the Fourth of July Riot, but most were acquitted and only four given brief sentences, after the jury had it shown to their satisfaction that the Chinese had provoked the attack by being deliberately and antagonistically present.

Those riots paled next to the famous incident at Lambing Flat, a goldfield in New South Wales named after the well-furnished city apartment where John Macarthur used to bring his pregnant ewes. By 1861, conflict between the Chinese and white diggers had already become commonplace there. The Europeans drove 500 Chinese men away in November 1860, and white gangs had killed two Chinese in early 1861. So it was the culmination of an escalating series of incidents when more than 2000 prospectors, of whom as many as four or five may have been sober, assembled on Lambing Flat, holding anti-Chinese signs and urged on by a band to provide that festive touch that always makes a race war go with a swing.

The makeshift army marched on the Chinese camp and attacked them with whips, picks, shovels and, of course, guns. More than a thousand Chinese fled the camp and hid out on a nearby farm. Those who didn't were beaten, maimed and sometimes killed. Miners ripped Chinese pigtails from scalps and murdered those who wouldn't reveal the location of their gold. Some were buried alive as they tried to hide their valuables down mine shafts. The camp itself was destroyed and looted. All in all, it was one of the most shameful acts committed by colonial white Australians in that particular week.

Naturally the police couldn't ignore an atrocity of this magnitude, and they took swift action against the thousands of rioters by arresting three of them. Incensed by this display of official near-justice, 3000 miners attacked the police, surrendering only when the coppers hit them with swords. Four policemen were wounded and one miner shot dead, the whole incident a stern cautionary tale for any future police chief who attempted to exceed his authority by trying to prevent mass hate crimes.

The NSW government, shocked by the violence at Lambing Flat, saw that something needed to be done about the intolerance and hatred being directed at Chinese immigrants, and so quickly passed a law making it harder for any to come in. One can imagine the loud and glorious sound of all the hands being dusted in the NSW legislature that day, a job well done.

Onerous restrictions hampering them in both New South Wales and Victoria, many Chinese prospectors headed to the fledgling diggings in Queensland, relieved to have finally found a part of the country free from racism.

But not all the unrest on the goldfields was racially based. The authorities' greatest challenge in this era was the fight against democracy.[76]

Give Me Liberty or Give Me a Discount

The American War of Independence. The French Revolution. The Russian Revolution. The Rebel Alliance. All famous instances from history when the people rose up against tyranny and oppression to demand justice and freedom, and to lay their lives down for their beliefs if necessary.

The Eureka Rebellion wasn't much like any of those, but it's pretty much the closest thing Australia's got, so it's worthwhile telling the

76 Still is, if we're honest.

story of when a few brave men briefly fought for their rights before everything went back to normal and people stopped caring about rights again.

Since the early days of the gold rush, miners had been disgruntled about licence fees. 'Why should we pay 30 shillings a month just for the right to dig a hole in the ground?' some diggers asked angrily. 'Because if we don't, the police will bash our skulls in,' said others, and the matter rested a while as the mining community digested the deep truth of this.

But the issue festered like a weeping sore.[77] The miners questioned why they should be taxed without representation – to which the answer was basically, 'because you are dirty peasants' – and began pushing for the right to vote and to buy land. Which honestly seemed a bit ambitious. I mean, obviously we can all sympathise with the principle, but when you're a penniless scrounger in the 1850s, panning for gold in a muddy creek, and you're demanding the fruits of modern democracy, you're starting to sound like the Little Mermaid singing about how unfair it is that she doesn't have legs.

Not that the goldfield authorities weren't a little bit oppressive. In fact, they had mostly got their jobs by responding to an ad:

Looking to travel? Want to see new places, meet new people,
and hit them over the head with a little club?
Are you a highly motivated self-starter with strong unfulfilled sadistic
impulses and a desire to abuse power in exciting new ways?
Why not become a DIGGINGS POLICEMAN?
Join the forefront of the fight against poor people
attempting to improve their lives!
Use officially sanctioned physical force to compensate

77 Also a big problem for a lot of miners.

for your personal failings!
Wear a nice uniform!
Previous experience in armed robbery or
protection will be highly regarded.

Nowadays people like this become trainers on *The Biggest Loser*, but back then the goldfields police force was the only outlet they had.

Suffice to say, the police and the diggers did not get along. The policemen were jealous of the diggers because they had a chance to become fabulously rich, and the diggers were jealous of the policemen's comparative lack of blunt force trauma.

In 1853, the law was changed to allow licence searches at any time, clamping down on miners who were reckless enough to go down a shaft without a licence in their pocket. Soon afterwards the Anti-Gold Licence Association was formed in Bendigo, but struggled to make headway due to constant argument about what its name meant. Were they an association expressing opposition to gold licences, or were they an association calling for licences for people who hated gold? The meetings frequently descended into chaos as the anti-gold licence campaigners clashed with the anti-gold licence enthusiasts, each side demanding to know whether it was actually the other side or not.

In June 1854, Sir Charles Hotham – nicknamed 'Hotham by name, Hotham by nature' due to his resemblance to a sweaty pig – became governor of Victoria. After touring the Ballarat goldfields, he determined that the people working there were nowhere near as bitter and resentful as they should be, and so ordered an increase in licence checks and general police douchebaggery.

The fuse of the miners' anger was lit, on 6 October 1854, by James Bentley, publican of the Eureka Hotel. Bentley was an ex-convict from

Van Diemen's Land and regarded with suspicion by many for basically the same reasons people regard Tasmanians with suspicion today. On the night of the sixth, Scottish miner James Scobie entered the Eureka with his friend Peter Martin. They were just simple gold-diggers in search of a refreshing drink with which to wash down the 50 drinks they'd already had that night, and there are some who say that the vast, Oliver Reedesque amounts of alcohol sloshing around inside the pair contributed to the argument that broke out between them and Bentley. It escalated when Scobie called Bentley's wife rude names, and when the drunken miners left the pub, Bentley and his friends followed.

What happened next is hard to determine with any clarity. Did Bentley kill Scobie? Who knows? The mists of history can cloud any event with ambiguity and doubt. Except in this case, Bentley definitely killed Scobie. I know that by pronouncing my certainty on this matter, I am risking the ghost of Bentley haunting me forever: but it is a risk I am willing to take for the sake of that strict devotion to truth that is every historian's loftiest aim.[78]

The mining community didn't respond well to Scobie's murder, and it responded even less well to the magistrate at Bentley's murder trial letting him off. It was generally believed that Bentley had bribed the magistrate. It's impossible to know for sure whether this was true, but in for a penny, in for a pound: he definitely did.

And so it was that on 17 October 1854, several thousand miners gathered at the Eureka Hotel to protest against Bentley's acquittal. These men were incandescent with anger, the injustice burning within them as fiercely as the Eureka Hotel itself did after they set fire to it.

One might have thought that, now that the Eureka had been burnt to the ground by an angry mob, things would've settled down,

78 LOL.

but history so often defies our expectations. If anything, arson seemed to make things worse. Three miners were arrested for the hotel fire, sparking a flurry of further meetings by the miners, who at this stage were so busy with meetings and riots that they weren't doing much mining at all – especially when you take into account all the drinking they had to fit in.

On 11 November, 10,000 miners gathered at Bakery Hill[79] to form the Ballarat Reform League, an organisation dedicated to defending diggers' rights. Admittedly the timing wasn't all that fortunate: it sort of looked like the main right they were defending was the right to burn down hotels, but there were other rights that they were always standing up for, like the right not to be murdered by publicans, and the right to dig for gold without being kicked in the head by a mounted policeman unless given seven days' notice in writing.

In many ways, the Ballarat Reform League represented the crystallisation of many of the issues that were coming to a head in the realm of public affairs in the Western world in the mid-19th century: the growing demand for universal suffrage; the weakening case for hereditary power structures; the eternal tension between the common man's right to set fire to buildings and the small businessman's right to murder anyone he wants to. These were thorny matters, and if events in Ballarat didn't quite resolve them, there was at least a fair amount of needless bloodshed, which is always fun.

The BRL resolved that 'taxation without representation is tyranny', which they totally ripped off from the American Revolution without paying any royalties or anything, and also committed to seceding from the United Kingdom if there was no redress, a commitment that caused a fair amount of hilarity in the corridors of power. Mind you, if Ballarat

---

79 So named because it was shaped like a vanilla slice.

had seceded, we might even now have a whole separate country sitting an hour outside Melbourne, its economy dependent upon tourists visiting Sovereign Hill and Kryal Castle, and a standing army of 14 guys with utes and a three-legged pitbull.

Back in this reality, though, secession was never very likely, although the miners were certainly ramping up the rhetoric. Three of their brethren had been convicted of the Eureka Hotel burning, causing three more to go to Melbourne to demand that Governor Hotham release them. Hotham answered this demand with what was described by observers as 'an obscene motion of the wrist', and the delegates returned to Ballarat dissatisfied.

Instead of acceding to the freedom fighters' demand that arson be made legal in Victoria, Hotham sent extra troops into Ballarat, where they were welcomed by diggers throwing stones and beating them up. They had been on the diggings so long that they had apparently forgotten one of life's most ironclad rules: people in canvas houses shouldn't throw stones at men with guns.

Lalor, You Got Me on My Knees

On 29 November, another meeting was held at Bakery Hill, under the new flag of the Southern Cross, representing the miners' independence and love of astronomy. Speaking at this meeting was one Peter Lalor, an Irish engineer who had come to Ballarat to strike it rich but thought that armed insurrection might be a fun way to break up the monotony. Lalor was a strong believer in civil liberties and the sound of his own voice, and gave an inspirational speech that day, in which he declared:

> *Three score and six years ago, our forefathers sent a bunch of thieves and murderers to this terrible hot place and they all*

started starving to death, and long may we honour them as we fight against tyranny and red tape. And yes, I reckon that men asleep in bed will think themselves accursed that they were not here, trying to strain tiny bits of gold out of big piles of mud and being harassed by policemen with God complexes. It is time, my fellow stupid miners, to cry havoc, and let slip the dogs of war, and I wish I meant that literally, because a few big vicious dogs would be pretty handy to have right now. Anyway, where was I? Oh yes, the Southern Cross. We swear by the Southern Cross – and thanks, by the way, to Richo's wife Betty for running up that flag for us last night, it's come up a treat – we swear by the Southern Cross to stand up for our rights to dig for gold and shoot at each other and abuse Chinese people and get stinking drunk and occasionally burn other people's property, without taxation without representation, because taxation sucks and representation is pretty sweet. I have a dream that one day miners everywhere will not be judged by the absence of their licences, but by the content of their cradles, as long as they are white. The miners, I mean, not the cradles. If anyone can keep their cradles white on the diggings, tell me your secret, ha-ha! Ummmmm anyway, yep, let's fight for our rights and stuff, boys. Hang around after this meeting for the raffle, drinks at bar prices.[80]

Even today, Lalor's speech retains its power to inspire and energise and confuse, and eyewitnesses who were at Bakery Hill that day recalled the hair on the back of their neck standing on end, shivers running up their spine, going weak at the knees, powerful abdominal cramps,

80 I'm paraphrasing a tad here.

throbbing headaches, fever and persistent nausea. Yes, the water at Bakery Hill was of a very poor quality, but that doesn't mean Peter Lalor wasn't a fine speaker, and his inflammatory rhetoric soon saw him elected leader of the Ballarat Reform League – his first order of business was to 'shoot the bloody arses out of those poncy soldier pricks'.

Following Lalor's speech, the miners all burnt their mining licences. What was it with these guys and burning stuff? As repressive as the government was, you have to feel a bit of sympathy with them: it can't be easy to keep control of thousands of pyromaniacs with shovels.

Robert Rede, the Gold Commissioner, immediately ordered a licence search for the next day, which was kind of a dick move. 'C'mon, man, you know we just burnt them all,' said the diggers. 'Can't you for once in your life be cool?' But Rede was a man who didn't know the meaning of the word 'cool'. Or of the words 'sweet', 'nice', 'pleasant' or 'cuddly'. To be blunt, he was a real Bligh. And Lalor was to be his Macarthur, except without the beautiful jumpers and lingering scent of lanolin.

And so the goldfields police swooped on the diggings, demanding to see licences. Those who offered a pile of ashes were arrested immediately. Those who requested an extension were told they needed to call during business hours. In response, the miners formed an angry mob, which made people wonder if they had any other tricks. 'Is forming angry mobs all you *do?*' asked the sarcastic teens watching proceedings.

In any case, the diggers had decided that a man should stick to what he's good at, and they were damn good at forming angry mobs. So the next day[81] they went ahead and formed yet another one, and while they

81 Notice how fast things moved in those days? If this had happened in the 21st century, everyone would still have been waiting for a Senate committee to hand down its report three years after the first riot.

were at it, they also formed a stockade. This they were slightly less good at, and what they had wasn't exactly an impenetrable rebel fortress, more a collection of planks propped precariously against one another in a vaguely fence-like shape.

Inside the stockade, the agitated miners gathered up all the weapons they could find – guns, knives, shovels, pickaxes and sardonic humour – and did some military drills, which was sort of cute, like toddlers putting on a fashion show. They also took the 'Eureka Oath', in which they declared, 'We swear by the Southern Cross to stand truly by each other and fight to defend our rights and liberties, for up to 15 minutes if weather allows.' After that, a lot of them went back to their claims, having realised with a growing sense of dread that Lalor wasn't just trolling. The ones who were left prepared for the ordeal ahead with some heavy drinking, the basic training of choice on the Australian frontier. They then lay down to sleep it off, which turned out to be less of a tactical masterstroke than they might have supposed.

At 3am on Sunday, 3 December 1854, around 300 policemen and soldiers, determined to uphold law and order in the colony and enraged by reports that Americans were making fun of Australia for having hardly any proper violence in its history, crept up on the stockade and charged.

The battle of the Eureka Stockade was over in about ten minutes, ranking it just ahead of the Battle of Apathy Gorge, and just behind the Franco–Wagga Wagga War, on the list of shortest ever military conflicts. Some scholars claim that the battle might have lasted longer if the miners had been awake, or good at fighting, or not outnumbered two to one: there's no way to know if any of these theories are accurate. All we know is that after most of the miners had gone home for the night, and the rest were passed out drunk, the brave defenders of the colonial government gallantly shot the bejeesus out of them. The miners soon surrendered, which the troops graciously accepted by continuing to shoot and bayonet them. Eventually they stopped after Captain Charles Pasley made an executive decision not to be a psychopath.

Six soldiers and police were killed in the battle. Estimates of the dead on the miners' side vary. Peter Lalor wrote that 22 had died, but others claimed the death toll was even higher, possibly as many as 60 when taking into account those who died of their wounds after the battle and those who were killed by bits of the poorly constructed stockade falling on them.

Lalor himself was wounded in the arm and hid under some fallen planks, in the manner of so many heroic freedom fighters throughout history.[82] The arm was amputated, and Lalor was taken to Geelong, in a double blow to his dignity. A reward was offered for his capture, but Lalor was never arrested, unlike several of his comrades who never had planks to hide under. They were acquitted, though, after successful deployment of the Government Is a Bastard defence.[83] The only man jailed for his role in the Eureka Rebellion was Henry Seekamp, editor of the *Ballarat Times*, who had published articles suggesting that miners were cool handsome guys with a fresh sense of style. These articles were ruled seditious, which seems a bit unfair in light of the fact that all the people who actually did proper sedition were let off.

Also, two men were sentenced to a week in prison for contempt of court after they applauded the not-guilty verdict for the rebels – Chief Justice William á Beckett ruled that clapping was an attempt to influence the jury, because Chief Justice William á Beckett was an

82 E.g. the famous story of how Pancho Villa secreted himself in a service station toilet to avoid the Federales.

83 Sadly, this one no longer works, even though it's still true.

imbecile who didn't understand the concepts of 'before' and 'after'. Imagine how dumb the assistant chief justice must have been.

The Hotham government continued to pursue Peter Lalor, but there were just so many one-armed Irishmen in Victoria, it was like finding a needle in a haystack. Eventually Hotham, in one of the gold rush's most famous orations, said, '*FINE!*' He declared an amnesty and then died, leading to much high-fiving among the mining community.

Commissioner Rede, meanwhile, was removed from his post and sent to live out the rest of his career in rural Victoria like a common racehorse.

Lalor had much greater fortunes than his enemies: after amnesty was declared he came out of hiding and was acclaimed a hero. In 1855 he was elected to the Victorian Upper House, and in 1856 to the Lower House, which sounds like a demotion but honestly it isn't. During his political career, Lalor lived up to his famed egalitarian ideals by supporting a Land Bill that favoured the rich, and by using low-paid Chinese workers to break a strike over wages and conditions at a mine of which he was a director. Still, Lalor's legacy as one of Australia's earliest freedom fighters is secure, and in a way the fact that he was an elitist anti-union bigot makes it even more impressive that he was able to inspire the common people of the goldfields to get themselves shot.

The Eureka Rebellion had major implications for law and government in Victoria. Mining licences were abolished and replaced by the 'Miner's Right', a fee of £1 a year. In 1857, miners were granted parliamentary voting rights when a bill was passed in the Victorian Parliament enabling universal white male suffrage, which in a time as racist and sexist as 1857 was about as democratic as anyone could realistically hope for. The bill made Victoria the first colony in Australia to grant universal white male suffrage – and was voted against by Peter Lalor, the people's champion as usual.

In a more far-reaching sense, the Eureka Stockade echoed down the ages as a symbol of Australian independence and the earliest stirrings of a nation's thirst for democracy, except for the people who say it's not that at all. There is no doubt that Eureka was a blow for freedom against tyranny, a working-class rebellion against tyrannical upper orders and a cry for justice for the oppressed; at the same time, it cannot be denied that it wasn't any of those things. It is, one might say, a tricky debate to resolve.

But if the truth is, as so often in historical analysis, murkier than a poorly maintained fish tank, we can at least be sure of this: some guys did not want to pay some fees, and in the end people got killed. And that's a pretty big deal.

ESSAY QUESTIONS

1. Explain, using diagrams, how you would have built a much better Eureka Stockade.
2. Discuss the problem of overpricing at Sovereign Hill. Couldn't they cut costs by sacking some of the people who just walk around in costumes? There's too many of them, I reckon.

SURVIVOR: ARMED ROBBERY

In which bands of desperados roam the bush in search of riches and glory but find only death and horses

IF THERE'S ONE THING that unites all Australians, of all ages, races and creeds, it is our love of violent criminals. Today, one can see this unique strain of the Australian identity in our popular media: in every major paper, even Adelaide's *Sunday Fulminator*, headlines are constantly cheering on lawbreakers of all kinds and urging readers to greater disrespect for law and order. It's all a part of our knockabout larrikin anti-authoritarian streak that we occasionally remember we're supposed to have. And it all began with the bushrangers.[84]

The first bushrangers were escaped convicts who fled the early colonies under the mistaken impression that living in the Australian bush was somehow preferable to being in prison. These fugitives were also known as 'bolters' due to their remarkable speed and deeply conservative political views, but originally they were associated merely with those who had slipped through the law's fingers and were able to live rough in the bush until they inevitably died from a snake bite or a spider bite or sunstroke or getting chlamydia from a koala. The 'bushranger' label came to refer to those who had not just broken up

84 Well, I guess in a way it all started with the time the continent was literally settled by criminals, but go with me here.

with the law, but were also hanging around its house making rude hand gestures and leaving insulting notes in its letterbox.

The first bona fide bushranger was John Caesar, a convict of African descent nicknamed 'Black Caesar' due to that being what people called him. Transported for theft on the First Fleet, Caesar utterly disproved theories of rehabilitation in the field of corrections by continuing to steal things on a regular basis. Escaping captivity, he led his gang in a series of thefts that shocked all sensitive and clean-living inhabitants of the settlement – of which, fortunately, there were not many. Governor Hunter offered five gallons of spirits as reward for Caesar's capture, and his faith in the reliable alcoholism of the colonists was well-founded. In February 1796, one John Wimbow shot Caesar at Liberty Plains.[85] Caesar's career was brief, but his influence would be enormous.

In the early morning of the bushranging era, Van Diemen's Land – later dubbed 'Tasmania' after Van Diemen was revealed to be not the sort of man you want to give a whole land to – was fertile ground for countryside-roaming ne'er-do-wells. The most prominent Van Diemenish bushranger was Matthew Brady, known as 'Gentleman Brady' for his suave and attractive way of inflicting post-traumatic stress disorder on those he met. Brady was transported to Sydney in 1820 for stealing and escaped to Van Diemen's Land in 1824, where he spent the next two years as a bushranger, terrorising and charming the local populace in equal measure with his irresistible combination of violence and sexiness. He was known for his reluctance to rob or insult women, even when they were extremely overweight or unfashionably dressed, and gained a reputation as one of the island's politest and most considerate criminals: not that this was all that tough a competition to

85 Now known as Auburn, after the original name became too ironic for anyone to bear.

win; you could be in the top ten just by not eating anyone. Nevertheless Brady's manners impressed, and his capacity for always knowing exactly the right suit to wear to any particular robbery, and habit of offering everyone he shot a complimentary mint, made the business of pursuing and arresting him a terribly bittersweet experience.

In 1826, Brady was betrayed by one of his own men and captured by a bounty hunter by the name of ...

John Batman!

That's right! The guy who invented Melbourne, whose name was literally BATMAN, was also a BOUNTY HUNTER. In other words, he fought crime as a citizen vigilante.[86] *Just like actual Batman*. If you delve deeper into John Batman's life, you'll probably find out he had a grappling-hook gun and infrared opera glasses. Seriously, how is the city not named after him? It's a disgrace.

Brady was hanged in Hobart in 1826 alongside four other bushrangers, including Thomas Jeffries, who was famous for eating people. Brady objected to being executed with a cannibal, but in Van Diemen's Land it wasn't that easy to find five convicts who had never eaten anyone.

Bushranging wasn't all about the opposing extremes of gentlemanly thievery and serial cannibalism, of course: most bushrangers inhabited the wide middle ground between the two. The first bushranger to really etch his name into legend was

Jack Donohoe

His real name was Jack Donahue, which is the source of much speculation about why he was called Jack Donohoe. He was born in Dublin in 1804 and transported to Sydney in 1825 after being convicted of 'intent to

86 When he wasn't fighting blacks as a citizen racist.

commit a felony' by the British Mind-Reading Court. In Sydney he was twice sentenced to 50 lashes, probably for something stupid like stealing a lettuce or spilling gravy on an officer's socks or something – they loved whipping people back then, and the main outcome of this enthusiasm seems to have been the creation of bushrangers.

Sent to work on a farm at Quaker's Hill – which modern-day readers will be familiar with as the location of basically nothing – Donohoe, as was the style at the time, escaped with two other convicts, Kilroy and Smith. The trio became known as 'The Strippers'[87] due to their modus operandi of robbing wealthy land owners while wearing tearaway Velcro trousers,[88] and quickly became known as the sexiest and most rhythmic outlaws in New South Wales. Servants in the colony would help the Strippers by supplying food, shelter and information on their employers, whom the gang would then rob in order to purchase tassels and sequinned thongs.

In December 1827, the Strippers were arrested after a tip-off from a civic-minded hen's night, and three months later they were sentenced to death. Donohoe, the little scamp, escaped again and started romping around the country west, north and south of Sydney in the company of the 'Wild Colonial Boys', the first criminal gang in Australia to truly recognise the value of effective branding. If they hadn't been called the Wild Colonial Boys, they might be remembered as just another bunch of dumb kids who rode around the place pointing guns at people and taking their stuff – but with a great name like that, they could hardly help but be immortalised in folklore. It's a similar situation with the Sex Pistols.[89]

It was due to his nimble PR campaign that Jack Donohoe became

87 Actual historical fact.

88 Non-actual historical fact.

89 And the Christian Democrats.

the first bushranger to have a popular song written about him. 'The Wild Colonial Boy' told Donohoe's story, explaining in an infectious, radio-friendly manner how great it is when a young man robs people and then gets shot to death. Unfortunately – again, like with the Sex Pistols – the authorities banned the song for being seditious (at this stage, people didn't know how patriotic bushranging was and just thought it was illegal). The ban caused different versions of the song to be written: an Australian version where the Wild Colonial Boy is called 'Jack Doolan', and an Irish one about 'Jack Duggan'.[90] The song explains how Jack used to rob the rich to give to the poor, which just goes to show that songwriters are pathological liars.[91] A sample of the lyrics:

Jack drew a pistol from his belt,
And waved it like a toy,
'I'll fight, but not surrender,'
Cried the Wild Colonial Boy.

This, at least, was accurate. In the end, Donohoe did fight, and did not surrender. On 1 September 1830, his gang was accosted by troopers at Bringelly near Campbelltown – the beginning of the now firmly established trend of people regretting going to Campbelltown – and a fire fight ensued. Donohoe was recorded to have called on the troopers to 'Come on, using the most insulting and indecent epithets'. It should be remembered that it was 1830, so this might have just meant he called the policemen 'scallywags' or told them to stop being so naughty. We sometimes forget that less than 200 years ago, men were still challenging each other to duels because someone refused to apologise

90 You've got to think the authorities probably weren't completely fooled by this.
91 See also: 'I Am the Walrus'.

for saying 'damn', so we can't apply our own pretty awesome standards of obscenity to the Wild Colonial Boy.

Whatever he called them, they certainly followed his instructions to the letter, firing on him with gusto. Trooper Muggleston was the man to finish the affair, shooting Donohoe through the head, one of the most romantic ways to die. His willingness to be shot in the head rather than cave in to societal pressure not to be shot in the head was part of what earned him the soubriquet 'Bold Jack Donohoe'. His courage is even more admirable when you realise he was only 163 centimetres tall and was described as wearing a 'cabbage tree hat'; no idea what that is, but it doesn't sound like something that would bolster the confidence of the average man.

After Donohoe's death, lovers of courageous rogues mourned, while lovers of not-being-robbed-at-gunpoint celebrated. One enterprising Sydney entrepreneur produced a line of pipes in the shape of Donohoe's head, complete with bullet holes in the forehead. Fashionable Sydneysiders took great pleasure in buying Donohoe's head and smoking it, proving that people in the past were basically a pack of revolting ghouls.

Donohoe was a major influence on the bushranger craze, inspiring hundreds of eager youngsters who dreamt of one day having their own bullet-riddled heads smoked. Such as

Captain Thunderbolt

Captain Thunderbolt was perhaps the most prominent personality of the Age of Captains, a period during which bushrangers with delusions of grandeur gave themselves silly names to strike terror into their enemies' hearts, assuming that their enemies suffered from an irrational fear of mid-level military officers.

Thunderbolt was born Fred Ward in 1835, and as a young man in New England[92] displayed great promise as a horse and cattle thief. On 22 December 1863, needing some cash for last-minute Christmas shopping, he robbed a toll-bar[93] at Rutherford, New South Wales, where he announced that his name was Captain Thunderbolt. There's a story that the toll-bar operator said, in reference to Ward's knock on the door, 'By God, I thought it must have been a thunderbolt', and Ward replied, 'I am the thunder and this is my bolt' – referring to his gun, obviously: this wasn't the opening scene of a porno.[94] The story has no basis in fact, as Ward actually dubbed himself 'Thunderbolt' in honour of his favourite scene from *The Sound of Music*.

Thunderbolt took to the northwest plains of New South Wales with his bushranger's moll, Mary Ann Bugg, who was quite the kickass action hero herself. Some disapproved of Bugg's lifestyle as an accessory to robbery under arms, but what really scandalised 1860s society was that she wore trousers and refused to ride side-saddle. 'Has the woman no sense of propriety?' gasped well-to-do matrons, fanning themselves in a comical fashion.

Thunderbolt reignited his bushranging career in 1865 with accomplices Patrick Kelly and Jemmy the Whisperer, a fearsome outlaw who would lure victims to him by speaking in a barely audible voice, until his listeners had to come closer to hear him better, and then headbutting them in the face.

Thunderbolt, Kelly and the Whisperer[95] dissolved in January 1866 – for all Thunderbolt's mastery of bushranging, he had a terrible HR

92 Obviously there was already a New England in America, so it might be more accurate to call this 'New New England'. Or 'New England: X-Treme'.

93 I dunno: some kind of pub with boom gates?

94 Though it could be: all we need is someone with the guts to write it.

95 Not to be confused with the breakfast radio team of the same name.

department and suffered from appalling staff turnover. 'I just can't seem to hang on to my accomplices,' he whined to Mary Ann, who was too busy having several babies to care.

Yet Thunderbolt's bushranging exploits continued until 25 May 1870, when after an armed drinking session at the Royal Oak Inn, Captain Thunderbolt staggered out to Kentucky Creek near Uralla and was shot dead.

There were claims by some in Uralla that it was not, in fact, Fred Ward who was killed at Kentucky Creek, and that it was instead his uncle William whom the police gunned down. This means it is possible that Captain Thunderbolt survived and may be living among us today. So if you ever run into an 180-year-old man who walks with a limp and keeps looking longingly at passing mail coaches, that might be Fred Ward himself, and you should shake his hand and congratulate him on his longevity.

Captain Thunderbolt is commemorated by Thunderbolts Way, a road between Gloucester and Inverell, in recognition of how much Fred Ward always loved roads between places. At the intersection of Thunderbolts Way and the New England Highway at Uralla, there's a statue of Thunderbolt on his horse, a reminder of the proud independent spirit of the people of New England and their love of illegal activities.

Thunderbolt wasn't the only captain to make his name in the harsh Australian bush: there was also Kasey Chambers. And before her, there was

Captain Moonlite

Captain Moonlite was the greatest of all Australia's misspelled bushrangers. He was born Andrew Scott in Ireland and came to Melbourne with a plan to become a priest, but decided to pursue a more respectable profession, so took up bank robbery.

On 8 May 1869, Ludwig Julius Wilhelm Bruun, agent of the London Chartered Bank in Egerton, near Ballarat, was forced to open the bank's safe and hand over the contents to a mysterious masked man who called himself 'Captain Moonlite'. It would have been impossible to find out who the masked man was, were it not for the fact that Bruun knew Scott and recognised his voice. As a novice in the crime game, Scott had yet to learn the fundamental inadvisability of robbing your friends, or if you do, the value of disguising your voice, Batman-style.[96]

Moonlite's first arrest came in 1870 over the improper purchase of a yacht that he attempted to sail to Fiji. It is at this point in Moonlite's biography that most historians begin to identify a certain tendency towards attention deficit disorder. If he had only concentrated on getting very good at one thing – being a priest, being an engineer, being a bank robber, sailing illegally obtained yachts to Fiji – he might have really made something of himself, but he always seemed to get distracted. He was put in gaol for 12 months, spending some of it in Parramatta Lunatic Asylum[97] after pretending to be insane, another hobby that he never really followed through on.

After being released from prison, Moonlite was arrested for the Egerton bank robbery, and proceeded to put in a most entertaining performance at his trial before Judge Redmond Barry, well known as the judge who seemed to preside over, like, every bushranger's trial ever, as well as the trial of the Eureka rebels – it's possible he was the only judge in Australia in the 19th century.

At that trial, Moonlite conducted his own defence and stretched

96 The real Batman, I mean, not John Batman. Though he might have disguised his voice too: it seems like the kind of thing he'd have done.

97 Now known as 'Westfield Shoppingtown'.

the case out for eight days, perhaps hoping that if the trial lasted long enough, everyone else would just get bored and go home.[98] He cross-examined Bruun for seven hours, testing the bank agent with 'shrewd and pertinacious questions' such as, 'Where exactly were you on or about the night of April 14th, 1654?', 'How many joeys does the average kangaroo give birth to in a year?' and 'If two trains leave Dandenong at 8.14am, one travelling at 80 miles an hour and the other travelling at 73 miles an hour, which one will arrive first at Ulladulla if the first one has to stop to pick up a consignment of breadfruit in Wangaratta?' The gallery applauded loudly Moonlite's amusing banter and pithy asides. They applauded even more loudly when he was sentenced to ten years' hard labour.

Because he was a particularly disobedient prisoner, Moonlite wasn't allowed out of prison until he'd served seven years of his sentence: a cruel near-adherence to a judge's decision that shocked decent society.

Following his release, Moonlite assembled a new gang, including James Nesbitt, a young man who had met Moonlite in prison and who was, in all likelihood, his boyfriend.[99] Moonlite wore a ring made of Nesbitt's hair during his final trial, and once wrote that 'Jim's sisters are my sisters, his friends my friends, his hopes my hopes'. The existence of further letters wherein Moonlite claims to rob banks 'so I can have coins to bounce off Jimmy's buns' is somewhat disputed in the academic community. Claims that Moonlite and Nesbitt had planned to buy a King Charles spaniel together are even more dubious.

The Moonlite gang kicked off proceedings at Mansfield in Victoria, but soon crossed into New South Wales in search of work and standard rail gauges. It was in New South Wales that Moonlite's gang committed

---

98 A.k.a. 'The Derryn Hinch Defence'.

99 True fact, and kind of sweet, I think.

their most celebrated act, the takeover of the Wantabadgery sheep station – so named because its owner, Claude McDonald, had famously always wanted a badger – near Wagga Wagga. The gang invaded the station after the McDonalds made the mistake of refusing the gang food and shelter, although to be fair the gang had made the mistake of being a gang of bushrangers, which history should have told them never ended well. So it proved at Wantabadgery, where Moonlite's men were interrupted in the midst of their carousing by the arrival of mounted troopers: the biggest buzzkills of the 19th century.

James Nesbitt tried to create a diversion to allow his captain to escape, but instead created a diversion allowing his captain to be captured. The troopers shot Nesbitt, and Moonlite rushed to his side: according to newspaper reports, 'his leader wept over him like a child, laid his head upon his breast, and kissed him passionately'. In all likelihood he also looked to the sky in slow motion and screamed, '*NOOOOOOOOOOOOOOOOOO!*' Historians are divided over whether the scene was more like the end of *Titanic* or the end of *Love Story*, or maybe the end of *King Kong*, but it was definitely incredibly poignant, and someone should probably make a movie out of it with Hugh Jackman as Captain Moonlite and some guy from *Home and Away* as Nesbitt.

Moonlite's decision to make Nesbitt's death properly tearjerking spelt doom for the gang, as the troopers moved in and took him into custody. Captain Moonlite was hanged on 20 January 1880, having never learnt to spell 'Moonlight', a tragedy of inadequate education systems. Before he died, he stated:

> *My dying wish is to be buried beside my beloved James Nesbitt, the man with whom I was united by every tie which could bind*

> *human friendship, we were one in hopes, in heart and soul and this unity lasted until he died in my arms.*[100]

The government of the time, which had recently passed stringent cartoonish villainy laws, refused this request. A hundred and 15 years later, however, Moonlite's remains were exhumed from Rookwood Cemetery and placed in Gundagai, next to Nesbitt. So there is a happy ending to the story, if you ignore the bit where one guy was shot to death and the other one hanged. A happy ending for their corpses, anyway.

Captain Moonlite is today remembered as one of the most stylish bushrangers out there, and has a firm place in Australian history as 'the one who isn't Captain Thunderbolt'. Which is at least better than 'the one who isn't Captain Moonlite', a title that goes to Captain Starlight,[101] a man whose greatest achievement was accidentally drinking poison and dying.

Dan Morgan

Dan 'Mad Dog' Morgan, who was born John Fuller but changed his name so that his nickname would be alliterative, was one of the most feared bushrangers of the 1800s, and surpasses even Ned Kelly in ferocity and number of Dennis Hopper films made about him. Whereas men like Matthew Brady and Captain Thunderbolt took pride in their reputations as 'gentleman bushrangers', Morgan revelled in his own notoriety as 'the complete and utter prick bushranger'.

---

100 Admit it: you wish someone would say that about you.

101 Not to be confused with the fake Captain Starlight from the novel *Robbery Under Arms*, who was based on Harry Readford, whom many consider 'the real Captain Starlight', not to be confused with the real Captain Starlight. So this clears that up.

A well-known engraving of Morgan by Samuel Calvert, from 1864, depicts him as a grim-faced, full-bearded man with menacing eyes, a pointy nose and no legs: though contemporary reports indicate that he did, in fact, have legs, so it's possible Calvert just forgot to finish the picture. In contrast, a photograph of Morgan taken after his death shows him as a horizontal man who is dead – Calvert's engraving doesn't include these details, suggesting that Morgan's tendency to lie down and die developed later in life.

But first there was mad-dogging to do. Under the name 'Dan Morgan', but also other aliases including 'Jack Morgan', 'John Smith', 'Dan the Breaker', 'Down-the-River Jack' and, perplexingly, 'Billy the Native', he set new standards in unproductive name-changing. But even between filing the deed poll paperwork, Morgan managed to get in some solid crime-doing during the gold rush period, when bushranging was particularly popular due to the recent revelation that gold was worth a lot of money. In 1860 he was riding about the Riverina area of New South Wales stealing horses, which were then so valuable that many people called them 'the gold nuggets of the mammal world', with thousands of immigrants flooding into the country to pan for ponies.[102]

Morgan popped up again in 1863 in the company of 'German Bill',[103] an accomplice well known for being German and being called 'Bill'. In August, Morgan and Bill were ambushed by police. Morgan responded by shooting Police Magistrate Henry Baylis, and then shooting Bill so that he could escape while the police attended to the wounded German. This was one of the first public indications that Mad

102 Obviously this is a lie.

103 Not to be confused with 'Billy the Native', who was actually Morgan himself. German Bill was not, as far as we know, a native, unless he was a native of Germany. Then again Morgan wasn't a native either, so don't go too far down the rabbit hole of looking for logic in bushranging nicknames.

Dog Morgan was, to put it mildly, a cold, cold bastard. His nickname was, if anything, an insult to actual mad dogs: Old Yeller might've caused a bit of trouble, but he never bit another dog in order to cause a diversion. Dan Morgan is lucky that history doesn't remember him as Mad Dick Morgan.

Having proven his credentials as a total psycho, Morgan decided it was time to take his game to the next level, leave behind the small-time realm of malicious wounding and chase his lifetime dream of murdering people. Affronted at the fact that the reward for his capture was only £200, he descended upon Round Hill Station on 19 June 1864, drank all their rum and started shooting in the endearing way that drunk men have. He told the manager, an unhappy man by the name of Sam Watson, to stand still so he could kill him, which did not provide Watson with a strong incentive to do as he was told. After shooting Watson in the hand, Morgan ordered station hand John McLean to ride for a doctor to show his compassion. He then decided he might've showed a bit too much compassion and dialled it down by shooting McLean in the back. This seemed to strike a nice balance between kindness and cruelty that was typical of Morgan's unpredictable treatment of his victims: it was no wonder they called him 'Erratic Behaviour Morgan'.

Shortly after that, Morgan killed Sergeant David Maginnity, and the reward hit £1000. To celebrate, Morgan killed Sergeant Thomas Smyth. This was in the days before Ned Kelly (see next chapter), so the general public didn't yet know that police murderers were courageous patriots and they found Morgan a rather intimidating figure, as did the government: in March 1865, they passed the *Felons Apprehension Act*, which made Morgan an outlaw – to me it seems like all the people he'd robbed and killed would've already done that, but they were sticklers for technicalities I guess.

The colonies were living in terror of the Mad Dog: from Wangaratta to Burrumbuttock he launched attack after attack on the squatters of the borderlands. But even the maddest dog must eventually be put to sleep. On 8 April 1865, Morgan bailed up the Macpherson homestead at Peechelba Station in northern Victoria. The next morning Morgan left the house to get his horse and was shot in the back by John Windlaw, which – no matter what you may think of the rights and wrongs of his career – is simply no way to treat a houseguest.

After death, his body was publicly displayed at Wangaratta, a town that was apparently full of incredibly gross people who enjoyed looking at dead bodies. Locals took bits of his hair and beard as souvenirs, and his head was cut off and sent to the professor of anatomy at the University of Melbourne. Yep, history is morbid and creepy, and you wouldn't want to hang out in it.

Mad Dog Morgan cemented his place in folklore by his daring, by his striking air of menace and by being 100 per cent batshit[104] insane. He was the bushranger you would least want to meet on a country road, because he would probably threaten to shoot you if you didn't hand over all your money, and then after you handed over all your money he would shoot you. On the other hand, if you were a friend of his ... he would probably still shoot you. Morgan didn't really have many friends. Not after he'd shot them, anyway. But you can't deny that he was a magnetic, colourful personality, and in his defence he only murdered people who were alive a long time ago, so nobody cares much about them anymore.

Mad Dog Morgan also gained a reputation as 'the travellers' friend', although God knows how, because honestly that is pretty stupid.

104 Not to be confused with Batman.

Ben Hall

Ben Hall was known as 'Brave Ben Hall' or sometimes 'Bold Ben Hall': violent disagreements frequently break out between historians over which one is more accurate. But either way, Hall is definitely a top-of-the-table talent when it comes to complimentary adjectives: 'brave' and 'bold' both beat Dan Morgan's 'mad', Jack Donohoe's 'wild' and Captain Starlight's 'cretinous'.

The story of Ben Hall is one of the most romantic in Australian history. Not romantic in the sense of *The Notebook*: more like romantic in the sense of season three of *Underbelly*.[105] It is a tale of heartbreak, despair, violence and betrayal, and the best part is that there are certain bits that are true.

Hall was born in Maitland, New South Wales, in 1837, and was agreed by most contemporary observers to 'have his entire life ahead of him'. But little did the newborn baby Ben Hall know what was in store. In fact, little did he know anything, being a baby.

When he was 19, Hall married Bridget 'Biddy' Walsh. There were early signs of impending tension when Bridget altered her wedding vows to read, 'I promise to love, honour and obey you, and ditch you for a sexy stockman when I get the chance', but Hall saw this as simply a manifestation of his new bride's quirky sense of humour. He and Bridget had a son named Henry in 1859, and shortly afterwards Hall leased the Sandy Creek cattle run in partnership with his brother-in-law John Maguire, later to gain fame as a reliable medium-pace bowler.

Hall's troubles began in 1862, when Biddy left him for the stockman[106] James Taylor, citing his sweetly mellow voice and

105 But sadly with less frontal nudity.

106 And possibly also ex-policeman, which is not really true but makes the story better.

understated guitar accompaniment as being far superior to Hall's. The happy couple moved to Humbug Creek, which seems appropriate.

Why the Halls' marriage fell apart is a matter for conjecture. Was Biddy simply a flighty shrew who cared not for Ben's broken heart? Was Ben a callous lothario who had tormented Biddy with repeated infidelities? Was James Taylor just really good in bed? The answers to these questions are lost to history, and our knowledge of the saga is the poorer for it, although our freedom to make things up is much, much richer.

Ben Hall's life here took on a startling similarity to a burning rubbish bin rolling down a hill into a sewer. After the departure of his wife, he began hanging around with a bad crowd, to wit: Frank Gardiner, notorious bushranger and handsome man. This wasn't a good move on Hall's part, but who could resist Gardiner's deep, soulful eyes?

Hall was arrested by Police Inspector Sir Frederick Pottinger for an armed robbery carried out by Gardiner's gang in 1862, but the charges were dismissed. From here on, Inspector Pottinger would become the Javert to Hall's Valjean,[107] pursuing him relentlessly and not even caring about what a sweet, sensitive young bushranger he was.

Due to peer pressure,[108] Hall took part in the robbery of the Lachlan Gold Escort and was again arrested, only to be released again for lack of evidence. Suffering financially from his legal troubles – which is an ironic problem for a man who has just helped steal a wagonload of gold – Hall was forced to give up the lease to his property. Unlike most people, who would find that the loss of everything important in their life and the sudden onset of poverty would naturally steer them away

107 You people better have seen *Les Mis*. That is a *very* good reference.

108 Sadly, *Degrassi Junior High* would not be invented for another 125 years, or else the whole tragic saga could have been avoided.

Governor Arthur Phillip in a pensive mood, seconds after being told of New South Wales's crippling wig shortage.

Robert O'Hara Burke dies, having been denied one final go on his friend's invisible chair.

The Welcome Stranger nugget, inspiration for the Picnic bar.

Gold rush miners using the now-discredited 'standing still on a pile of dirt' method of gold extraction.

A group of WWI diggers take a break from being shot to death to enjoy their new confident national identity.

Legendary, courageous New Zealand stretcher bearer Dick Henderson, who served in WWI for three years, painted while engaged in his favourite activity: being mistaken for John Simpson Kirkpatrick, who served in WWI for three weeks.

A WWII poster considered by some historians to be conclusive proof that women existed as long ago as the 1940s.

Bust of Sir Robert Menzies, Australia's first and so far only earless prime minister.

Australian diggers on the Kokoda Track, participating in their office team-building exercise.

Prime Minister John Howard demonstrates his ability to control all metals. AFP Photo/Greg Wood.

Kevin Rudd greets the Australian people upon becoming prime minister. AAP Image/Lukas Coch.

from crime, Hall sadly descended further into it.

He continued hanging around with the bushranging no-goodniks, slouching around by the shops, making rude remarks to passing grannies and spitting on the footpath. It was no surprise that Hall, having been marked as an undesirable, was coming into frequent contact with the police. 'You're up to no good,' the police would say, and Hall would reply, 'Why can't you coppers get off our backs, man?' The situation would become heated extremely quickly. Inspector Pottinger, wishing to take the heat out of the situation, decided that burning down Hall's house would probably fix everything.

In the end, this turned out to be a miscalculation. If anything, having the police set fire to his home made Hall even less inclined to respect the law. He had lost his wife, lost his son, lost his property and lost his home, and seeing the reasons *not* to be a bushranger dwindle down to nothing, Hall set out to gain sweet revenge on the authorities who had blighted his life by stealing lots of money and eventually getting killed. That'd show them.

Hall became viewed as a heroic figure, fighting against corrupt and unjust officialdom, and even the most law-abiding among us has to admit he had a very honest face. He robbed and raided, but he never killed anyone,[109] and he was known for his courtesy and kindness towards everyone who wasn't a policeman. Hall assumed the mythical status of an Australian Robin Hood, except he didn't use a bow and arrow, and he was motivated less by a desire to rob the rich to feed the poor than by a desire to rob the rich to make the pigs look like idiots. No wonder Inspector Pottinger was always stamping his foot and going, '*Ooh*, that darned Ben Hall!'

---

109 His friends totally killed people though, and it's not like he rang 000 or anything when they did.

Hall demonstrated his idiosyncratic approach to crime in the taking of Canowindra, when his gang took over the pub in the NSW town and imprisoned the whole population inside it. Although they were captives, they were not badly treated,[110] and the bushrangers gave them food and entertainment. What kind of entertainment isn't recorded, but one can easily speculate that, knowing what we know about Hall and his men, it was probably something along the lines of a karaoke competition or an impromptu performance of *Grease*: unless they went the more sedate route and set up a Scrabble tournament, as bushrangers were known to do from time to time.

At the end of the Canowindra incident, Hall's men set the hostages free, paid the pub's landlord for his goods and compensated the townspeople for their time, just to rub in with steel-wool thoroughness how great they were, especially compared to the dumb police – who, in the case of Canowindra, spent the duration locked in their own station's cell. The message was further reinforced by a later incident in which Hall's men stripped three policemen of their clothes, tied them to trees and lectured them on police misbehaviour: an incident that not only embarrassed the police force and proved the unconventional non-violent tactics of the Hall Gang, but that was also hilarious and caused job applications for a position in the gang to flood in.

Hall returned to Canowindra not long afterwards to hold the town hostage for another three days of fun and frolics, and a wonderful time was had by all. The children of Canowindra were by now calling him 'Uncle Ben', and several townsfolk had invited him to go fishing with them on the weekend. At the time of his death there was a motion before the town council to rename Canowindra 'Benville'.[111]

---

110 Except in comparison to people who haven't been imprisoned.

111 If anyone from Canowindra is reading: there's still time to do this.

Of course it couldn't last. Hall's gangmates began to cause trouble by killing policemen, upsetting the dreamy, romantic bushranging heartthrob, who had always lived his life according to a strict moral code. It was a moral code that did allow for armed robbery and assault, but it was a strict one nonetheless. Up till then, Hall's gang had been interested only in humiliating the police – locking them in their own cells, tying them to trees, publishing witty satirical cartoons and so on. The murders turned them into the kind of dull, unoriginal gang that just killed police like all the other gangs, and the bushranging critics denounced the disappointingly safe and derivative direction Hall's work was moving in. 'He seems to have run out of fresh ideas, and taken refuge in cliché,' tutted the *Bushranger Fanciers' Monthly*.

What was worse, Inspector Pottinger remained hot on their trail, relentless in his obsessive chase. 'Who are those guys?' Hall asked Gilbert in exasperation as he yet again saw Pottinger's men crest a nearby hill, the inspector's distinctive straw hat standing out at the band's head. There was only one thing for it: he would have to move to Bolivia.

Or, at least, he should have – he might have lasted longer. Instead, Hall merely resolved to leave New South Wales, realising he couldn't keep evading the police indefinitely and that housing prices were simply out of control. The gang prepared to move to Queensland, where they would find more opportunities, nicer weather and SeaWorld.

Local man Mick Coneley offered the gang his assistance, which was extremely welcome, but the Hall Gang soon realised they should have asked Coneley exactly what kind of assistance he meant, when he revealed that his assistance would be taking the form of a report to the police on the gang's location. Maybe they should have been more specific about what they were looking for, as it might have saved a bit of unpleasantness: 'This wasn't what we wanted at all!' they cried angrily at Coneley, who was shocked at their ingratitude. 'This is the last time Mick Coneley does someone a favour,' he grumbled.

The coppers tracked Hall down and approached his camp at dawn on 5 May 1865. Eight policemen surprised Hall, who ran to his horses but never made it. The police shot him in the back as he ran. Hall reportedly called out to his friend Billy Dargin, an Aboriginal tracker assisting the police, 'Shoot me dead, Billy! Don't let the traps take me alive!'

Dargin did not comply, possibly knowing even then that the story was made up and Hall never actually said that, but Hall needn't have worried in any case. As he fell to the ground, the policemen kept on firing, pumping 30 bullets into his body. 'Better safe than sorry,' seemed to be the motto of this particular band of policemen, not wishing to spoil the ship for a ha'porth of tar, or the extra-judicial execution of a bushranger for want of a few extra bullets. Within a few seconds, Bold Ben Hall was dead several times over. His vow that they would never hang him had been fulfilled in what has to be called a less than satisfactory manner. Inspector Sir Frederick Pottinger celebrated with a brief joyous dance.

A lot of questions were asked about whether the killing of Ben Hall was necessary or even legal. At the very least, some argued, the policemen should be reprimanded for the massive blowout in the department's annual bullet budget. But nothing was done, because to any questions about the propriety of the operation, the police force simply pointed out that Hall was a bushranger and that dying in a hail of bullets was in his contract.

Many years later, in the 21st century, Hall's descendants pushed for the inquest into his death to be reopened to determine the legality of his execution, but the push failed due to an unfortunate confluence of 19th- and 21st-century attitudes: people in the 19th century didn't care about due process, and people in the 21st century don't care about people in the 19th century.

But Hall's legacy lives on. He is second only to the Great Kelly in the pantheon of Australian bushrangery, and his good manners and relatively non-violent exploits helped establish him as even more of a gentleman bushranger than the approximately 63 previous gentleman bushrangers had been. The image we have of Hall – of a man victimised by corrupt authority till he fought back in the only way available – strikes a chord with all of us: it's easy to see ourselves in his place, taking up pistols and leaping astride a horse to start a life in the bush, after the drive-through forgot to put our chips in one too many times. The story of Ben Hall is the story of all of us who have ever been let down by society and retaliated by threatening to shoot people unless they give us money.

When you look into Ben's sad, wistful eyes in the old photograph, you can't help but whisper, 'I feel you, brother. It's you and me against the world.' In fact, why not celebrate him today by tying a nude policeman to a tree in your own neighbourhood?

But no matter how romantic Ben Hall's tale, he will never achieve the stature in the public consciousness of the one indisputable bushranging colossus.

ESSAY QUESTIONS

1. Which of these is the best name for a bushranger: a) Captain Orange Juice; b) Major Explosions; or c) Staff Sergeant Asteroids?
2. What is a cabbage tree hat? Would you ever wear one?

My Helmet Rules

In which the original metalhead rides out against the people's oppressors, and a funny hat enters the annals of legend

Edward 'Ned' Kelly is the most famous bushranger of all, a legendary figure whose story has been told myriad times on the page, on the stage, on the screen and in song, and whose enduring popularity is a constant reminder of Australians' innate love of the underdog, anti-authoritarian attitude and willingness to embrace any murderer with the courage to wear an amusing hat.

Ned Kelly was born in Beveridge, Victoria, in 1854, the son of an Irish pig thief[112] turned gold-digger who swore that his children would have all the things he never had growing up, e.g. pigs. As a child, Ned was given a green sash as a reward for bravery, after saving another boy from drowning in a creek: in an example of the fundamental unfairness of colonial justice, this wasn't taken into account at his trial later in life, even though by any reasonable standard, saving a person's life should really cancel out at least one of the murders you commit later on. It's possible Ned just had an incompetent lawyer who neglected to bring up the fact he was owed a freebie – one of the many tragedies of Ned's life.

112 A pig thief from Ireland, that is: he didn't steal pigs of any particular nationality.

The Kelly family was in frequent contact with the police, who were a friendly lot and liked to keep in touch with their pals, usually by arresting them. Ned himself first tangled with the law at 15, when he was accused of assaulting and stealing from a Chinese man named Ah Fook. Fook claimed that Ned had beaten him with a bamboo stick and taken ten shillings[113] from him. Ned denied the charge, saying that he'd confronted Fook for abusing his sister, upon which the Chinese man had started to beat *him* with a bamboo stick. Nobody seemed willing to place the blame on the true culprit: the bamboo stick.

Ned was charged with highway robbery, which was unfair as it didn't even happen on a highway, but the charges were eventually dismissed. A mutual resentment had begun to simmer, though, between him and the police – in particular one Sergeant Whelan, who hated the young Kelly for his devil-may-care attitude and precocious capacity for growing facial hair, and was resolved to bring him down one way or another, becoming very much the Pottinger (Javert) to his Hall (Valjean).

In 1870, Ned was charged three times with acting as an accomplice to bushranger Harry Power, and three times the charges were dismissed due to lack of evidence. This may have been because the police were fabricating the charges just to have an excuse to harass a Kelly, or it may have been because the Kelly family were strong-arming potential witnesses. The Kellys were known to be fond of strong-arming people, and the police were known to have a deep love of fabricating charges and harassing people, so it's difficult to tell where the truth lies. On the other hand, Ned's later adventures do create the impression that he was a big fan of bushranging.

Here Ned's story takes a slightly unexpected turn, as he was

---

113 In today's money, half a sixpence.

imprisoned for six months for assault and sending calves' testicles through the mail.[114] To be fair, he only sent the calves' testicles as a favour for a friend, but Victoria was in the grip of a brutal police crackdown on livestock gonad distribution, and Ned felt the brunt.

After serving his testicle time, Ned went home and got in a fight with a policeman, having failed to read the popular pamphlet *What Not to Do Immediately After Getting Out of Prison.* And being a man committed to his craft, he didn't only fight with Constable Hall: he rode him like a horse. Hall had come across Ned riding a stolen horse – Ned claimed he had no idea it was stolen, but it's an open question whether we can trust the word of a known testicle-mailer. Hall tried to arrest the young man, and when that didn't work, to shoot him, but Ned beat him, sat on him and stuck his spurs into Hall's legs.[115]

Ned's actions hurt his defence: although he maintained he didn't know that his friend had stolen the horse, it was a lot more difficult to convince the jury that he didn't know Constable Hall wasn't a horse. He was sentenced to three years' hard labour for receiving stolen goods and aggravated policeman-riding.

In 1874, he was released and became bareknuckle boxing champion of the district, for want of anything better to do. But sadly, a promising boxing career never fully flowered. In 1877, Ned was arrested for public drunkenness and ended up in a scuffle with his police escort, in the course of which Constable Lonigan grabbed him by the testicles (but did not, by all accounts, attempt to post them to anyone). Lonigan's actions would have far-reaching repercussions, and not just for Ned's testicles.

Already Ned Kelly had endured about as much police harassment as any sensitive career criminal could stand, but the final straw that

114 He really did. Sometimes history is just weird.

115 Again, this is absolutely true freaky history.

broke the calf's balls was an incident at the Kelly house on 15 April 1878. Constable Alexander Fitzpatrick went to the house to arrest Ned's brother Dan for horse stealing, an oppressive charge to lay upon the young man given that for the Kellys, stealing horses was really more a traditional cultural practice than a crime. Fitzpatrick did not have the warrant for Dan's arrest with him, and Dan refused to go. Fitzpatrick drew his gun, to which the Kelly matriarch, Ellen, gave a retort along the lines of 'Nice gun, dickface.'

What actually happened at the Kelly house is the subject of much conjecture. Fitzpatrick claimed that the Kelly family, armed to the teeth,[116] set upon him, Ned shooting him in the wrist and Ellen hitting him with a coal shovel. Ned, however, asserted that he was 200 miles away at the time, and that a drunken Fitzpatrick had turned up to harass his family and then given himself injuries that he blamed on the Kellys.

Who was telling the truth? Who knows? Probably Fitzpatrick *was* drunk, but this was the 1800s and pretty much everyone was drunk all the time because drinking water gave you diarrhoea.[117] Ned may not have been there, but then again he may have, and shooting people in the wrist was definitely the kind of thing he liked to do, when he wasn't too busy riding them like horses or sending them reproductive organs. Likewise, Ellen Kelly was a proud and fiery lady who would always stand up for her family in the face of injustice, but also probably enjoyed the odd shovel-bashing just for fun.

Whatever the truth, the fact is that Ellen, her son-in-law and the Kellys' neighbour were all gaoled for their part in the incident, and both

116 Many have cast doubt on this story, pointing out that the Kellys were known to never carry guns in their teeth.

117 The world as a whole didn't really sober up until about 1904.

Ned and Dan became wanted men. Later on, Constable Fitzpatrick was dismissed from the police force for drunkenness and perjury, but that's probably a coincidence.

Burning with the injustice of it all, Ned and Dan took to the bush with their friends Joe Byrne and Steve Hart, who weren't wanted by the police but figured what the hell, it was boring not being a fugitive. Together the four formed the 'Kelly Gang', so named because Dan and Ned had two votes and Joe and Steve only one each. The four men took an oath, affirming their dedication to the core principles of the Kelly Gang Philosophy:

1. Resistance to tyranny in all its forms
2. Belief in the inalienable rights of all men
3. Shooting and stealing things
4. Huge, luxuriant beards

With these principles established, the Kelly Gang set out to strike terror into the hearts of all who were foolish enough to try to live a peaceful and happy life in their vicinity. They began as all great freedom fighters do: with multiple police murders.

With the gang camping in the Wombat Ranges,[118] the Victorian police sent two parties to apprehend them on 25 October 1878, the idea being to close in on the gang from two sides, trapping them. One party was made up of Sergeant Kennedy and Constables McIntyre, Lonigan and Scanlan. They set up camp at Stringybark Creek, having planned their assault meticulously in every detail, with one exception – they forgot the part of tracking bushrangers where you keep an eye out for any bushrangers who might be around.

---

118 Named after their discoverer, Sir Cecil Wombat.

Due to this minor oversight, McIntyre and Lonigan were making tea late in the afternoon of October 26 when the Kelly gang strolled up and told them to throw their hands in the air like they just didn't care. McIntyre obeyed. Lonigan, being more eager to get shot in the head than his comrade, tried to make a break for it and instantly had his wish granted. 'Oh Christ, I am shot,' Lonigan cried, having the irritating habit of constantly stating the obvious.

Finally, Ned had his revenge for Lonigan's heinous squirrel grip. 'What a pity,' said Ned. 'What made the fool run?'[119]

'Dunno,' McIntyre replied. 'Maybe it was those guns you were pointing at him.'[120]

'No need for that tone,' Ned reproved him. 'You've got to admit it's pretty stupid to try to run away from men with guns.'

'Run away, stand still, what difference does it make? You're going to shoot us all anyway,' said McIntyre gloomily, his natural nihilism rising to the surface.

'That hurts, McIntyre,' Ned said, with genuine pain in his voice. 'I thought we were friends.'

'What?'

'Calm down. Have a cup of tea.'

And so Constable McIntyre had a nice cuppa and a smoke, and the policeman and the gang sat down and got to know each other a bit better. 'Kind of sucks that you're a policeman,' said Ned. 'Policemen are rubbish.'

McIntyre nodded in agreement, though there is a slight possibility that this was because he had so many guns pointed at him.

'Do you promise,' Ned asked in a kindly fashion, 'to quit the force

---

119 Authentic historical dialogue™.

120 Less authentic historical dialogue.

after we let you go?'

'Of course!' McIntyre cried. 'I was thinking of doing it anyway, to be honest, so this is kind of a relief really.'

'Great, then that's settled.' They shook hands and rejoiced in the pleasure of new friendships. It was a shame that the party had to be broken up by the return of Kennedy and Scanlan to the camp. 'Oh well, back to the grind,' sighed Ned.

The gang hid, and Kennedy and Scanlan rode over. McIntyre told Kennedy to give it up, they were totes rumbled. 'There are Kellys, like *everywhere*,' he emphasised. This was backed up by Ned yelling, 'Hands up!' from his hiding place.

In one of history's greatest conversational miscalculations, Sergeant Kennedy assumed it was Lonigan yelling out as a hilarious joke. Grinning broadly, he put his hand on his gun, only to feel several bullets whizz past his nose. He realised the comparative lack of humour in the situation, and gave up. Scanlan, on the other hand, stayed true to his assigned role as Official Police Moron, jumped from his horse and tried to get to a tree to hide behind. He was, instead, gunned down as quickly and easily as Lonigan had been.

'What the hell is *WITH* you guys?' asked Ned. 'Do you think we *LIKE* shooting you to death?'

'Well, you do seem to,' said McIntyre.

'Okay, yeah, we do like it a lot, but still: if you didn't keep running away we wouldn't do it nearly as often.'

'You'd run away too if you were being chased by a man with such a magnificent beard.'

'Flattery will get you everywhere,' Ned simpered coyly.

It was a sweet moment, but it was the Kellys' mistake to let Kennedy's continental charm affect them, because McIntyre took advantage of the distraction to jump on the sergeant's horse and bolt. After the nice tea they'd had together, Ned didn't like to shoot the fleeing policeman. Kennedy, on the other hand, Ned did like to shoot – and he totally did.

With three cops taken out, and all the other cops in the world to go, the Kelly Gang began to get down to some serious marauding. They bailed up the Gooram Gooram Gong Wool Station at Euroa and robbed the town's bank, all the while treating their prisoners with respect and courtesy as they made a late bid to become the 140th gang to be referred to as 'gentleman bushrangers'. They didn't quite achieve that aim, but public sentiment was coming around to their side, and against the police, as the public became more and more aware of how annoying the police were.

Ned Kelly was riding high as a people's hero when he robbed the bank and held up the police station at Jerilderie in New South Wales. It was here that Ned handed over the famed 'Jerilderie Letter' to a Mr Living, who promised to get it published. Living instead gave the letter to the police, so who's the real villain: the bushranger or this little twerp who broke his promise? Exactly.

The Jerilderie Letter was 56 pages and 8000 words long, Kelly totally ignoring the fact that this is far too long for a letter. Ned dictated it to Byrne, who was in the gang mainly for his penmanship. It wasn't really a letter, of course – it was more like one of those 'open letters' that dull people write for bad newspapers. Some call it Ned's manifesto, others call it his confession and still others call it a mad idiot blathering on endlessly about God knows what. It begins: 'Sir, I wish to acquaint you with some of the occurrences of the present past and future.' Which could lull the reader into thinking it's a kind of educational pamphlet. 'Good on him for acquainting us,' a person might think. 'I really need to brush up on the occurrences of the present past and future.' Unfortunately Ned quickly reveals that all the occurrences he wants to discuss are occurrences that happened to *him*. It was all me, me, me with Ned Kelly – you've never met a bushranger so self-obsessed.

The letter consists of three main points that Ned wished to convey to the public:

1. Bushranging is awesome, and when I do it I am awesome.
2. I am extremely pissed off at a lot of people because they are all stupid and arseholes.
3. If you don't do what I say, I am going to blow your freaking heads off.

There was also some stuff about rights for the Irish, referring to:

> *many a blooming Irishman, rather then subdue to the Saxon yoke, were flogged to death and bravely died in servile chains, but true to the shamrock and a credit to Paddy's Land.*

Nobody had any idea what he was talking about: common opinion was that he was speaking Gaelic. But, in fact, Ned was crying for justice for his people, who had since the First Fleet been condemned to abuse, harassment, bigotry and being forced to speak in stupid accents in films. The Irish in Australia had had enough, and Ned planned to change public perceptions of the Irish community by making it clear how capable of violent crime they were.

He reserved much of his most ferociously blithering invective for the police, calling them:

> *a parcel of big ugly fat-necked wombat-headed big-bellied magpie-legged narrow-hipped splaw-footed sons of Irish Bailiffs or english landlords.*

The police immediately issued a statement flatly denying that any of their currently serving officers were magpie-legged, a controversy that rages to this day. There was also a complaint lodged with the Anti-Discrimination Commission from the Irish Bailiffs Anti-Defamation League, who didn't see why Irish bailiffs were any worse than any other bailiffs, or what was so terrible about their sons.

The Kelly Gang was on top of the world,[121] doing as they pleased and gaining fame and renown for doing so. But they had one problem: Aaron Sherritt, an old friend of Byrne's, had turned informant and was keeping the police up to date on the gang's movements and plans. The gang found this a bit beyond the pale, and they cooked up a hilarious prank to put Sherritt in his place: they would murder him.

The one thing standing in the way of the gang's plan to kill Sherritt was that four policemen were stationed at Sherritt's house to protect him. However, the one thing standing in the way of the police's plan to protect Sherritt was the fact that the four policemen were a bunch of wusses who stayed huddled together in the bedroom, quaking in terror, while Byrne came to the front door and put two bullets in Sherritt.[122] For 12 hours, Byrne and Dan Kelly kept the cops trapped in the Sherritt house, where history doesn't record exactly how many times they wet themselves.

After Sherritt's death, Ned decided that it was finally time to make a legendary last stand that would live on in the national consciousness

121 Though geographically on the bottom of it.

122 With a gun.

and look amazing in movies. Thus, he rode with his men to Glenrowan, having chosen the town as the most suitable location in the area to set up kiosks and a twice-daily live show. The Kelly Gang herded the townspeople into the local pub, as was the style of the time. Everyone had great fun, drinking, dancing, singing and playing 'hop, step and jump', a traditional Irish game where participants have to nominate their favourite way of getting out of the way of a bullet. It was a wonderful day for everyone, and sentiment in Glenrowan was unanimous: Ned Kelly threw the best parties *EVER*.

But even the greatest of parties can't last forever, and this one came to an end when Ned ordered the gang to put on their armour. This wasn't as crazy as it sounds, because they did have some armour, which *was* as crazy as it sounds. The gang, searching for a way to make themselves slightly harder to shoot that would also severely restrict their movement, had come up with the perfect solution: suits of armour that weighed more than 40 kilos and protected the head and torso but not the legs, because they had read somewhere that legs are immune to bullets.

A large force of police arrived in Glenrowan and, on the morning of 28 June 1880, began firing on the pub. The gang fired back. The police fired back at the gang firing back. This went on for some time, until nobody could see through the smoke anymore.

The police were waiting outside the hotel, occasionally firing their guns just to relieve the boredom, when a nightmarish apparition appeared through the trees from behind them. It was Ned Kelly, dressed in full armour, raining fire down upon his enemies. Sergeant Steele and Constable Kelly (no relation) fired at him, but the bullets simply bounced off his iron shirt. Was this a monster, an invincible juggernaut, a mythical beast from the depths of hell? Sergeant Steele tested the theory by shooting Ned in the legs – and, as it turned, it was none of those things: it was a man wearing a tin can on his head. Kelly went down, wounded in the leg, foot, hand, arm and groin. His armour had been remarkably effective, inasmuch as it had forced the police to shoot him in places that the armour didn't cover.

The last stand was done. Byrne had been shot while drinking, so at least he went out doing something he loved. The police set fire to the pub, where Dan Kelly and Steve Hart had, most likely, killed each other to avoid capture.[123] As the hotel burnt to the ground, the people of Glenrowan watched the golden age of bushranging going up in smoke.

Ned lived to stand trial before Judge Redmond Barry, full-time bushranger-judger, was convicted of the murder of Constable Lonigan and sadly granted no clemency on the grounds that Lonigan had once squeezed his nuts. Barry sentenced him to hang, and on 11 November 1880 – the date chosen to commemorate Prime Minister Gough Whitlam's dismissal – the sentence was carried out. On being informed of the appointed hour of execution, Ned reportedly said, 'Such is life', and he had a point. 'I suppose it has come to this,' he added while on the scaffold, and again he had really put his finger on the crux of the matter.

More than 30,000 people had signed a petition to have Kelly's death sentence commuted, which proves that even before the internet, petitions were completely useless.

Since his death, Ned Kelly has devoted himself mainly to rest and having his skull stolen. The end of the Kelly Gang was also the end of bushranging as a viable career path for youngsters looking for celebrity and early death. The bushranging era had been an exciting and entertaining one for all, but eventually a country must move on:

123 A remarkably effective, if counterproductive, strategy.

the increasing urbanisation of society, greater interconnectivity of communication and transport systems and the rise of a burgeoning middle class all conspired to break the bushranging business model.[124] It was now a lot more lucrative just to sell opium.

But bushrangers would live on in the Australian consciousness as a crucial part of the way we delusionally see ourselves. The iconic figure of the bushranger speaks to our rugged outback souls, which is a comforting thought when we are sitting in a cafe wondering which modern dance production to see tonight. We like to think that there's a little bit of the bushranger in all of us: in our self-reliance, in our defiance of authority, in our barely repressed willingness to shoot people in the face to get what we want.

We may have left behind the days when brave young men would live fast and die young in the bush, guns blazing and beards flowing, but as long as we keep in our collective memory the knowledge of how heroic crime can be when conducted on top of a horse or from behind a homemade helmet, the spirit of the Wild Colonial Boys will never die.

ESSAY QUESTIONS

1. Would modern criminals be more popular if they wore buckets on their heads? Discuss with specific reference to Carl Williams, Christopher Skase and Paul from *Neighbours*.
2. Would you kill a man if he squeezed your testicles? Give examples.

---

124 This is really impressive sociological analysis, in case you hadn't noticed.

Better Off Fed

In which the best and the brightest meet to invent a country, and cats are effectively herded

FORGING A NATION: A TRANSCRIPT OF THE PROCEEDINGS OF THE CONSTITUTIONAL CONVENTION, SYDNEY, MARCH–APRIL 1891

In 1891, a group of Australia's most patriotic and bearded men gathered in Sydney, having determined that the colonies were now mature enough to strike out on their own as a united nation, to thrash out the details of Federation, the grand experiment that aimed to prove that a group of extremely similar people could forge a common purpose and live sort of independently from their imperial masters. Together they created a commonwealth that took as its foundational principle the idea that any Australian, whether male or rich, white or Christian, is endowed with the same fundamental human rights. This is the record of their deliberations.

Present at the Convention:

HENRY PARKES (NSW): Well-known Father of Federation and personification of the concept of Time.

SAMUEL GRIFFITH (QLD): Queensland premier, chief justice and shearer-hater.

EDMUND BARTON (NSW): Australia's first prime minister, look it up.

ANDREW INGLIS CLARK (TAS): Taswegian MP, lawyer and failed author.

ALFRED DEAKIN (VIC): Repeat prime minister and racist.

JOHN QUICK (VIC): Politician with few achievements, but did know shorthand.

RICHARD BAKER (SA): Former South Australian attorney-general and Teddy Roosevelt impersonator.

SIR JOHN HALL (NZ): Former New Zealand premier who really didn't need to be here.

JOHN COCKBURN: South Australian premier and double entendre.

CHAIRMAN: Order, order! This Constitutional Convention will come to order. Gentlemen, we have before us a weighty task: to determine the shape and form of a new nation, created from the disparate colonies of this vast horrible continent. This is no small responsibility: future generations will have to live with the consequences of our decisions here today. If we fail, history will judge us harshly; if we succeed, hardly anybody will remember our names. It is a no-win situation, gentleman, so let's just get this over with. Mr Parkes, you have the longest beard, so you go first.

HENRY PARKES (Delegate from New South Wales): My dear friends, as premier of New South Wales, a failed businessman and a part-time shopping centre Santa Claus, I have a wide experience of the people and the spirit of these colonies. And let me tell you that at this moment in time, our continent has been gripped by an irresistible fever: typhoid. But we are also under the sway of a more metaphorical kind of fever, and its name is Federation. Gentlemen, we must federate with all possible speed. It is now 14 years since the Australian cricket team played the first ever Test match and, frankly, a country that has a cricket team before it has a government looks like a fool. Other countries are beginning to make fun of us. I propose that we move immediately to create a new nation, a nation called 'Australia', and leave behind our current title, 'The Non-United States of West New Zealand'.

SAMUEL GRIFFITH (Delegate from Queensland): Sir, you forget yourself! Federation may be an inevitability, but there's no need to disparage the honour of the Non-United States of West New Zealand. The NUSWNZ has been a great force for good in the world. As the Non-United States we have produced great criminals like Ned Kelly and John Macarthur. Let us never forget, even as we form a new nation, what wonderful things our loose assemblage of convict dumping grounds and faux-aristocratic kleptocracies has done.

PARKES: Point taken, Mr Griffith, but I do feel it's important not to dwell on the past, but look ahead to the future. We should set a timetable for Federation to be finalised no more than five years after I die.

CHAIR: Be it so ordered![125]

GRIFFITH: Although I am sympathetic to Mr Parkes's desire that we be united relatively soon after his failure to live long enough to see his most cherished dreams realised, I feel it necessary to point out that many difficulties present themselves, obstacles to Federation that must be overcome if we are to become a robust, vigorous,

125 The Chair definitely had a habit of exceeding his authority.

flourishing country that might one day host the Olympics, whatever they might be. For example, look at the American Civil War.

EDMUND BARTON (Delegate from New South Wales): What about it?

GRIFFITH: Well, there was one.

BARTON: So?

GRIFFITH: Well, it was bad.

CHAIR: Order! Order! Delegates will cease their awkward silence immediately.

[General discord]

GRIFFITH: If I may elaborate, Mr Chair, my meaning is simply that America's states federated, and before you knew it, they started killing one another. I think we all want to avoid such an eventuality.

ANDREW INGLIS CLARK (Delegate from Tasmania): I dunno. Their history books are heaps more interesting than ours. Maybe if we had a civil war it would spice things up a bit.

ALFRED DEAKIN (Delegate from Victoria): What are you talking about? We have *AWESOME* history! The gold rush, the rum rebellion, that time two guys had a fight over a frying pan: there's never a dull moment here in West New Zealand! I agree with Griffith – if we could devise a constitution that would minimise the chances of our citizens spending five years slaughtering one another in record numbers, that would be pretty sweet.

PARKES: I am, in general terms, also supportive of the principle of not slaughtering each other in record numbers. I propose making civil wars illegal!

[General agreement]

CHAIR: Then it is agreed: the Constitution of the new Commonwealth of Australia will feature strong protections against civil wars.

JOHN QUICK (Delegate from Victoria): Wait ... is that what we're calling it? 'The Commonwealth of Australia'?

CHAIR: Do you have a problem with that?

QUICK: Well, I dunno. It sounds a bit, you know ... pretentious.

DEAKIN: Yeah. I don't even know what it means, to be honest.

BARTON: It means we're a commonwealth. It means, you know, our wealth ... is common.

QUICK: How can wealth be common? If wealth is common, it isn't wealth. Basic economics.

RICHARD BAKER (Delegate from South Australia): But don't we want everyone to be wealthy?

QUICK: But if everyone were wealthy, then nobody would be.

BAKER: That's stupid. If everyone were wealthy it'd be great. Everyone I know is wealthy, and we love it.

QUICK: Yeah, I bet you love it, down in Nazi Town.

BAKER: You know very well we stopped calling Adelaide that over three years ago.

BARTON: Shut up, you guys. The point is, as a commonwealth, we assert that we are a united nation in which we all share equally.

DEAKIN: We don't actually mean that, though, do we?

BARTON: Duh! Of course not.

[General merriment]

QUICK: I still don't like it. I think 'Commonwealth of Australia' makes us sound like, you know, we think we're good.

BARTON: But don't we think we're good?

QUICK: Well, sure, but we don't want anyone to *think* we think we're good. One of the founding principles of Australia should be that we're not really very proud of ourselves.

DEAKIN: I agree. We don't want to look like wankers.

CHAIR: So, what do *you* want to call us?

QUICK: I was thinking something like, 'Australia or Whatever'.

DEAKIN: I love it!

JOHN HALL (Delegate from New Zealand): I reckon we just stick with West New Zealand. Seems to sum it up.

CHAIR: No one listen to him, he doesn't even go here.

DEAKIN: What if we called it, 'A Big Bag O' Australia'?

QUICK: 'Australia: A Real Country and Everything'.

PARKES: 'Australia: Now It's Personal'.

CHAIR: Shut up! It's going to be the Commonwealth of Australia. We are making a *real* country here, gentleman – it has to have a proper country name. And 'Commonwealth' makes us sound classy. Don't you want to sound classy?

[General reluctant agreement]

GRIFFITH: Gentleman, as premier of Queensland, it would be remiss of me not to raise the subject of racism in our new country.

CHAIR: Yes?

GRIFFITH: What kind of racism do you think we should have?

DEAKIN: It should definitely be the kind where everyone's white. Look at a map: right above us is a whole mess of Asians just itching to get in here. We should have the kind of racism that doesn't want them to. Can you imagine an entire country full of Chinese? It'd be ridiculous! Let's keep Australia white.

[Cries of 'Hear, hear!']

BARTON: Oh yeah, that sounds pretty sweet. What would be the point of having a country if we were going to let the Chinese in?

DEAKIN: Yeah. Or the Aboriginal people.

BARTON: They're actually already in.

DEAKIN: Oh. Well, can we do something about that? Like maybe we could put in the Constitution a bit about 'Aboriginal people have to go away'.

CHAIR: That might be a bit awkward.

BARTON: Look, I think it's okay to have the Aboriginal people stay, as long as we are completely clear about white being the best thing to be. As they say, 'a white Australia is a happy Australia'.

DEAKIN: Who says that?

BARTON: The guys down the pub.

DEAKIN: When you're right, you're right. I've met people of at least four different colours in my life, and I can definitely say the white ones are my favourite.

GRIFFITH: My only reservation here is that if we proceed down the all-white route, we might run into some issues with the sugar.

QUICK: Isn't the sugar already white?

GRIFFITH: No, I mean the sugar cane. The harvesting, you know. We've had a lot of success bringing in dark fellows to do the hard bits, and if we had a country where everyone had to be white, it might put a crimp in the profits.

CHAIR: Hmm, that is a point. We want to create a country that is just racist enough to keep the wrong sort of people *out*, but not too racist to stop us from bringing people to do the jobs we don't want to do *in*. What do you think, Mr Parkes?

PARKES: You can worry a bit too much about these things. If we set up a strong, robust country, where freedom and democracy is the birthright of every white man, I have enough confidence in the wisdom of my people to be sure that they will find a natural balance between isolationist xenophobia and colonialist exploitation.

BARTON: Well said, sir!

[General applause]

CLARK: I'm more worried about states' rights.

GRIFFITH: See, this is the civil war thing again. Tasmania can't have slaves, Clark, no matter how much you want some.

CLARK: No, no, I wasn't saying that. I mean, Tasmania is a little state.

PARKES: It's all right, Clark, no need to apologise.

CLARK: NO! I mean, since we're so little, how do we stop the big states from doing all kinds of awful crap to us?

BARTON: Well, we wouldn't.

CLARK: But what if you did?

BARTON: We *promise* we wouldn't.

DEAKIN: Everyone knows what New South Welshmen are like, Barton. Always trying to steal our rivers and our grand prixs. Never trust a New South Welshman – let's put that in the Constitution.

CLARK: But what about the Victorians?

DEAKIN: What?

BARTON: Ha!

CLARK: Well, you've got all that gold, and all those coffee shops and wine bars. How do we stop you screwing us over?

JOHN COCKBURN (Delegate from South Australia): Exactly. We need protection from the rapacious alpha colonies.

BARTON: Oh God, who even invited the South Australians? Don't you have a killing spree you should be on, Cockburn?

COCKBURN: Don't pronounce my name that way.

PARKES: Gentleman! The solution is simple. We simply have a bicameral parliamentary system, in which the Lower House is constituted of representatives elected by districts delineated on the basis of population, and the Upper House grants equal representation to each state in order to protect the interests of the smaller states against the tyranny of the majority, and act as a house of review for the actions of the Lower.

[Impressed silence]

DEAKIN: Did you just think of that?

PARKES: Yeah, it just kind of came to me.

GRIFFITH: Astonishing. Let's write that down.

DEAKIN: Obviously, though, the Lower House will be, like, the boss house. Right? The Upper House will just be sort of like commentators.

COCKBURN: No! The Upper House will be a genuine house of review: laws will need to pass it.

DEAKIN: Sure, sure. But not the important laws. I mean the Upper House will be mainly for the little laws that nobody cares about.

BARTON: Stop it Deakin.

DEAKIN: You stop it, Barton. You're only going to be prime minister once; I'm going to be prime minister three times. So I outrank you.

[Murmurs of agreement]

BARTON: But I'll be the *FIRST* prime minister. I'm going to be in *way* more trivia questions than you are.

[Murmurs of agreement]

CHAIR: Let's compromise. We'll agree that the Senate will have the power to defeat any Bill, but we'll also make sure that all Senators are allowed to trade away their constituents' interests for narrow personal crusades. That way we get proper oversight, but also the mechanism to avoid that oversight when it gets too annoying.

[Cheers]

DEAKIN: Now, about defence.

PARKES: What about it?

DEAKIN: The colony of Victoria strongly feels that we should have some.

BARTON: We already have some. There's a guy down my road has about five guns just on his own.

DEAKIN: I'm talking about an actual army. Remember that the French and the Germans are forever poised to attack us.

QUICK: I thought it was the Chinese who were poised.

DEAKIN: It's the French, and the Germans, *and* the Chinese.

GRIFFITH: You're starting to come off a bit paranoid.

DEAKIN: Look, if we unite as a nation, we will be stronger if we also have a united defence force. We can't let Australia fall into hostile hands.

BARTON: All right then, we'll have an army. And a navy. And an air force, once that's a thing that is possible to have. To defend ourselves against foreign incursions.

DEAKIN: And also to fight for Britain.

[General agreement]

COCKBURN: For Britain? But once we're federated, we won't be Britain anymore, will we?

PARKES: Of course not! But that doesn't mean we won't be British.

DEAKIN: Really, Cockburn, you're embarrassing yourself.

COCKBURN: But, I mean, our army ... it needs to fight for Australia.

PARKES: Yes. And it will do that by fighting for Britain. Isn't it obvious?

COCKBURN: I ... look, I'm not following this. We form a new nation, right?

OTHER DELEGATES IN DISTURBING UNISON: Right.

COCKBURN: And the new nation will have its own military, right?

OTHER DELEGATES: Right.

COCKBURN: And that military's purpose will be to defend this country, right? The country we're currently standing in? The one just south of New Guinea?

OTHER DELEGATES: Yep.

COCKBURN: So, if Britain was fighting a war on the other side of the world that our country had nothing to do with, the military that we formed to defend our country would obviously say that the defence of our country was its priority.

BARTON: Yes. So we would go join the war. That's how you defend a country, Barton: by fighting in other countries.

[Nodding]

COCKBURN: Of course. I see it so clearly now.

BARTON: Frigging South Australians, you have to explain everything to them 50 times.

PARKES: Let's discuss religion. I think we should have a bit in the Australian Constitution that says, 'Catholics are bastards.'

[General groaning]

BARTON: Parkes, do you *never* shut up about Catholics?

PARKES: I'm just saying. They suck.

CLARK: I hardly think that needs to go in the Constitution, though.

PARKES: But what if people forget?

DEAKIN: Look, I want to see a nation united, not divided. We want a country where people of all religions coexist peacefully, with mutual respect and understanding. It shouldn't matter, in our country, whether you're Catholic or Protestant.

CLARK: What about the other religions?

DEAKIN: I don't think there are any.

PARKES: Look, I agree we should coexist with mutual respect and understanding, but we can surely coexist with mutual respect and understanding while also hating Catholics.

GRIFFITH: Gentlemen, I think we are all, broadly speaking, in agreement.

QUICK: No, we're not.

GRIFFITH: Thank you. I propose that we take our draft constitution and put it to the people of our various states for ratification.

BARTON: The *people*? Can we really trust them?

DEAKIN: He's right – they're a dodgy lot. We need to specify that they not be involved in any important decisions.

BARTON: Or know exactly what's going on at any time. The Constitution needs to provide for a free and unfettered press, so that we can prevent the people from ever being fully informed.

DEAKIN: Right. We'll take this constitution to the people, but not let them know too much: we'll just promise them that it's a cracker and they'd be an idiot not to vote for it. And we'll let them know that if they don't vote for it they'll be murdered by the Chinese.

[Applause]

CHAIR: Excellent. Let's go through it. Griffith, you're generally credited by future historians as the drafter of the Australian Constitution – tell us what you've got so far.

GRIFFITH: Right. Let's see. Okay, first of all, we agree that the six colonies of the Australian continent will unite to form a single federation. We also agree that New South Wales and Victoria will always be the most important states, in return for which the other states will be permitted to develop aggressive inferiority complexes. We agree that each state will be assigned its own humorous stereotype, to wit: Queenslanders are ignorant racists, Tasmanians have sex with their siblings, South Australians are elitist serial killers, Victorians are pretentious snobs, New South Welshmen are greedy amoral philistines and West Australians don't exist in any real sense.

[General agreement]

DEAKIN: Don't forget the Northern Territory!

GRIFFITH: Oh yes. We agree that the Northern Territory is a terrible, scary place and doesn't really count for anything.

BARTON: And the Australian Capital Territory!

GRIFFITH: Yes, we agree that the Australian Capital Territory will exist, and we agree that we don't know why. We agree that the federal Parliament will have power to raise taxes, regulate trade, pass laws for the proper maintenance of law and order, subsidise dying industries, fund white elephants, fan the flames of mass hysteria in times of crisis and take Fridays off. On every day that Parliament sits, there will be a period set aside in the afternoon for Question Time, during which Ministers of the Crown will be required to insult the intelligence of the public and turn the concept of democracy into a grim farce. Members of the Opposition will be permitted, during this time, to abandon the concept of interrogation in favour of unfocused abuse, while Members of the Government will be permitted to sacrifice their last scrap of integrity by wrapping repellent sycophancy in the flimsy guise of questions.

[General high-fiving]

CLARK: And also, don't forget that Parliament will be moderated by a Speaker, who will be chosen from the ranks of the ruling party, because every constitution needs a few really bad ideas. The Speaker's job will be to kick Members of the Opposition out of the chamber and to deny that there was ever a point of order.

[Air punches]

GRIFFITH: The government shall be divided into three branches: legislative, executive and judicial. These branches shall be kept separate and independent of one another, except inasmuch as the executive will be the same guys who are in the legislative, and the legislative and executive will both have the power to stick their noses into the judicial whenever a newspaper tells them to. The legislature shall be divided into Houses, an Upper and a Lower, with the Lower dedicated to actual government and the Upper dedicated to weird tiny parties that nobody actually wants there.

[Cheering]

GRIFFITH: Elections shall be held every three years, or every two years, or whenever, and shall be subject to oversight by volunteer sausage cooks.

CLARK: Do the bit about states' rights!

GRIFFITH: Yep. States shall have the right to self-govern up to the point that the federal government would rather they didn't. States will have the power to raise revenue through traffic fines and taxes that nobody understands, and also through begging the federal government. States will also have the right to play one another at football and steal major events from one another, especially in the case that said events are unprofitable and widely disliked. States shall also have the power to grant favours to wealthy property developers whose parties the states have been invited to.

CLARK: That's my favourite bit.

[More general high-fiving]

GRIFFITH: We agree that the federal government shall have the power to maintain a standing army for the purposes of supporting the military adventurism of diverse foreign powers. The federal government shall also have authority for any and all character assassination of any citizen who might at any time criticise said standing army in any way. This should not be taken as denying the government authority for character assassinations in other circumstances: those powers shall be reserved.

[General drunken carousing]

GRIFFITH: Speaking of reserve powers ... the head of the government shall be the prime minister, and the first of these is to be Sir Edmund Barton, the well-known umpire. The head of state shall be Queen Victoria of the United Kingdom, Empress of India, and her successors if she ever bloody dies. The Queen's representative in Australia shall be the governor-general, to be appointed by the Queen on advice of the prime minister, from the ranks of the country's most elderly and uninteresting citizens. In the event of a constitutional crisis, the prime minister and governor-general shall be empowered to work together to make a massive trainwreck of everything.

CHAIR: Guys ... this is a pretty damn great constitution we've got right here.

GRIFFITH: Oh, I almost forgot. Parliament shall have the power to stop any and all boats it deems necessary to stop for the security of the nation – or just for its own amusement.

[Massive standing ovation]

BARTON: Gentlemen, we have today achieved something wonderful. A nation for a continent, and a continent for a nation.

CLARK: Wow, catchy.

BARTON: As the only man here without a huge silky beard, I propose a toast: to the people of Australia and their future relaxed somnolence in the face of even the most horrific abuses of power.

[Clinking of glasses]

BARTON: May our new nation be as rich and powerful as the Jim Beam we've been downing for this entire convention.

[Rousing cheer, retching, etc.]

DEAKIN: And may I, as the future three-time prime minister and Australia's most prominent racist religious maniac, propose a further toast: to the father of Federation, Henry Parkes, whose tireless work for unification and liberty for our nation has made him a living national treasure beloved of all Australians, particularly the children to whom he delivers presents every Christmas. Long may his memory be kept alive and his sleigh bells tinkle.

[More rousing cheers, thuds of men falling to the floor]

PARKES: I thank you all, gentlemen. It is indeed gratifying to see you, my esteemed colleagues and friends, coming together in such a spirit of reasoned cooperation to bring about a new age of freedom and democracy, and I look eagerly forward to my own impending death, as it will be shortly followed by the miracle of Federation.

CHAIR: I declare this Constitutional Convention adjourned. On behalf of all delegates, I will write to Queen Victoria and request that Australia be properly federated on 1 January 1901, to ensure that we can never have a proper holiday in celebration of it.

[General throwing of hats in the air]

POSTSCRIPT:

Sir Edmund Barton went on to become Australia's first prime minister and drink enormous amounts of wine, earning the nickname 'Toby Tosspot', which wasn't as funny back then as you might think. Later he became a justice of the High Court and took up appearing on stamps. The Barton Highway was named after him, as it is the highway that Australians most often forget the existence of.

Alfred Deakin became Australia's second, fifth and seventh prime minister, proving that he really did have trouble moving on in life. Later he suffered from memory loss, which may have been the reason he kept going back to a job he'd been kicked out of in the first place. As one of the first Australian politicians to make an eloquent case for being terrified of Asians, he holds a special place in white Australian hearts and is remembered in the name of Deakin University.

Sir Henry Parkes died in 1896, before seeing the united Australia that he longed for, but was given due credit for being the driving force behind Federation, and also for his wildlife conservation work, saving numerous endangered species by hiding them in his beard. He is commemorated by the name of the town of Parkes, which later became the home of Sam Neill, inventor of the moon landing. Henry Parkes was buried at his ancestral home in the North Pole, next to the toy workshop.

Sir John Hall served with distinction as prime minister of New Zealand, which never joined Australia's Federation and therefore is completely irrelevant.

Andrew Inglis Clark introduced the Hare–Clark electoral system to Tasmania, for which many have still not forgiven him. He was a generous man, once described as 'never too busy to mend a toy for a child', speaking volumes about the way in which he would neglect his professional responsibilities. He died in 1907 while trying to remember how his electoral system worked.

Sir John Quick wrote *The Judicial Power of the Commonwealth*, *The Legislative Powers of the Commonwealth and the States of Australia* and *Australian Literature from Its Beginnings to 1935*, and therefore had very few friends. He was the founding president of the Bendigo Cornish Association, but failed in his attempt to have Australia annexed by Cornwall. He died at the age of 80, making his surname pretty funny.

Sir Richard Baker was the first president of the Australian Senate – and, believe me, he never let you forget it. He helped develop the copper mining industry in South Australia, but at the time people didn't know how monstrously evil that was. He died in 1911 of wig poisoning.

Sir John Cockburn spent the last three decades of his life in England, which if you ask me is deeply suspicious. He was extremely active in the suffragette movement and frequently spoke at meetings of the Women's Suffrage League, even though they asked him politely to stop. He died in 1929 without ever convincing anyone not to pronounce his name like that.

Sir Samuel Griffith, after drafting the Australian Constitution, went on to draft Queensland's Criminal Code, which today remains largely unchanged due to Queenslanders' inability to join the rest of us in the modern world. He then went to England and sat on the Privy Council, injuring them severely. As Queensland premier he gained the nickname 'Oily Sam', due to his famously unappetising pasta.

Australia grew up into a fine, strapping young country, full of ideals and hopes and dreams that it grew out of. Today it spends most of its time screaming in terror and vomiting up coal.

ESSAY QUESTIONS

1. Who was the first prime minister? Don't look back at this chapter! You've forgotten already, haven't you? Ha!
2. What would you call your new country? Mine would be Benistan.

The Boering First Episode

In which adventure on the high veld turns out to be less fun than it sounds, and a homicidal Englishman becomes the newest Australian hero

---

For more than a hundred years, Australians have fought in wars, and if the world is agreed on one indisputable fact, it is this: Australia is better at fighting in war than any other country ever in the universe. Every wartime ally of Australia's has said they couldn't have won the war without us, and every enemy of Australia's has said that our presence was the reason they lost. Moreover, many nations that fought in wars not involving Australia are on record as wishing they'd had us there to help out. Both sides in the Russo-Japanese War tried as hard as possible to hire Australian troops, while George Washington, in a 1778 letter to Thomas Jefferson, wrote that 'this Revolution would already be done and dusted if only Australia existed and was on our side'.

What I'm saying is, our country has a military history so proud that other countries justifiably hang their heads and slit their wrists in shame over their inability to match up to our peerless reputation for producing fighting men and occasionally women.

It's often said that 'Australians fight in wars, but do not start wars', and that's also a point of pride for historically minded patriots. Although our fighting record is magnificent, we have always waited for a more powerful country to start a war before we take their side. Because not only are we brave and skilful, we are also smart enough never to get ourselves into a fight without first knowing we've got a very big friend standing behind us. It's this combination of battlefield guts, combat capabilities and strategic savvy that has made Australia the greatest military power in history, according to every reputable historian.

Doubtless there were many Australians serving the British Empire in various conflicts throughout the colonial period – the Crimean War, the War of 1812, the several hundred wars Britain fought against France – and certainly white Australians served bravely in the Frontier Wars against the Aboriginal people, bringing honour not just to their own country, but also to lovers of racist oppression and genocide everywhere. But the true history of Australian military supermen begins right before Federation, with the Boer War (1899–1902), which was actually the Second Boer War, following the First Boer War (1880–81).

As a war, the Boer War was not one of history's most important or sizeable, but it was nonetheless significant: first of all because it was the first genuinely rhyming war since the War of Eighteen Forty-Four – which was technically not even a war, but a dispute over opera tickets – and secondly because it was the first war in which Australia participated as a unified nation. In 1899 and 1900, troops came from Australia as representatives of their separate colonies, but following 1 January 1901, when Henry Parkes's grand dream of not living to see Federation came true, the Commonwealth of Australia entered the war as a single entity.

It was a momentous occasion for the new nation, and popular opinion was that it was a stroke of luck that there was already a war on when Federation happened, so Australia didn't have to wait around for one to happen along, but could slide straight in with a minimum of fuss. Mind you, at the turn of the 20th century, the likelihood of there being a war on was roughly on a par with the likelihood of a cricket team including a man with a moustache. Anyway, the Boer War was a seminal moment for Australia's emergence as a real nation, and it would never have happened if it weren't for a ferocious dispute over which European race had a greater right to exploit Africa's natural resources.

'Boer' is the Dutch and Afrikaans word for farmer, so what you were thinking is just an unfortunate coincidence. The word was used to describe the Dutch-descended settlers in southern Africa who had upset British sensibilities by standing in the way of the Empire's belief that the entire world belonged to them. Although the British refer to the Boer War as the 'Boer War', the Boers call it the *Anglo-Boereoorlog*,[126] the *Tweede Boereoorlog*[127] or the *Tweede Vryheidsoorlog*[128] – the variety of names testament to the many euphonious ways that Afrikaaners have of sounding like Orcs.

The war came about as a result of several issues on which the Boers and the British disagreed:

1. The issue of gold and diamonds, and the numerous British and Boer citizens who wanted them
2. The issue of voting rights for Britons in the Boer republics: the Boers objected to them because of the risk that if Britons had the right to vote, they might vote
3. The issue of Britain having a bunch of troops massed at the border, making the Boers nervous and slowing down their native-dispossession
4. The issue of the republics threatening to declare war on Britain

126 'The Fight with the English'.
127 'The Fight with the Tweed'.
128 'Count Dracula'.

if Britain didn't withdraw its troops, followed by the issue of the republics declaring war on Britain because Britain didn't withdraw its troops

The die was cast: once the Boers had declared war, war was practically inevitable. Shortly afterwards, when Britain brought in several contingents of Australians, the Boers' defeat became inevitable.

The first Australian troops to arrive in Africa were the NSW Lancers,[129] who landed at Cape Town on 2 November 1899 to the sounds of terrified screams and wails of despair from the Boers. On 22 November, the Lancers kicked the stuffing out of a bunch of wussy Boers at Belmont. At the Battle of Modder River, they again tore the Boers to shreds, a total victory only prevented by the fact that a column of British troops had been allowed to tag along.

As more units of Australians arrived from the colonies, the Boers became more and more terrified, and the Australian commanders became more and more frustrated that the Englishmen kept getting in the way of their swift and devastating conquest of the entire African continent. Major Australian triumphs were recorded at the Battle of Paardeberg, where the NSW Rifles captured Boer General Piet Cronjé, in revenge for which his descendant Hansie would one day throw a stump through an Australian door; and at the Relief of Mafeking, where Australian contingents did some heavy-duty relieving, mainly by letting Mafeking know its kids were okay and ringing up with good news about the mortgage application. Queen Victoria wrote to all colonial governments, saying, 'We are relieved', and there was much rejoicing.

But perhaps Australia's most heroic moment of the war was the

129 With sports suspension and airbags as standard.

Siege of Brakfontein on 4 August 1900. Koos de la Rey's 3000 Boers attacked the British outpost, which was defended by 300 Australians and 201 fairly irrelevant Rhodesian volunteers. De la Rey told the Australian commander, Colonel Charles Hore, that if he gave up all his supplies, he would let them all go unharmed. Hore, probably donning a pair of sunglasses and taking a cigarette out of his mouth, replied, 'Even if I wished to surrender to you – and I don't – I am commanding Australians who would cut my throat if I accepted your terms.'

Why had the British staffed the Brakfontein outpost with Australian murderers? Who knows? But, for once, a murderer-intensive strategy paid off. For the next 11 days, the 3000 Boers hammered the outpost, and the ragtag bunch of plucky Australians refused to surrender. De la Rey said afterwards, 'For the first time in the war we are fighting men who used our own tactics against us ... our men admitted that the Australians were more formidable opponents and far more dangerous than any other British troops.'[130]

So I guess that settles the question of who are the most formidable opponents. The world now knew what Australians had known for over a century: we are, essentially, a nation of invincible supermen. And the advent of Federation only enhanced our powers – united, we became more powerful than the Boers could possibly have imagined.

Australians were perfectly suited to fighting in the South African landscape, which was similar to their own. Our rugged bushmen and experienced riders were far better at operating in the hot, dusty African terrain than the feeble British, raised on cobbled streets, their growth stunted by diets of jellied eels and suet sandwiches, their pasty complexions prone to melting right off their bodies under the harsh glare of the southern sun. Britain's army was, essentially, a horde of

130 He was laying it on a bit thick, don't you think?

revolting little goblin-men, and God knows how the war would've turned out without the tall, muscular, painfully handsome Australians there to teach them how horses work and tell them to duck when someone shot at them.

In fact, the Australians fighting in the Boer War were so freakishly good at it that public opinion began to turn against the war. 'I feel sorry for those Boers,' sad Australian civilians would say. 'It seems unfair that they have to fight us – after all, they're only human.' This ambivalence would only be intensified by the most notorious incident in Australia–Boer interactions: the tale of Breaker Morant.

Breakers Gonna Break, Break, Break, Break, Break

Harry Morant was an Englishman – so there's one strike against him already – who came to Australia as a teenager and worked as a roustabout (or, as the English would say, 'merry-go-round'). He drank heavily, cut a swathe through the colony's female population and rode horses. In fact, he rode a lot of horses and gained a reputation for being what his fellow bushmen called 'a horse rider'. Few men, it was said, could ride a horse like 'the Breaker': a nickname given to him in recognition of his terrible washing-up skills. He was also a prolific poet, although this doesn't necessarily mean he deserved to die.[131]

The Breaker volunteered for military service in South Africa and excelled, thrilling his superiors with his wonderful horsemanship and clever wordplay. In 1901, he joined the Bushveldt Carbineers, an irregular unit that nonetheless always tried its best. Morant's military career went awry, however, when he became an enthusiast of the 'shooting prisoners' school of tactical warfare. It soon became apparent that nothing enraged Breaker more than being surrendered to – it

131 It doesn't necessarily mean he didn't, though.

really brought out the summary executioner in him. The routine was usually the same: Morant's men would come across a party of Boers; the Boers would run up a white flag and hand over their weapons; Morant would take this as a personal insult; the Boers would be shot in the head; everyone would sit around and ponder the moral complexities of war.

Of course, not everyone Morant killed was an unarmed Boer soldier. He also killed a clergyman who had comforted the unarmed Boer soldiers before they died. So don't let anyone tell you that Breaker Morant didn't know the meaning of variety.

After his killing spree, Morant and his subordinates Lieutenants Handcock and Witton were court-martialled. During the proceedings, their lawyer Jack Thompson gave a spirited defence, but the old proverb 'In a murder trial, the guys who killed a bunch of people are always under pressure' rang truer than ever. The three men were convicted and sentenced to death by Bud Tingwell, though Witton's sentence was commuted to life imprisonment because he had a sweetly boyish face.

On 27 February 1902, Breaker Morant and Lieutenant Handcock were executed by firing squad. Before being shot, Morant famously bellowed, 'Shoot straight, you bastards', and it's hard to feel much sympathy for a man who could be that rude to people who were, after all, just doing their jobs under difficult circumstances.

The case of Breaker Morant was extremely controversial. During his trial, he claimed that he'd acted on orders from the top to take no prisoners. Many people – on the basis that 'I was only following orders' has always been considered an excellent defence to accusations of war crimes – believe that Morant and his men were wrongly convicted.

After being released from prison,[132] George Witton wrote a book, *Scapegoats of the Empire*, in which he claimed that he, Morant and Handcock had been scapegoats of the Empire: Witton had yet to learn the value of not giving away your book's plot in the title.

Was Breaker Morant a good soldier following orders, made to shoulder all the blame for widespread British war crimes in South Africa to help facilitate a looming peace treaty, or was he a callous murderer whose lust for revenge drove him on a savage and unforgiveable killing spree? These questions remain unresolved, but the answer to both of them is 'yes'.

In subsequent years, the legacy of the Breaker Morant case had a profound effect on the Australian psyche and ideas about independence from the Empire. While Australians had long felt a natural kinship with the mother country, many asked why we should stand beside the British if they were simply going to go and execute us every time we committed mass murder.

In 2010, a petition was sent to Queen Elizabeth calling for a pardon for Morant, Handcock and Witton. The petition was motivated by the discovery of new evidence revealing that the petitioners had too much spare time.

The Boer War ended in 1902 with the Treaty of Vereeniging, which absorbed the two Boer republics into the British Empire and led to the formation of the Union of South Africa, in which both British and Afrikaaners learnt to peacefully coexist and recognise their real enemy: racial equality.

Australia's military history was to kick it up a notch just a few years later.

---

132 Life imprisonment still didn't mean what it said, apparently.

ESSAY QUESTIONS

1. Can you shoot straight, you bastard?
2. 'Australians fight in wars, but do not start wars.' If this is true, don't you find it a bit suspicious?

If You Are the One

In which a young country desperate for an identity finds one in the last place it looked, and a generation's sacrifice gives everyone an acronym that they can believe in

World War One, also known as 'The First World War', 'WWI', 'The Great War' and 'Blackadder Goes Forth', was a complex international conflict that came about as a result of several interconnecting causes:

1. The competing imperial ambitions of European superpowers
2. The power vacuum left by the decline of the Ottoman Empire
3. Evil Germans
4. Unresolved territorial disputes
5. Arms races, etc.
6. Wacky diplomatic misunderstandings
7. A guy shooting another guy
8. The world's crippling complex international conflict shortage
9. Rasputin, Russia's greatest love machine
10. Australians' urgent need for a nation-defining moment that would forever be remembered as our national coming of age

This last was probably the most important of all. Diplomatic cables from the early 1900s show that leaders of all the great European powers were extremely concerned about the issue of Australian identity. 'Australians just don't know who they *are*,' wrote Kaiser Wilhelm to British Prime Minister Herbert Asquith in 1910. 'Is there anything we can do to help them out?' Asquith replied promptly, asking, 'Do you think a colossal international war would give them a bit of a boost? I do hate to see them looking so down in the dumps.' Wilhelm replied with a picture of a thumbs-up, possibly history's first emoji.

Yes, there were major issues in Australia over the question of national identity. We had become a country in 1901, but were we a *nation*? Yes, we were: 'country' and 'nation' mean the same thing.[133] But still, what did it mean to be Australian? The storied deeds of Ned Kelly and Breaker Morant had provided us with one possible answer: Australians were murderers. But was that enough? The perception persisted that despite Federation, Australians were still not citizens of a proud, independent country, but of a far-flung outpost of Empire, still clinging to Mother England's apron strings like a crying baby clinging to a dolphin's back. If we let go, would we drown?

Australia's identity crisis had become almost unbearable when the blessed relief of World War One came along. On 4 August 1914, Britain declared war on Germany, causing Prime Minister Joseph Cook to declare that 'when the Empire is at war, so also is Australia', which is a slightly suck-uppy thing to say, but he was under a lot of stress. In September, Cook was replaced by Prime Minister Andrew Fisher, who emphasised that he was in agreement with Cook that going to war would be a real blast. And the young men of Australia agreed, signing up in their thousands for a chance to see the world, meet new people and watch their feet gradually rot off their legs while they were being shot at.

133 Look it up: it's true.

Of course, signing up was exactly what the young men of Australia *had* to do, because the government couldn't force them to fight like a really *ballsy* government would. Prime Minister Billy Hughes, who became the country's first ferret leader when he succeeded Andrew Fisher in 1915 on a platform of making the country angrier, did his best to change this. Believing that no civilised nation would ever welcome the prospect of war, and that therefore it needed someone to force it to, Hughes put the question of conscription to the Australian people twice, through plebiscites in 1916 and 1917. Both plebiscites were defeated due to the majority's belief in freedom of conscience and the minority's belief that a 'plebiscite' was a kind of dinosaur.

World War One was fought by Australia against Germany, Turkey and British incompetence. There were times, in fact, when Britain was so inept that Australia regretted letting them help fight the war in the first place. And yet, despite the fact that every single British general was a lunatic with a mental age of six who insisted on pointing his cannon the wrong way and ordering troops to charge into machine-gun fire nude and armed only with fresh fish, Australia still managed to win the war pretty much on its own.

The most important battle of the war was

Gallipoli

A crucial turning point of the war, in Gallipoli an outnumbered Australian force was ordered to commit suicide by stupid Englishmen, but instead conquered Turkey. It all began when the Ottoman Empire, known as the 'sick man of Europe', agreed to join the war on Germany's side in return for a share of Germany's vast paracetamol reserves.

This outraged the Allies (Australia, Britain, Russia, New Zealand, Norfolk Island), who had maps proving that most of Turkey was in

Asia and that therefore the name 'sick man of Europe' was incredibly misleading. An attempt to sue the Ottomans for false advertising went nowhere, as did British ships trying to bring supplies to Russia through the Dardanelles strait, because there were a whole bunch of Ottomans[134] in the way.

Winston Churchill, First Lord of the Admiralty and legendary woman-insulter, hatched a cunning plan: 'What if,' he mused, sucking amiably on a cigar, 'we attacked them?'

There was silence in the Admiralty lunchroom. 'Is ... is that it?' asked an admiral.

'It's not that original an idea, is it?' asked another admiral.

'Well, I didn't hear any of *you* come up with it,' Churchill pointed out, tapping ash onto his secretary.

'Do you have any particular strategies in mind?' asked the first admiral.

'Yes!' Churchill boomed, taking a shot of bourbon. 'I think we should send troops ... by ship!'

Again an awkward silence descended. A small timid admiral piped up. 'Well, yes. That does seem the best way to get them there.' Churchill beamed at this endorsement of his master plan.

'And once the troops get there, what do they do?' asked the second admiral.

Churchill chuckled. He was ready for this one. 'They shoot ...' he paused to maximise the drama, 'at the Turks.' He burped for emphasis.

The admirals stared at the First Lord as he quaffed some more whisky. 'Mr Churchill,' one said, 'you are a terrible First Lord of the Admiralty.'

'That may be so,' Churchill shot back, 'but *you* are ugly, and in the

134 Ottoman Turks, that is: not ... well, you know what I mean.

morning I'll be –' He never finished his thought, instead falling off his chair and going to sleep on the floor.[135] And so, to the peaceful sounds of Churchill's walrussy snores, the Gallipoli campaign began.

The main aim of the assault on the Dardanelles was to dig a series of trenches in which to die in enormous numbers over the course of a painfully protracted stalemate. In this, the Allies were spectacularly successful.

The ANZACs (standing for Australian and New Zealand Awesome Coolguys) landed at Gallipoli on 25 April 1915, a date that is still celebrated each year in Australia as Kickarse Army Day. They immediately began gunning down Turks left and right, and would have taken the peninsula in a matter of minutes were it not for orders coming through from British High Command that the campaign should switch to Bumbling Incompetence Mode with all possible speed.

Pinned down by Turkish fire and beset by incompetent British officers, it was a miracle that Australia managed to win Gallipoli so easily, but then miracles are what tend to happen when you put an Australian in a uniform and give him a gun.[136] At the battle of **Lone Pine**, the Australian 1st Infantry Brigade inflicted major casualties on the Turks and took possession of the lone pine, one of the most daring tree-acquisitions of any Allied unit during the war. They also captured about 150 metres of ground, which made all the difference when they needed somewhere to play football later on.[137]

The Australians suffered casualties of almost 3000 at Lone Pine, but the Ottoman casualties were as many as 7000, so you can't be

135 This and more legendary zingers can be found in *The Wit of Churchill: 101 Winnie One-Liners to Wow With*.

136 Just ask Glenn McGrath.

137 Which happened surprisingly often during World War One, a.k.a. 'The Drop Punt War'.

unhappy with that. General Sir Ian Hamilton certainly wasn't, calling the Australians' efforts 'a desperate fine feat', before riding to Harrenhal to take command of the Lannister forces. Seven Australians won the Victoria Cross, a special military honour reserved only for soldiers who kill more enemy combatants than Queen Victoria did.

ANZACs also distinguished themselves at **The Nek**, a narrow strip of ground that connected 'Russell's Top' – a ridge named for its resemblance to the haircut of a man called Russell – to 'Baby 700', a knoll that looked like an extremely fat infant. The Battle of the Nek came about when the ANZACs' commander Major General Alexander Godley, who had been dropped on his head as a baby more than 50 times, ordered the Australian 3rd Light Horse Brigade to charge headlong at a heavily defended Turkish position in order to test his theory that being shot multiple times by a machine gun could cure lumbago. Struggling due to not actually having any light horses,[138] the Australians had to run at the Turkish trench carrying unloaded rifles with fixed bayonets, following an artillery bombardment that finished too early and achieved nothing, in accordance with government policy. After the entire first wave was gunned down, the commanders sent in three more waves in order to be sure that it was the bullets causing the soldiers to fall over and not a mass outbreak of contagious epilepsy.

In all, 600 of the Light Horse charged the Ottomans, of which 234 were killed and 138 wounded. But they did manage to kill eight Turks as well, so we can probably call that one even. And we got an award-winning and seminal moment in domestic cinema out of it, which is more than you can say about Turkey, whose technical victory at The Nek did nothing to launch Mel Gibson's career.

---

138 Had they done some research before the war, they'd have known that horses are very heavy creatures (*Zoology Today*, Issue 48, Nov 1976).

At the Nek, the world found out that Australians were the kind of fearless, indomitable warriors who would not stop advancing even when they had literally zero chance of achieving anything but their own rapid and horrible deaths. The world considered the possibility that this made Australians a bit stupid, but after some thought realised it made them incredibly brave, especially considering they were only committing suicide because some pencil-necked chinless English moustache rack had told them to. And the alternative to jumping over the trench to get shot by the Turks was disobeying orders and being shot by the British, so it's not as though the world was exactly their oyster.

The fact is that, even for earthbound demi-gods like the average Australian soldier, life at Gallipoli was pretty tough. Partly it was the artillery bombardment and machine-gun fire. Partly it was the appalling living conditions: squatting for months in filthy trenches, sinking into mud when it rained, living on weevil-infested biscuits and barely edible knitted goods from home. Partly it was the constant barrage of psychological trauma that came from watching friends get maimed and killed beside you, while also having to live with the indelible memory of the men that you yourself had maimed and killed. But more than any of those, it was all of them put together. 'War is all hell,' William Tecumseh Sherman famously said, and he never even had to follow orders from an Englishman.

And yet, Australians everywhere had cause to be grateful for Gallipoli – except, obviously, for the Australians who died there. What that eight-month campaign at Anzac Cove gave us were authentic national heroes, true patriotic icons who didn't even have to put kettles on their heads. Men like

Albert Jacka

Albert Jacka was the first Australian to receive the Victoria Cross during World War One and was therefore better than the others, who dillydallied far too long in receiving theirs. He won the medal after engaging a unit of Turks who had taken a section of a trench. Diving in with no thought of personal safety, Jacka shot five and bayoneted two of the enemy, causing the others to abandon the trench with loud cries of 'WTF?' He held the trench single-handedly overnight, keeping the Turks at bay by firing at them with one hand, while with the other he sipped a cup of tea and read a magazine. He was recommended for bravery by his commander, instantly becoming a national hero. Melbourne businessman John Wren gave him £500 and a gold watch for being the first Australian VC-winner of the war, and the Australian media showered him with acclaim, declaring that never before in the history of Australian combat had killing seven men looked so awesome.

Jacka went on to even more glory. He gained rapid multiple promotions, fought in France, won the Military Cross at Pozières and a bar to the MC at Bullecourt, killed several bears with his bare hands, cleaned the Augean stables in a single day and stole fire from the gods. Upon his return to Australia, he was given 50 of the peasantry's most beautiful maidens, 7000 cattle and a magical sword. He is rightly considered 'the Bradman of shooting and stabbing dudes'.[139] And yet, it is possible that Jacka was only the second-greatest Australian hero of Gallipoli, after

Simpson and His Donkey

This is one of the greatest Australian war legends, much beloved by

139 Some even say that it is Bradman who was 'the Albert Jacka of *not* shooting and stabbing dudes'.

writers everywhere because it's mostly untrue and nobody really cares. Simpson and His Donkey was born John Simpson Kirkpatrick in England in 1892 – at that point he didn't yet have the donkey from which he took his name. After deserting from the merchant navy in Australia in 1910, Simpson, still without a donkey, romped around the country cutting cane and mining coal and basically being a suspicious-looking drifter, until World War One broke out and he joined the army because he thought it seemed like a cheap way to get back to England; as, like all true Australian heroes, he desperately wanted to leave Australia forever.[140]

Simpson enlisted as a stretcher bearer because of his great physical strength, but when he arrived at Gallipoli he started using a donkey because of his great physical laziness. Many other stretcher bearers carried wounded men back from the front lines without help from any ungulates whatsoever, but we don't remember them: we remember the man so unwilling to put in a day's honest work that he outsourced his job to a donkey.

Anyway, Simpson ran through a few donkeys at the front: none of them ever gave informed consent, but he pushed them out there anyway. He'd already shown his love of desertion and slacking – why not add animal abuse to the mix, I suppose was his thinking. The donkeys were wounded and killed, but still Simpson went on, dragging innocent animals into the hell of modern warfare, singing and whistling[141] as he went about his gruesome work.

Simpson became a legend on the beach at Gallipoli for what those ignorant of his dark donkey-hating heart considered his uncommon valour. The public were amazed by his rescue of 300 men and other

140 He was the Nicole Kidman of his day.

141 He really did. Tasteless.

stories that weren't true. In fact, few Allied servicemen can match Simpson's sterling record of fictional feats.

Simpson and his donkey were at Gallipoli for three weeks, and then he got shot and died – unlike New Zealand's Dick Henderson, who also used a donkey to carry the wounded to safety, but managed to keep working through the whole war and live until 1958 without a single person ever giving half a grasshopper's bollock about him. So ill-treated was Henderson by history that when the Kiwi artist Horace Moore-Jones painted his famous *The Man with the Donkey*, working from a photograph of Henderson, he thought he was painting Simpson, and the heroic New Zealander had to watch as his picture helped reinforce Simpson's fame around the world.

Simpson, on the other hand, continued to induce historical orgasms in all who heard his story, or at least the loose collection of dubious claims that people called his story. In 1997, the RSPCA gave his donkey a posthumous Purple Heart, which today still stands as the most pointless act in military history, just ahead of World War One itself.

Some people have petitioned for Simpson to receive a Victoria Cross, but at the time of writing the authorities continue to have actual work to do.

Victory at Gallipoli

After eight months of brutal trench warfare at Gallipoli, Allied forces withdrew in December 1915, due to Australia having won the battle so overwhelmingly that High Command was afraid if they kept going there might be nobody left alive in Turkey by Easter. During the evacuation, the British Army showed, not for the first or last time, that running away from a battlefield was something at which they excelled, although even that might not have been achieved so efficiently if it weren't for the Australian contingent, who sped up the retreat by hurling artillery and tanks back onto the boats with their bare hands, and in some cases improvising oars out of tree trunks to row battleships with damaged engines away from the Dardanelles.

In the end, casualties from both sides at Gallipoli numbered more than 350,000, with both Allies and Ottomans counting over 50,000 dead each. These poor souls are remembered each year on 25 April when thousands of young Australians travel to Anzac Cove to pay tribute by performing the traditional Leaving of the Empty Beer Cans, a solemn ritual that represents the deep connection today's Australians feel to their forebears and also to their beer. The reverence shown by modern-day Aussies to the site of the original ANZACs' sacrifice is a testament to our nation's almost superhuman gall in demanding that a foreign nation host a yearly memorial service dedicated to our invasion of them.

But it would be a mistake to think that Gallipoli was the only theatre of the Great War. A fault of many Australian history books is that they give the impression the Gallipoli campaign constituted the bulk of Australian involvement: in fact, though most historians do estimate that about 90 to 95 per cent of World War One took place at Anzac Cove, there were other bits of the war here and there, including

The Western Front

Fromelles. Pozières. Ypres. The Somme. Names that every Australian recognises as being of places in another country somewhere. All were important locations of battles on the Western Front of World War One, where for four years the mighty German war machine was battered and humiliated by the astounding abilities of the ordinary Aussie digger.

Records indicate that several times over those four years, the Germans tried to quit the war, but Australians kept chasing them and dragging them back to beat them up some more.

The **Somme** was one of the bloodiest battles of the war, which is why soldiers sometimes referred to it as 'the bloody Somme'. It lasted from July to November 1916 and involved an Allied assault on German lines in France. It's known for featuring the first use of tanks in war, and for featuring thousands of men massacring one another for long periods of time. At the end, Allied forces had gained six miles, representing an average of half a millimetre per horrific wound suffered. Australian troops' main responsibilities during the Somme were to kill huge numbers of Germans, and to be stronger and more handsome than other soldiers.

The Battle of **Bullecourt** took place from March to May 1917 and was won by the Australians due to their mind-boggling bravery and indefinable charm. It was notable for being a battle where thousands of men massacred one another for long periods of time.

Ypres[142] is a city in Belgium, but that shouldn't be held against it. The Battle of Ypres, also known as the Battle of Passchendaele in honour of the soft drink that Australian soldiers drank while fighting, was a failed campaign due to British commanders' pigheaded insistence on allowing non-Australian troops into the field. In the end, the Allied divisions got stuck in the Belgian mud, which was particularly thick, rich and hazelnut-flavoured, and were unable to capitalise on the Australians' many valuable and well-dressed gains. The Battle of Ypres lasted from September to November 1917 and stood out from many other battles of the time because it featured thousands of men who massacred one another for long periods.

---

142 Pronounced 'Ypres'.

The second Battle of the Somme, known to historians as the First Battle of the Somme due to historians' perverse desire to make life harder for everyone, included the First Battle of **Villers-Bretonneux**, a little town that was captured by the Germans in 1918, but then recaptured by two Australian brigades, who according to eyewitness reports walked straight into the town square and began punching the German tanks in the face. To this day, there is an annual Anzac Day ceremony held at the Australian War Memorial at Villers-Bretonneux, which is always a moving occasion, if unable to match the Gallipoli ceremony for alcohol consumption. On the other hand, the Second Battle of Villers-Bretonneux was part of the Battle of the Lys, not to be confused with the Second Battle of the Somme, which was the third battle of the Somme. All of these battles were particularly memorable for the long periods of time during which thousands of men massacred one another.

Eventually Australia's exploits on the Western Front brought about the end of the war, after ANZAC infantry units harried the enemy with 'Peaceful Penetrations': small-scale raids that allowed the capture of German positions and eventually forced Germany to withdraw from the war due to pregnancy.

But although the diggers' valiant battles at Gallipoli and throughout France and Belgium sent the Kaiser whimpering back to his Kaiserhole, it should not be forgotten that Australians also performed acts of great heroism in **Sinai and Palestine**. During that campaign, thousands of men massacred one another for long periods of time, but it never really felt the same.

The Legacy

What was the legacy of Australia's involvement, and victory, in World War One? In many ways it was the war in which Australia grew up.

Just as a boy cannot become a man without a period of indiscriminate slaughter, so Australia needed to be baked in the kiln of war before it could emerge as a genuinely independent pot. The Great War provided Australians with a new way of seeing themselves, based on three important facts:

1. The young men of this young nation had proven themselves not only the equal of the fighters of any other land, but actually so much better than them that every other country looked like a bunch of little asthmatic babies. We therefore began to see ourselves as deserving of a place on the world stage.
2. Where previously, despite Federation, Australians had still considered Britain their 'true' homeland, and Australia itself to be more a sort of purgatory in which they had to work off their sins, the war showed them that the British were just as stupid and incompetent and clueless and prone to throwing huge numbers of innocent people into gigantic meat grinders as anyone else. Thus the umbilical cord became much easier to bite through, and we were able to see ourselves as a country in our own right.
3. A lot of Australians were now dead, so we were able to see ourselves as a country of dead men.

Taken together, these facts helped sculpt a new identity for Australia, one that survives to this day and makes no more sense now than it did then. What, then, is this identity? Is Australia a nation of soldiers? A nation of heroes? A nation of British lapdogs? A nation of invaders of sovereign nations? A nation of clean-limbed young men stupid enough to volunteer for the army? Australia is all these things and, for all I know, more. And we have World War One to thank for that.

World War One had a few other consequences as well:

1. Massive advances in military technology
2. An almost incurable outbreak of poetry
3. World War Two

But before the latter brouhaha could come along to set the world alight once more with death and hatred, Australians would be confronted by the Depression, as well as the horrors of a war on their own doorstep.

ESSAY QUESTIONS

1. What is the correct pronunciation of 'Ypres', and why don't you know it?
2. How many miniseries can be made about Gallipoli?

Depressed

In which a nation gets down in the dumps, but finds solace in the cracking of balls and the galloping of fetlocks

If there is one quality that has always defined Australians, it is happiness. The convicts were happy as they were starved and beaten by their overseers, the bushrangers were happy as they were gunned down by the police, the ANZACs were happy as they invented Australianness – throughout this country's history, we have been a cheerful lot, merry and carefree and almost idiotically optimistic about a future that is almost certain to be disappointing.

But there was a time when Australians were not so joyous. That time was known as the Great Depression,[143] in recognition of its superiority to previous depressions that had always felt like a bit of a letdown. During that time, sadness and despair stalked the land like two enormous stick insects, making everyone feel nauseous with their unnaturally elongated bodies and horrible alien heads. God, stick insects are disgusting, but not as disgusting as the Great Depression, although it's a close-run thing.

When the Depression first came to Australia, many people flat-out refused to participate in it. 'This is an American thing,' they said,

143 Everything was great back then.

sneering, 'we don't need any of that rubbish here.' They refused to hang out Depression decorations and would turn away the children who came to their doors asking for Depression treats. 'What's next?' they would ask. 'Basketball and Christianity?'

And, of course, they were right: the Depression *was* an American invention, originally imported to Australia to exterminate cane toads, but it soon got completely out of hand.

The story of the Depression begins in ancient Mesopotamia, when the concept of currency first arose. But space limitations prevent us from tracing the saga from that point, so let's fast-forward to 28 October 1929, known as 'Black Monday' because it was the day that people everywhere started setting fire to themselves. On this day, the US stock market lost 13 per cent of its value, and Black Monday was followed by Black Tuesday, named after Black Monday, when the stock market lost another 12 per cent. As time went on, it became apparent that the market lost a quarter of its value and that nobody knew where it had gone. Sorcery was suspected.

What did the stock market crash mean for the world? To understand this, one must first understand what stocks are. And since nobody knows this, there's not much point in trying to grasp the whole thing. Essentially the point is this: millions of people had been putting all their money in shares, not realising that shares are imaginary things invented to ruin our lives, and when the chickens came home to roost they quickly began pecking everyone's eyes out.

There's academic disagreement on what exactly caused the Great Depression. In *The General Theory of Employment, Interest and Money*, John Maynard Keynes posits that decreased aggregate expenditure caused economic activity to decline and unemployment to rise, leading to a sub-optimal point of equilibrium. What this means is that it's up to the government to stimulate the economy during downturns with increased spending – so you wonder why Keynes couldn't have said that in the first place, the nerdy blowhard.

In contrast to the Keynesian explanation, the monetarist theory states that the Depression was caused by a monetary contraction, which sounds both painful and distressing. On the other hand, some say that a combination of Keynesian and monetary factors contributed to the Depression. There are also those who contend that the Austrian School is correct, although that seems unlikely, them being Austrian.

The point is, things got very bad. Nowhere was it worse than in Australia, where the export industries on which the country relied were crippled by nobody having any money to buy our stuff. Those who once rode on the sheep's back suddenly found themselves underneath the sheep, clinging to its belly, banging their heads on the ground with every step. Those who rode on wheat's back had it even tougher, but they'd been pretty uncomfortable in that position in the first place.

The Wall Street crash happened in the first week of James Scullin's government in Australia. I'm not saying Scullin necessarily had anything to do with it. I'm just saying that it's kind of a suspicious coincidence, from which the reader can draw his or her own conclusions.

Scullin, who photographic evidence indicates was played by *Mad Men* star John Slattery, was in fact a hard-working and idealistic prime minister who came to office with many ambitious plans for making Australia a better place, but unfortunately all of those plans depended to a greater or lesser extent on there being any money anywhere. But beginning with the stock market plunge, his term in office was marked by skyrocketing unemployment and diving commodity prices. The Scullin government was deeply in debt and, against all of its members' well-honed political instincts, something had to be done.

Scullin took advice from the Bank of England's Otto Niemeyer, who recommended spending cuts and balancing the budget in order to repay government debt. Alternatively there was the plan of Scullin's Labor Party colleague, NSW Premier Jack Lang, who believed that the best way to address mounting debts was not to pay them. 'After all,' Lang reasoned, 'we're the government, we can basically do whatever we want.' It's surprising that Lang isn't more revered by modern-day politicians really, with that attitude.

As it was, though, nobody outside liked Lang, because he looked like Geoffrey Rush's overbearing father from *Shine*, so the federal government instead went with the idea of slashing spending and raising taxes, on the basis that the best way to combat a situation where people don't have enough money is to make sure they have even less.

Not that it was Scullin who put that plan into action, however, as the country, exasperated with their prime minister's failure to personally direct the course of the global economy, turfed him out, and Joseph Lyons became prime minister at the start of 1932. This marked the beginning of Australia's recovery from the Great Depression, as the business community responded favourably to Lyons' calm demeanour and reassuringly wavy hair. Bit by bit, the Lyons government devalued the Australian pound, stimulated the manufacturing sector and, perhaps most importantly, sat around waiting for the rest of the world to get better: a strategy that worked spectacularly well. Lyons remained PM for seven years and became known as the 'Great Gradual Recoverer', a label that spoke well of his considerable abilities but was hard to fit on a poster. Meanwhile, Scullin went to bed and sulked, while Jack Lang was dismissed by the governor after his plan to have the governor arrested didn't quite come off.

The Great Depression didn't only affect politicians, although obviously as the most sensitive and highly strung members of society they were particularly hard hit. The spike in unemployment, which at one point reached 32 per cent, meant that quite a few ordinary people also had a difficult time. Proud men, finding themselves unable to provide for their families, were consumed with shame and ignominy and hardly even noticed, because they were also starving to death.

People dealt with the privations of the Depression in different ways. Some coped by going to soup kitchens or charity agencies for help. Some coped by killing themselves. Each approach had its own pros and cons. Unemployed people from the city flocked to the country in search of work. Unemployed people from the country flocked to the city in search of work. They all had a good laugh when they figured out what had been going on, but it was only a brief interlude of mirth. In general, the Great Depression was a bit of a downer.

Many thousands were made homeless by the economic slump. Shanty towns sprung up outside cities. The destitute filled the refuges and public parks of Australia's cities. Some families moved into caves, desperation forcing them to abandon dignity and comfort and natural human fear of bears. Massive queues formed outside any business advertising even a single job vacancy, even if it was just for a call centre or hosting cosmetics parties.

At times the hunger, homelessness and sad men sitting on the ground with heartbreaking cardboard signs around their necks even spilled over into violence, with angry mobs rioting in Sydney and Melbourne to express their disenchantment with the country's decline. The governments responded by throwing up their hands and crying, 'Dudes! Economics is *complicated*! We've got *NO* idea what to do!'

Indeed, the Depression was an era of gloom, pessimism, widening social fractures, intractable frustrations and award-winning black-and-white photography. There was a very real risk that the economic devastation laying waste to the land would lead to an irreparable splintering of the community itself. Could the country hold together? And if it couldn't, would recovery ever be possible?

Keeping Our Chins Up

The Roman poet Juvenal once wrote of the people's capacity to be placated and kept from political agitation by 'bread and circuses'. Perhaps he was writing about Australia during the Great Depression. Obviously he wasn't: he died in the second century AD. But if he was a time traveller or something. You know what I mean.

Point is that though bread was rather thin on the ground during the Great Depression – or not even that, since any bread left on the ground, however thin, would quickly be snatched up and eaten by the starving masses – and with *The Voice* yet to go to air, the Australian people found diversion and solace in circuses. And by circuses, I mean sport.

As a country that had a cricket team before it had a government, Australia has always rejoiced in the magic of sporting success and its ability to make a person forget that genuinely important things exist. If there's one thing that Australians pride themselves on living vicariously through, it's sport: some consider sport an even better expression of Australian identity than warfare.[144] And if there ever was a time when the populace desperately needed champions, it was the Great Depression, when a man would gratefully latch on to any athletic triumph that came along if it helped him forget that he was eating his shoelaces.

---

144 Unlike truly patriotic Australians, who understand that sport *is* warfare.

The biggest game in town at the time, of course, was cricket, these being the days before communists infiltrated the country and spread the rumour that other sports were better. And it so happened that the Depression coincided with the emergence of the most freakish cricketer ever to tuck a single to backward square leg. Was this purely luck? It so often happens that times of crisis give birth to their own redemptive compensations: see how it took the Great Fire of London to bring about the magnificent rebuilding of that city, or how Vincent van Gogh's intolerable inner pain resulted in the incomparable beauty of his art, or how it required the tragic sinking of the *Titanic* to make possible the movie *Titanic*. In the same way, perhaps it's possible that the unique conditions of the Depression were themselves responsible for the legend of Donald George Bradman, the smiling diminutive run machine who made Freemasonry cool again.

On 6 January 1930, Australians first got an inkling that Bradman could be the man to make the Depression bearable. Playing for New South Wales against Queensland, in the days when the general public was still aware that state cricket teams existed, young Donald pummelled the Queensland bowlers – who themselves rapidly became subject to a great depression – for 452 runs. He was 21 years old and had broken the world record for the highest first-class innings, making the runs in just 415 minutes and off only 465 balls. The cricketing world rocked slightly on its axis. The Queensland team chaired Bradman off the field, having decided that he was to be their new god.

The presence of greatness in the land was a fillip to public confidence, but as money matters continued to press painfully upon Australian minds, everyone knew that the country would not be able to truly enjoy life until that greatness was put to work for the only purpose that real Australians can see nobility in: humiliating the English.

And, like characters in a heartwarming stop-motion Christmas special, Australians saw all their dreams come true in the winter of 1930, when the Australian cricket team headed to England to avenge their own humiliation at English hands the year before. Once landed in the mother country, Bradman proceeded to fulfil the predictions made by the town elders back in Bowral. 'One day,' the old cobbers would say, 'that lad will give an entire country post-traumatic stress disorder.' So it proved, as the man whom unimaginative fans had already nicknamed 'The Don' slammed centuries from Southampton to Glasgow and redefined the concept of 'unnerving human automaton' for everyone. At Leeds he hit 309 in a single day. At Lord's he claimed that 'every ball went where I wanted it to'[145] in his 254. Unfortunately these were the days before televised sport, so Australians didn't actually see Bradman's astonishing feats in the 1930 Ashes, although contemporary reports indicate that the public took his word for them. It was a more trusting time.

Bradman returned to Australia as probably the greatest non-murdering hero in Australian history to that point. And he wasn't even finished. Over the next couple of years, he slapped both South Africa and the West Indies silly with his humble slice of wood. It got to the point where the next time England came to Australia, they turned for leadership to Douglas Jardine, a man who took up cricket after being thrown out of his local branch of the Royal Animal-Torturing Society for being too anti-social. The Bodyline series, in which the English countered the threat of Bradman by thoroughly testing the thickness of the Australian players' skulls, was if anything an even greater respite from the misery of the Depression than Bradman himself, as it gave the public an opportunity to indulge itself in seething anger, hatred of foreigners and gleeful self-righteousness all at once.

---

145 In some cases to different counties.

Bradman wasn't the only champion cricketer to lift Australian spirits during the Depression: Clarrie 'The Gnome' Grimmett, Bill 'Tiger' O'Reilly, Bill 'Puddin' Ponsford and Bert 'Bert' Oldfield were just a few of the superstars who occasionally stood near Bradman. But the Don was the man who brought the punters through the gates and, once they were in, convinced them to look in the direction of the field. More importantly, he was the man who made the relentless grind of poverty bearable. 'We may be poor,' Australia said. 'We may be hungry, we may be homeless, we may be sewing our own clothes from the skins of cats who unwisely wandered into our caves – but we have Our Don Bradman, and that makes the future seem bright.' Indeed, many modern commentators have expressed the opinion that it would be worth having another Great Depression if it meant we got another Bradman, a view aired especially stridently every time Shaun Marsh gets back into the Test team.

Do not allow yourself to fall under the misapprehension that the only comfort to Australians under the thumb of the callous global economy was the Bowral Bunker Buster. It was also a source of relief, at a time that evidenced the failures of humankind, to be reminded of how much better than people animals are. And so the nation turned its eyes to perhaps the greatest athlete to ever grace these shores without actually knowing he was an athlete: Phar Lap.[146]

Phar Lap was a racehorse, having committed some grievous sin in a past life. Like most great Australians, he was from New Zealand, although unlike most great Australians, he had his testicles removed at the age of two.[147] Free from the distractions that gonads inevitably

146 His name coming from the Thai word for 'animal cruelty'.

147 Great Australians who did *not* have their testicles removed at the age of two include Weary Dunlop, John Farnham and Skippy the Bush Kangaroo.

bring, Phar Lap proved to be one of those horses that racing experts technically describe as 'able to run very fast, even with a little dude sitting on them'. The racing fraternity soon grew to revere him – apart from those members of the fraternity who tried to shoot him[148] – as a champion. But his legend grew to encompass more than racing folk: the general public took him to their hearts as enthusiastically as if he'd been a human being engaged in a proper sport. With the Depression laying national spirits low, the people were crying out for a horse – and in Phar Lap, it's fair to say, they found one.

Phar Lap, also known as 'Big Red', 'Bobby', 'Red Terror', 'Wonder Horse' and 'Aguirre the Wrath of God', won numerous races, which in many ways is a good thing for a racehorse. Thousands cheered his every victory, as he filled the country's dog food factories with the corpses of the vanquished.

In 1932, Phar Lap went to Mexico, which proved to be just as good an idea as most people's trips to Mexico are. When he won the Agua Caliente Handicap, North America's richest race,[149] it seemed like nothing could stop him from conquering the world except a sudden and suspicious death from duodenitis-proximal jejunitis, and it's funny I should say that.

Whether the Americans poisoned Phar Lap to prevent his domination of their corrupt racing industry can't be known with certainty, although let's be honest, it's the sort of thing they might have done. But whether Phar Lap was murdered or simply fell prey to the 1930s belief that horses ran faster when given regular meals of arsenic, his reign as the world's greatest jockey-seat was over. His legend, though,

148 This actually happened on 1 November 1930. The Depression made everyone a bit edgy.

149 Is it weird that the richest race was in Mexico? It's weird, isn't it?

lived on, and when the broken men of Australia lined up to beg for a minimum-wage dung-shovelling job, they knew that no matter how low they sunk or how much of their self-respect they abandoned, there had once been a horse who ran much faster than most horses ran, and it would give them a warm, happy feeling in the spot in their stomachs where food would normally go.

Phar Lap's heart was sent to Canberra, his skeleton to Wellington and his skin to Melbourne, where even today visitors to the Melbourne Museum can look into his cold dead eyes and feel the silent accusation he directs at all humans for their horrific mistreatment of his equine brothers and sisters throughout history. Yes, the racing industry is our greatest shame, and its part in helping us through the Depression cannot be understated.

Other sporting achievements that soothed the sting of the Depression included the Empire Games in 1938, which were held in Sydney and resulted in Australia winning more medals than any of the various loser countries who surprisingly even bothered showing up. In particular, Australia won more medals than England and New Zealand put together, giving birth to the popular Australian phrase 'stick that up ya'.

There were other consolations for Depression-era Australia: the screen exploits of the dashing Tasmanian sex offender Errol Flynn, the funny-page antics of quintessential Aussie juvenile delinquents Ginger Meggs and Fatty Finn – and, of course, polio. All these pleasures made the irredeemable misery of the Great Depression one of the happiest periods of most Australians' lives. It was a testament to the resilience of our national character that we were able to carry on with a smile and forget about our problems in a pretty irresponsible way.

ESSAY QUESTIONS

1. What was Don Bradman's Test batting average? Come on, you know this. Really? God. Pathetic.
2. Is the Keynesian or monetarist explanation of the causes of the Great Depression more convincing, and can you illustrate this with examples from the movie *Working Girl*?
3. Is it offensive to people with clinical depression to refer to an economic slump as a depression, or is it offensive to economic slumps to refer to people with mental illness as depressed? Is this the most profound question you've ever heard?

Duty and the Beak

In which birds of a feather flock together, and rugged sons of the soil learn that if war is hell, ornithology is a nightmare

The Emu War – also known as 'The Great Emu War' in recognition of the fact that it was pretty great – is a pivotal moment in Australian history that is most notable for being something that actually happened. If it wasn't the most brutal war the country ever fought in, it was, at the very least, the most hilarious.[150]

The emu (*Dromaius novaehollandiae*[151]) is, of course, one of Australia's most iconic animals. If the kangaroo symbolises the wide-open spaces and natural athleticism of this country, and the koala represents our laidback attitude and general cuddliness, the emu is the embodiment of the Australian people's psychotic aggression and terrifying, insane eyes.[152]

In the early 1930s, that aggression and those eyes were proving problematic for the farmers of Western Australia – or to be more exact, the mouths and stomachs attached to the aggression and eyes were proving problematic. Twenty thousand emus had migrated to the Campion region, where they found out that this new wheat stuff that

150 With the possible exception of the War on Drugs.

151 The Greek *dromaius*, meaning 'mad bastard', and the Latin *novaehollandiae*, meaning 'who wants to kill you'.

152 Our political system is of course represented by the platypus.

all the chicks were talking about was pretty damn good. It is unknown whether the emus were unaware of the fact the wheat was meant for human consumption, or whether they knew and just didn't care, but anyone who's ever met an emu would probably have their suspicions.

This was really the last straw – in some cases literally – for the farmers, who had been having a hell of a time already. Many of them were veterans of World War One[153] who had apparently become so addicted to suffering and deprivation that they thought farming sounded like a fun way to spend their lives. When the Great Depression arrived, the government decided to stimulate the economy by promising subsidies to wheat farmers to increase their crops. They then decided it would stimulate the economy even more if they didn't give them the subsidies. 'Nothing boosts economic growth like a whimsical prank on the agricultural sector,' the government chortled.

And so, with wheat prices plummeting and farmers going broke and threatening not to let anyone have any wheat at all if people weren't nicer to them, the last thing anyone needed was 20,000 emus. In fact, if we're honest, there are hardly any situations where the sudden arrival of 20,000 emus will improve matters, and this was no exception.

For their part, the emus could hardly believe their luck: with huge areas of bushland cleared for crops, and increased water supplies for livestock, it appeared to them that the humans had deliberately adapted the landscape for an emu lifestyle. 'This is brilliant,' they burbled to each other. 'We should have done this years ago.' So the birds settled in for some heavy-duty pillaging of the land. They ate the wheat, and what they didn't eat they knocked down and trampled on. They tore holes in fences, letting in rabbits, who were often even more destructive than

---

153 Also known as a 'Great War', but believe me nowhere near as good as the emu one.

the emus – indeed, among country folk the rabbit is known as 'the emu of the burrow'.

Seeing their crops destroyed and their rabbit-proof fences de-rabbit-proofed by these sociopathic mutant charity bins, the farmers of Western Australia decided to make a stand. 'Today it is our wheat: tomorrow it will be our wives,' they declared. 'Stop this menace before the entire country is speaking Emu.' And so, in a notable moment of calm and proportionate reflection, they called in the army.

The army, which was kicking around the house at a loose end, leapt at the chance to go back into combat. World War One had ended 14 years ago, and World War Two wasn't due to arrive for another seven, so the military was bored out of its mind, and the emus were a perfect way for soldiers to work off their excess energy and get them out of their parents' hair for a few hours. Minister of Defence George Pearce, who had as it happens campaigned in the last election on a platform of shooting birds, called in Major G.P.W. Meredith of the Seventh Heavy Battery of the Royal Australian Artillery. Major Meredith immediately narrowed his eyes, grabbed his best men and two Lewis guns[154] and swore that if it was the last thing he did, he would get those feathery bastards. A cameraman also came along, to document the glorious victory of the men of the Seventh Battery.

Ask your average man in the street what the best way to kill thousands of emus is, and after getting over his alarm at being accosted by a stranger with such a bizarre question, he would probably say that high-powered machine guns were a good start. And indeed, Major Meredith and his superiors were supremely confident of success in their campaign against the emu occupation – wartime experience had taught them just how effective shooting was as a means of making

154 A gas-operated machine gun invented by rugby league legend Wally Lewis.

things dead, and if 20,000 men could die in one day on the Somme, 20,000 acromegalic turkeys should be a doddle. Yet history has a way of making brain-dead apes of even the wisest of prognosticators, and in spite of the confidence of all involved in the operation, history went on to record one beautiful fact about the Emu War:

The Emus won.

It was not only the most surprising and most humiliating defeat ever suffered by the Australian Defence Force, but it was also the first and, to date, only one to be inflicted by members of the family *Dromaiidae*, as well as the first war involving Australians to be voted by audiences as one of the Top 50 Greatest Sketch Comedies of All Time. Major Meredith was shocked, but in hindsight it should have been obvious that no mere military men could hope to be a match for nature's most perfect fighting machine: the emu.

The first setback came on 2 November 1932, when Meredith's men attempted to ambush 50 emus, only for the emus to split up and run in different directions. This was an unnerving development for the soldiers – back in the war, the Germans had never split up: they'd all stayed in the one spot to be shot at like decent chaps. The Lewis guns managed to bring down a few birds, but already the emus' fiendishly cunning tactics were looking ominous for the hapless humans. If they were up against a foe so unsportsmanlike as to get out of the way of the bullets, what chance did they have?

On 4 November, Meredith planned another ambush on a flock of 1000 emus gathering at a dam: supposedly for a drink, although in hindsight it's possible they were just creating a diversion so that the larger emu force could carry out a major assault elsewhere. Waiting to see the whites of the emus' eyes, the soldiers fired. Twelve emus were killed, but the rest once again scattered to all parts, escaping to regroup at Emu Headquarters. At this point the gun jammed, making further attack impossible. At the time, Meredith wrote the jamming off as a poorly timed accident, but it now seems likely that the emus were deploying saboteur birds to tamper with the ADF's equipment.

Meredith continued to pursue the emus, travelling south where, according to papers of the time, the emus were 'reported to be fairly tame'. He quickly discovered that a 'fairly tame' emu was like a 'reasonably gentle' serial killer. The major even tried mounting one of his guns on a truck to better maintain the pursuit: this move failed due to the rough terrain that caused the truck to bump and jolt so much that the gunner was unable to fire. Not that it mattered, as the emus were faster than the truck anyway.[155]

Meredith was faced with an enemy that moved faster than his troops, split into multiple smaller units when threatened, making it impossible to focus his assault on any one spot, and even when hit by the machine guns didn't seem to mind very much. He commented, 'If we had a military division with the bullet-carrying capacity of these birds it would face any army in the world. They could face machine guns with the invulnerability of tanks.' The really inexplicable thing is that despite the combat-readiness of the average emu being explicitly documented in this way, at the time of writing the ADF still stubbornly refuses to enlist emus in any branch of the armed forces. They'd be better value than the Joint Strike Fighter.

Six days into the Emu War, the Australians had fired 2500 bullets and killed, at most, a couple of hundred emus – and possibly as few

155 Many historians now believe the truck was purchased from the Acme Corporation.

as 50. On the bright side, Meredith's official report stressed, the army had recorded no casualties at all. Some of the most unsung heroes of Australian military history are the men who managed to read this report with straight faces.

The troops withdrew, demoralised and sunburnt. The emus, giggling to themselves, immediately resumed tucking into the wheat, with the difference that they were now not only destroying crops, but also leaving insulting notes behind afterwards. The farmers, suffering from chronically low standards, begged for the military to return. George Pearce, now known as the 'Minister for Doing Whatever Farmers Tell Him to Do', duly sent Meredith back in: this was done on the basis that he was the most experienced man in the army with regard to emus, due to seeing so many of them in his recurring nightmares.

After a few weeks more of killing some emus while seeing many more run blissfully off into the distance cackling with laughter and arranging their tail feathers into rude shapes, Meredith and his men came home, shaking and gibbering with the trauma of what they had been through.

Some believe that the campaign may have had a different conclusion if the army had been willing to consider less conventional tactics, like infiltrating the emu command with heavily disguised intelligence operatives – or using nuclear strikes. Alas, the military's capacity for innovation extended only to deciding to fight birds, not to thinking too hard about how. So the Emu War was, overall, a failure for the Australian Army, but it did provide valuable data for ornithologists, who had always believed that emus were properly classified as flightless birds: the war proved that, in fact, the emu is a strange and unholy hybrid of a rhinoceros, a velociraptor and Satan.

The other positive to take from the Emu War was that it was

responsible for possibly the greatest exchange ever to take place in the House of Representatives, which went as follows:

MR THORBY: Who is responsible for the farce of hunting emus with machine guns mounted on lorries? Is the Defence Department meeting the cost?

PRIME MINISTER LYONS: I have been told that the Defence Department will not be paying the bill.

MR JAMES: Is a medal to be struck for this war?

Surely, no matter what the cost, the fact that this discussion, on the subject of a war between humans and emus, is in Hansard, makes it all worth it.

ESSAY QUESTIONS

1. Could you kill an emu if asked? Provide diagrams.
2. Listen to John Williamson's hit song 'Old Man Emu'. Do you find the line 'He can run the pants off a kangaroo' problematic? Why/why not?

The Second Course

In which the world once again calls on Australia to save it from tyranny, and global fascism is defeated by an unstoppable alliance of rats, angels and rabbits

'Fellow Australians, it is my melancholy duty to inform you officially that in consequence of a persistence by Germany in her invasion of Poland, Great Britain has declared war upon her, and that, as a result, Australia is also at war.'

With those words, Australian Prime Minister Robert 'Badger-Brows' Menzies ushered his country into a conflict even more cataclysmic and conducive to excellent movies than World War One. The world, and Australia, would never be the same yet again.

World War Two, also known as 'The Second World War', 'WWII', 'World War One Part Two', 'Hitler's Bogus Journey' and 'Bedknobs and Broomsticks', was the third overseas war in a row that Australia won, foreshadowing a similar streak at the Cricket World Cup. As stated earlier, World War Two was caused by World War One, but union rules require me to state that the causes of the war were complex. They included:

1. Hitler wanting to conquer the world
2. The world not much wanting Hitler to conquer it

3. Japan needing a hobby
4. Spike Milligan's humorous journals
5. France forgetting to set its alarm clock and not waking up until it had already been occupied
6. Mussolini seeking a grand stage on which to prove Italian troops' ability to be humiliated
7. Franklin Roosevelt's secret wheelchair
8. Indiana Jones's failure to bring home the Holy Grail
9. A growing surplus of bullets, requiring some kind of outlet to dispose of them
10. Neville Chamberlain's frantic quest to find Germany the perfect birthday present

All of these factors combined and mingled and intertwined and simmered on low heat until one thing became quite clear: Adolf Hitler was out of his tiny mind and there was only one way to stop him – Australians. But between the declaration of war on 3 September 1939, and Weary Dunlop strangling Hitler in his bedroom in 1945, a lot of water had to flow under a lot of bridges.

Menzies wasn't kidding when he said that declaring war was a 'melancholy duty': earlier in 1939, he had told an audience in Perth that 'history will label Hitler as one of the really great men of the century',[156] and it must have been quite a wrench for him to go to war with such a super chap only a couple of months later. He probably sent Hitler a note to apologise: 'Dear Adolf: soz about the war, the Poms made me do it. ☹'

Initially, Australia's participation in World War Two was inextricably

---

156 Leading to much heckling from the people of Perth, who at the time were notoriously anti-genocidal maniacs.

linked to that of Britain, because all that 'forging a new identity' stuff from World War One was just a little gag. Australia truly entered the war several hours after Menzies' announcement, firing across the bows of a ship that was trying to leave Melbourne without permission. This showed the Menzies government's vigilance. 'No freighter will leave for Tasmania without its crew being scared out of their minds on *our* watch,' they vowed.

Early in the war, Australian forces were deployed mainly in the Mediterranean and Middle East, where troops were urgently needed to laugh at the Italians. In this they were wildly successful – many witnesses spoke in awe of the diggers' booming *basso profundo* guffaws, echoing across the Mediterranean every time an Italian ship accidentally sank itself or two Italian soldiers were comically knocked unconscious by running into each other at high speed.

These were the happy days of the war, when the azure waters of the Mediterranean and the balmy nights were rich with the sweet scent of romance, and travel agents offered package tours to the area for families looking for a relaxing holiday with free entertainment. In January 1941, the Australian 6th Division, which was not even fully equipped yet, took 40,000 prisoners at Bardia in Libya, where the Italians, paralysed with terror by the sight of the Australians' inferior numbers, surrendered within two days. Two weeks later, 25,000 more Italians gave themselves up at Tobruk. It was estimated that within two months, the entire population of Italy would be prisoners of the Australian 6th Division. Sadly, though, at this point Germany ruined everything by sending its own army to clean up the Italians' mess and transform the North African campaign from a breezy vacation to an actual theatre of war.

On the downside, the German assault led to many deaths and

helped prolong the global nightmare that was World War Two. On the upside, it allowed an excellent demonstration of the by now well-established fact that Australian soldiers were inherently better than everyone else.

The Rats of Tobruk

'Never send an Italian to do a German's job.' That was the motto of Erwin Rommel, nicknamed the 'Desert Fox' due to his classically handsome features and sand-filled hair, and he lived up to it when he rampaged through North Africa in Operation *Sonnenblume* (literally, 'My son's flowers').

In February 1941, having spent the past couple of months cruising around Libya slapping Italian heads, most of the British contingent in Africa became bored and went to Greece in search of a good retsina. This was a major miscalculation, as those Allied troops left in Libya were soon fleeing the *Deutsches Afrikakorps* (literally, 'Germans' African corpses') to the Egyptian border. The only hope to prevent Hitler taking control of Africa and uncovering the Ark of the Covenant was, as usual, Australia, whose brave diggers took up their positions in the port city of Tobruk in preparation for an astonishing yet predictable display of superlative masculinity.

The siege of Tobruk began on 10 April, when Rommel surrounded the town[157] and ordered tank, infantry and artillery units to begin highlighting the Australians' courage. This they did with ruthless Teutonic efficiency. In later years, military historians would question whether the outcome of the war may have been different if the Nazis had committed fewer resources to making Australians look good. But hindsight is 20/20: at the time, Hitler and his advisors saw the

157 Not personally: this isn't a fat joke.

mythologising of Australian invincibility as a non-negotiable aim of the war, and their concentration of effort reflected this.

From April to November, the Germans continued to try to get into Tobruk, and the Australians continued to tell them that they couldn't. Rommel attacked with tanks, with planes, with gunboats, with watertight epistemological arguments: nothing would dislodge the indomitable Aussies from their posts. In response to the German attacks, the Australians launched several daring raids of their own, causing the Germans to become extremely depressed and lock themselves in their bedrooms for days at a time, listening to Wagner and writing sad poems.

Probably the most memorable of the Australian raids was the Twin Pimples Raid, because it was called the 'Twin Pimples Raid'. Try saying 'Twin Pimples Raid' a few times yourself and note how difficult it becomes to forget. It's one of the great and undeniable joys of history that the Twin Pimples Raid exists: any time you're feeling down in the dumps, just think about the Twin Pimples Raid for a bit and feel the blues melt away.

The Twin Pimples Raid itself was some kind of attack that the Allies made on some Italians on a hill or something. Does it really matter? When you've got an incident called the 'Twin Pimples Raid', who wants to ruin it with detail? But if you really want to seem erudite at parties, just say, 'The current situation is very reminiscent of the time that the Australian Engineers raided the Twin Pimples from behind.' Your friends will be amazed.

The Allied command made several attempts to relieve the defenders of Tobruk, but they proved difficult to relieve, having a lot on their minds at the time. The first attempt was Operation Brevity, so named because it ended before anyone did anything. The second was Operation Battleaxe, so named because it was personally led by Field

Marshal Montgomery's mother. Finally there was Operation Crusader, so named because it was the Pope's idea, which finally succeeded in raising the siege.

The men who defended Tobruk in 1941 were affectionately dubbed 'The Rats of Tobruk' for their heroism: the rat being the most heroic animal that science had discovered up to that point. It kicked off a brief craze for rodent-based nicknames of military heroes, including the famous Squirrels of Dunkirk, the Beavers of Iwo Jima and the legendary Capybaras of Omaha Beach.

The first man to use the term 'Rats of Tobruk' was Lord Haw-Haw, the loveable aristocrat who was employed by the German government to show radio audiences the playful side of Nazism. It's possible that he intended it as an insult – maybe he was jealous of the Australian soldiers' well-toned bodies and devastating wit.

The Rats of Tobruk are commemorated today by the Rats of Tobruk Association, which works to ensure the survival of the Rats' legacy through events and monuments. And, I guess, occasionally releasing actual live rats into crowded public spaces to keep the public's minds focused – at least, that's what they would do if I were in charge.

The Rats, with their typically Australian strength, efficiency and sexual magnetism, were the heroes of the North African theatre of the war, but what of the Pacific theatre? Here we find numerous tales of Aussie bravery in the face of Japanese brutality and American laziness, but perhaps the greatest story of the war in the Pacific was that of the Kokoda Track.

Kokoda

The Kokoda Track runs for 96 kilometres through Papua New Guinea's Owen Stanley Range. It was built in the 1890s to provide a place for

Australian football teams to conduct off-season bonding exercises, but also played a crucial role in World War Two, when the Japanese war machine landed on New Guinea and attempted to take Port Moresby for what they claimed were strategic reasons, but was probably just Japan being Japan – they pretty much spent the whole war being deliberately annoying to everyone.

The lead-up to the Kokoda campaign was similar to the lead-up to the Gallipoli campaign, in that it involved Winston Churchill being a gross selfish man-pig. After the fall of Singapore, Churchill, who was now British prime minister and had even more latitude to drink in the bath and shout at everyone, gave Australian Prime Minister John Curtin a call.

'John!' he bellowed down the line.

'Jesus Christ,' said Curtin to himself; to Churchill he said, wearily, 'Hello, Winston, what can I do for you?'

'I was having my pre-dinner vodka, and I thought to myself, *Why not have three?* And then I thought, *Wouldn't it be great if Little Johnny Curtin gave me his army to play with?*'

'That's nice, Winston, but we need our army right now, because Japan is coming to attack us.'

'Ugh, Japan!' Churchill splashed. 'Don't get me started on Japan, with all their noodles and karate and the, the ... where was I?'

'You were asking for my army.'

'Yes! I was thinking, if I had the Australian Army to order about, it'd really help me with Hitler, and the, you know ... we could fight them on the beaches, and Australians love the beach so ...' Churchill began to snore down the phone.

'Winston. Winston!'

'Uh, what?'

'You can't have our army, Winston,' Curtin said patiently. 'I'm bringing them home to protect their country. You'll have to do without them.'

'That's not *FAIR*!' Churchill shouted. 'I need armies to order around. It's part of my thing.'

'You're being very selfish, Winston.'

'I may be selfish,' Churchill retorted, 'but you have stupid glasses, and in the morning I'll be ... *zzzzzz*.' The line went dead.

Curtin sighed and called up US President Franklin Roosevelt. 'Hi Franklin,' he said brightly. 'Let's talk about fighting the Japanese.'

'I'm *NOT* in a wheelchair!' Roosevelt screamed. 'Who said I was?'

And so, the defence of New Guinea began. General Douglas Macarthur determined to halt the Japanese advance in New Guinea and ordered his Australian minions to secure Kokoda in order to defend against the Japanese landing.

On 29 July, the Japanese captured the Kokoda airstrip after a fierce battle in which the Australian defenders inflicted significant casualties on the invaders: the Japanese reportedly believed that they had overwhelmed a force of 1200 Australian troops, when the defenders numbered only 77. This illustrates two profound truths about the war:

1. Australians are basically gods.
2. Japan can't count.

An attempt to retake the airfield failed, and Australian forces retreated down the Track, and then retreated again, and again, and again. The terrain was harsh and the climate was taxing, but the Australians' suffering was alleviated by the fact that they all had malaria, which took their minds off things. There were also the Japanese troops, of course, who had started to make real nuisances of themselves what with all their shooting and killing and mutilating and occasionally eating people.[158] The suffering of the desperate diggers was so intense that it really makes the modern Australian appreciate the sacrifices made by Kevin Rudd and Joe Hockey when they walked the Track.

Although the Japanese continued to attack the withdrawing Australian forces, they were unable to score a decisive victory thanks to the unprecedented heroism that came as naturally as breathing to the average Australian. Heroism such as that of Private Bruce Kingsbury, who saved the day at the Battle of Isurava by charging the enemy, in the teeth of intense machine-gun fire, and with his single gun slashing a path through the Japanese lines. Sadly, Private Kingsbury's Victoria Cross was to be awarded posthumously, after a sniper bullet took him down as he charged. His final words were said to be, 'Do not fail ... to commercialise ... my sacrifice.'[159]

Throughout the Kokoda campaign, the Allies were forever precariously on the edge of catastrophic defeat. That they avoided disaster and, after exhausting the Japanese, were able to surge back and retake Kokoda, was a feat probably beyond soldiers from any other country, who are almost without exception feeble and cowardly, though to be fair the Australian fighting man sets a mighty high bar.

But the incredible achievements at Kokoda weren't only due to Australian indomitability: a massive debt is also owed to the native Papuans, who aided the Allied forces in their withdrawals. Helping sick and wounded soldiers walk the Track, carrying stretchers bearing those who couldn't walk, and going above and beyond the call of duty

---

158 This makes them sound really bad, but they had to eat something, and Menulog hadn't been invented yet.

159 This joke brought to you by Woolworths. Lest we forget.

– especially as it wasn't their duty in the first place – to care for their charges, the PNG nationals played a major part in saving the Allied campaign. In recognition of their assistance, Australians dubbed them the 'Fuzzy Wuzzy Angels', to signify that the Aussies were both deeply grateful and deeply racist.

Some say the fact that the Australian Army coerced the locals into helping them by executing and torturing those Papuans who didn't want to help takes some of the gloss off the Kokoda campaign, but it should be noted that this fact only impacts negatively on our perceptions of the Australian forces if we acknowledge its existence, which would be a fairly un-Australian thing to do.

Following the exploits of Kokoda, General Thomas Blamey, commander of the Australian military forces, visited the 21st Infantry Brigade and informed them that they had been defeated by an inferior force with inferior numbers. He then observed that the Japanese were like gorillas, staying in their holes, while the rabbit who runs away is the rabbit who gets shot. The troops interpreted this as Blamey saying that they had run away like rabbits, although it would've been just as plausible an interpretation to assume that the general had succumbed to dementia while visiting a zoo.

Later when Blamey visited the wounded in hospital, they nibbled on lettuce and whispered, 'run rabbit run',[160] so it's possible they had dementia too. Whether it was beneficial for Blamey's mental health to see large numbers of bed-ridden men imitating rabbits, when he clearly already had a dangerous rabbit obsession, is questionable. After the incident, many Australians pilloried General Blamey for his habit of harshly criticising his subordinates and seeking scapegoats for every failure, giving him the insulting nickname 'Thomas Blamey'.

160 Yet another patented Real Historical Fact™.

Winning the War

If the Kokoda Track was Australia's Dunkirk, and Tobruk was Australia's Rorke's Drift, and the invasion of Madagascar was, I don't know, Australia's Agincourt or something, then one could definitely say that drawing parallels to events from English history as a means of explaining Australian history has its limits. But whichever inappropriate comparison you wish to make, you can't deny that D-day – the day on which Allied forces landed at Normandy in 1944, named 'D-day' because of Dwight Eisenhower's incurable stammer – was a pretty major part of the war.

Only 3000 or so Australians participated in the Normandy landings, just a fraction of the more than 150,000 troops overall, which makes it even more incredible that this tiny contingent of Australians won the war practically single-handed. Much as the Australian minority at Gallipoli broke the back of the German war machine, even though the Germans weren't actually there, D-day's plucky band of diggers tore through Hitler's forces like a dose of particularly violent salts.

A good depiction of the situation was the film *Saving Private Ryan*, in which an intrepid squad of American GIs trek across Europe to rescue a single soldier to save his mother from heartbreak, leaving the Australians to do most of the actual fighting. Most of the US forces, in fact, were engaged in missions of this sort after D-day: roughly half the American troops who landed at Normandy were despatched to bring back comrades whose brothers had all been killed; most of the other half were engaged in finding and preserving priceless artworks stolen by the Nazis. Of the remainder, most were assigned to the chocolate and nylons task force, responsible for winning the gratitude of nubile French women.

Of course, it wasn't all Americans and Australians invading Europe

– some estimate there were as many as 50 or 60 British troops involved as well. These men were mainly responsible for making the tea and sewing uniforms to be placed on the various corpses that were used to make the enemy believe that the invasion was taking place somewhere else.[161] There were also several Canadians who chopped down the trees on Omaha Beach and fought any bears that happened to stray onto the battlefield.

All this meant that the heavy lifting of the liberation of Western Europe fell to the Australians, who penetrated deep into occupied territory, driving the Wehrmacht out of France and pursuing the Germans to the gates of Berlin, which they then hooked up to a tow truck and pulled off its hinges. As Australian infantry marched ruthlessly across Europe, scattering Hitler's finest before them, the RAAF flew above, shattering German infrastructure from the air, and the Royal Australian Navy bombarded the Axis from the sea or, when impatience got the best of them, drove their battleships up onto the beach to chase the enemy around.

Australia's rampage culminated, on 8 May 1945, in V-E Day (named after the Allies' obsessive insistence that everything that happened in the war needed to be commemorated with initials), when members of the Australian Special Forces infiltrated a cinema and shot Hitler in the face before burning the building down.

The war in Europe was ended, although there was still the war in the Pacific to be won: which it was on V-J Day (see above), 15 August 1945, when the Japanese finally surrendered after America, having dropped two atomic bombs on Japan already, threatened to send a

161 In the end, the British created approximately 80 fake men to fool the Nazis, distributing cadavers in places as diverse as Norway, Spain and Fiji, resulting in the worldwide dispersal of confused German forces.

division of Australians to Tokyo if they didn't give up immediately.

World War Two was over, but the memory of the way Australia saved the world would never die. Today many historians believe that the war was one of the more memorable and significant events of the 20th century. It led, for example, to:

1. The deaths of both Prime Minister Curtin and President Roosevelt, thus causing citizens of both their countries to associate war with negative memories
2. The non-death of Prime Minister Churchill, thus allowing him to drink even more and act even more rudely to women at parties
3. The embarrassment of Germany, which spent the next 20 years staring awkwardly at its feet and looking as though it was about to say something, but then not
4. The baby boom, one of history's greatest tragedies, in which all our grandparents had sex
5. Women playing baseball
6. George Bush Senior
7. Keith Miller refusing to bowl bouncers at Bill Edrich, thus enraging Don Bradman and giving Ian Chappell more excuses to tell boring stories on TV
8. Hit TV show *'Allo 'Allo!*
9. Some wonderfully artistic propaganda posters that later went on display in museums and made modern observers wonder if everyone in the 1940s had brain damage
10. Yossarian being assaulted by Nately's whore in *Catch-22*

In terms of Australia specifically, World War Two was the moment when the country came of age for the 15th or 16th time since

Federation. The fact that John Curtin had looked, in time of greatest need, to America as our greatest ally, instead of our traditional BFF Great Britain, was hugely significant, as it meant that we were no longer bound by the apron strings that we hadn't been bound by since Gallipoli or possibly Breaker Morant. The United States was now the most important factor in the defence of Australia, and our traditional connection with the United Kingdom was as past its prime as Winston Churchill's bathwater. The decision to align our interests with a colossal military superpower became known as 'The Obvious Doctrine'.

And so, war over, Australians settled down for a long, comfortable peace. They got a whole five years under their belts.

ESSAY QUESTIONS

1. In your opinion, was Hitler good or bad?
2. Discuss, in no more than 10,000 words but no less than 8000, James Coburn's accent in *The Great Escape*.

Australia's Next Top War

In which an increasingly confident nation finds a variety of fun new wars to dabble in, and a succession of Asian getaways produce steadily diminishing returns

Having survived the dreadful devastation of World Wars One and Two, Australia was finally ready to settle down and concentrate on getting into some more wars. Although the exploits of our brave diggers had allowed us to forge a real national identity, there was always the risk that it might fade away if we didn't keep refreshing it with regular fighting.

But where should we send our army next? By this stage, Europe felt terribly old hat, and so naturally Australia looked to the excitement of Asia and the modern, efficient wars it promised to deliver. Of course, we know now that becoming involved in a land war in Asia is a terrible idea, but in 1950 *The Princess Bride* was still 37 years away, so everyone was very optimistic.

My Brilliant Korea

The Korean War was fought from 1950 to 1953, and then again in prime time from 1972 to 1983. Australia's involvement is the subject of much debate: some historians describe it as forgettable and insignificant, while others claim it was boring and pointless.

The war itself was caused by Soviet-backed North Korea becoming restless and claustrophobic and seeking a bit of legroom by taking over South Korea, or as it is more popularly known, 'the good Korea'.[162] Robert Menzies, who had been given another shot at the Australian prime ministership after promising the electorate that he had been practising very hard, again showed his sincere love of throwing thousands of his countrymen into deadly combat situations overseas by committing troops in support of UN Security Council Resolution 82 (this resolution called for North Korea to get their hand off it and requested that UN members give them a good slapping).

The Menzies government began a recruitment drive to find a thousand experienced military men to go to Korea to stick it up them. The drive was named 'K-Force' in recognition of the Australian populace's mental age of ten.[163] Overall, 17,000 Australians would serve in the Korean War, of whom 339 were killed, which is how the war gained its Australian nickname, 'The Relatively Unimpressive War'.

The Korean War ended in 1953 after North Korea agreed to restrict its future actions to comically unrealistic threats, and the United States agreed to make fun of North Korea's president in various movies. Australia's biggest gain from the war was the signing of the ANZUS Treaty, which committed Australia, New Zealand and the United States to full military cooperation with whatever the United States wanted.

After the Korean War, Australians entered a period of existential angst, worried that they might never see another major war in which to forge their identity and carry on the proud Australian tradition of etc. etc. They needn't have been so gloomy, though – it was only nine

162 It's okay, we can call it that: they won't be able to get this book in North Korea.

163 K-Force should not be confused with *K-Zone*, which is a children's pop culture magazine and is worse than war.

years later that they got another chance to run their manhood up the flagpole, with

The Vietnam War

The Australian experience in Vietnam can be perfectly summed up in the words of the classic Redgum song 'I Was Only 19': 'What's this rash that comes and goes? / Can you tell me what it means?' Indeed, for many years Vietnam was a painful itching sensation on the epidermis of Australia's national psyche. There are those who believe that we should never have gone to Vietnam – but, to be fair, it was the only war available at the time, and beggars can't be choosers.

The Vietnam War was caused by communism, just like pretty much everything back then. North Vietnam, in what was clearly shameless plagiarism of North Korea's idea, attacked South Vietnam, causing the United States to come to the South Vietnamese's defence, and the US president to pull the rope that rang the bell in Australia's servants' quarters.

In 1962, Prime Minister Menzies, as feisty as ever despite being 800 years old, sent 30 military advisors in response to the South Vietnamese government's urgent request for advice. The advisors assessed the situation and advised South Vietnam to ask for a whole bunch of soldiers. This proved to be good advice, or – depending on your point of view – very, *very* bad advice.

By 1965, the United States had committed 200,000 troops to Vietnam, and Australia had sent a force to keep an eye on the Americans and stop them getting into trouble. The Australian force was bolstered by conscription, a cunning policy calculated to create the greatest army in the world by ensuring that most of its members didn't want to be there. Under the *National Service Act of 1964*, all 20-year-old males[164] had to be available for military service. If they won the conscription lottery, they were required to serve for two years, followed by three years on the active reserve list, followed by 20 years singing folk songs about their experiences. The conscription lottery was one of the best-value lotteries in Australian history: it was almost absurdly easy to win. Sometimes you suspected the government of rigging it.

Conscription was extremely controversial in Australia, as many of the new generation, who had no memory of how much fun the two world wars had been for everyone, didn't especially want to be forced into the army against their will, even when they were informed that it would prevent Southeast Asia from being overrun by Russian dominoes. Some youths protested against conscription by burning their registration cards, an act of defiance that made it quite clear the government wouldn't be able to bend this generation to its will without a lot of meaningless empty gestures being made first.

To avoid conscription, a man needed to prove his status as a genuine pacifist, which he could do by passing a test requiring the claimant to listen to Les Murray reading his own poetry for ten minutes without punching him. So very few managed to legitimately dodge the draft, and many were forced to go on the run to avoid serving. We had come very far indeed from the days when fit, healthy youngsters would lie about their age to get an opportunity to die in a trench.

'Still, we're here now, we might as well make the most of it,' said the diggers in Vietnam, and presumably they did just that. The fact that 'the most of it' was one of the most nightmarishly disastrous military adventures of modern history is hardly their fault; it is, in fact, America's.

---

164 Preferably human ones.

Although handicapped by the hopelessness of their allies, Australians fought valiantly in Vietnam. In August 1966, Australian D Company won the Battle of Long Tan, despite having only 108 men while the Viet Cong had as many as 2500. Indeed, if Gallipoli was Australia's Waterloo, and Tobruk was Australia's Bosworth Field, and Kokoda was Australia's Masada, then surely Long Tan was Australia's Gallipoli. At Long Tan, Australia finally came of age and gained a real national identity, although it didn't take and had to be replaced by a new one two years later, this time based mainly on Billy Thorpe.

In 1968, Western forces were blitzed by the Tet Offensive, a major campaign by the North Vietnamese named after the clucking noise you make with your tongue to indicate disapproval of the foreign armies invading your country. The Americans and South Vietnamese were surprised by the Tet Offensive, never having expected North Vietnam to attack during school holidays.

Later in 1968, the Australians had their fiercest engagement of the war in the Battle of Coral-Balmoral, which was fought, unconventionally for the time, on a picturesque island off the coast of Scotland. Twenty-five Australians were killed at Coral-Balmoral, compared to around 300 North Vietnamese, which is the usual ratio of good guys killed to bad guys killed maintained by the supernaturally talented Australian military forces throughout history. Other major Australian actions in Vietnam included Binh Ba, in which Australia destroyed the village in order to save it; the battle of Long Khanh, in which the Australians lost an Iroquois helicopter and had to pay for it by doing chores for the rest of the war; and Hat Dich, which was not only a battle, but also a serious medical deformity.

Sadly, even the Vietnam War couldn't last forever, and eventually the Australian government began to get sick of people ringing them up and telling them to get the hell out of there. They never knew how those people got their number, but the calls were incredibly annoying and starting to distract from the serious business of government, of which there presumably was some. In addition, Western troops were becoming less necessary due to the policy of 'Vietnamization', which was Richard Nixon's strategy to end the war by gradually turning everyone in the world Vietnamese.

And so, finally, Australian Prime Minister William 'The Startled Lemur' McMahon announced that he was sick of listening to protest songs and would begin withdrawing troops from Vietnam as soon as Sonia could find his reading glasses. It's now generally agreed that McMahon's withdrawal from the war was one of Gough Whitlam's greatest achievements, as he was a much nicer man than McMahon.

Vietnam had a profound effect on Australian society, dividing the nation between those who felt that the war was a crucial part of the global fight against peace, and those who believed joining protest marches was a good way to get laid. Many of the latter thought that the conflict between North and South Vietnam was simply not Australia's fight: their opponents countered by pointing out that if Australia sat around waiting for their own fights to come along, they'd never get to do a war, and how would that be any fun? There was a further division between the people who supported the troops and urged the continuation of the war until the job was done, and many of the troops themselves, who wanted to come the hell home.

The war also caused a deep political schism, with the Labor Opposition arguing against both the war itself and the policy of conscription introduced to help prosecute it. In many ways, this marked the end of the love affair between the Labor and Liberal parties, and they've never got along since.

The return of Vietnam veterans to Australia was also the cause of much friction, as those who believed the war immoral refused to honour them as war heroes – having forgotten that in war, it's not whether you win or lose, it's how many foreigners you kill. Some branches of the RSL refused to admit Vietnam veterans, for which the veterans were eternally grateful,[165] but other segments of society judged the veterans harshly for their apparent complicity in war crimes and their failure to generate sufficient patriotic mythology. Of course, conscription had meant that many young men had no choice about whether they went to war or not, but Australians believed that the Anzac spirit meant accepting responsibility for the choices others made on your behalf.

Since then, our understanding of what Vietnam veterans went through has become far more sophisticated, as expressed by Cold Chisel's hit song 'Khe Sanh'. Every Australian who hears those lyrics cannot help but feel a pang of familiarity: for there but for the grace of God go we. And it is thanks to those who spoke up about what they saw in Vietnam that Australian governments today vow that Australia will never again launch into full-scale war on such dubious pretexts unless it seems like a good idea at the time.

From Vietnam to Today

Since the end of the Vietnam War, Australia has continued its proud history of sending men overseas with guns to scare the crap out of people with their sheer manliness. In recent years it's even started to send women occasionally, and they've proved to be as manly.

Australia's military engagements in the recent past have included Iraq, Afghanistan, Iraq again, Afghanistan a bit more, some more Iraq just to be sure, and Syria. Why such a concentration on that region of

---

165 Except on $12 Parma Night.

the world? Military and historical experts agree: it's a coincidence.

Australia also did itself proud in East Timor, where our diggers assisted in the birth of a new nation by preventing our cherished ally Indonesia from slaughtering everyone. During this deployment, Australian troops had several violent encounters with our cherished allies, in which frank and forthright expressions of enduring friendship and cooperation were offered on both sides. Sometimes the Australian-Indonesian alliance became so excessively warm and reciprocal that shots were fired, which just goes to show how passionate soldiers can be when it comes to international camaraderie.

In all its engagements, the Australian Army has lived up to those ideals that infused it way back in 1901, when the first Commonwealth troops ventured onto the high veldt with dreams of glory fizzing in their brains and the desire to shoot prisoners pulsing through their trigger fingers. From Brakfontein to Gallipoli, from Tobruk to Kokoda to Long Tan and beyond, the honest, humble, physically and mentally perfect Aussie digger has done us proud, with his dedication to duty, scarcely believable bravery, scrupulously fair approach to battle and refusal to countenance failure winning admiration and terror worldwide. Whether playing a cheeky game of two-up, displaying an anti-authoritarian attitude towards superiors or blowing a man's head clean off, the loveable larrikins of the Australian Defence Force have made their mark – and, thanks to them, so has our wonderful war-obsessed country.

ESSAY QUESTIONS

1. Explain how the concept of 'destroying the village in order to save it' could be effectively applied to Karl Stefanovic.
2. Do you support the troops? Which ones? Name names.

The Menzies Centuries

In which a soufflé rises twice, a statesman threatens to live forever and reds are ruthlessly extracted from under beds

As a child, Robert Gordon Menzies would watch the caterpillars crawling along the branches of the trees near his home in the Wimmera, marvelling at how they were able to transform themselves from sluggish, earthbound grubs into beautiful butterflies, spectacular explosions of artful colour soaring above the earth. In the invertebrate's life-cycle, young Menzies saw echoes of his own vaulting ambition. 'Someday,' he vowed to himself, 'I will glue two of these caterpillars above my eyes.'

But too many people think that the Menzies era was all about eyebrows: there was so much more to it. It was a time of stability, a time of prosperity, a time of comfortable middle-class certainty and reassuring Cold War paranoia. During the Menzies years, Australia became one of the richest countries in the world, and finally came to realise life's one essential truth: everything is fine.

Menzies was born in 1894 in the Victorian town of Jeparit,[166] to James and Kate Menzies, the children of immigrants who had come to Australia in search of gold. James Menzies was a prominent member of the Jeparit community, which wasn't difficult as only about four people

166 Source of the old joke 'Jeparit? I never touched it!'

lived there. James was a storekeeper, a lay preacher, twice president of the shire council and co-founder of the Jeparit branch of the Australian Natives' Association, a body that worked to advance the cause of white men in the most ironic way possible. In 1911, James Menzies was elected to the Victorian State Parliament and created a sensation by collapsing from nerves during his maiden speech. Young Robert learnt a profound lesson from his father's experience: 'I resolved then and there,' he later wrote, 'to never collapse from nerves during my maiden speech.' And his resolve held firm for his entire life.

Menzies was 19 and held a commission in Melbourne University's militia unit[167] when World War One began. As thousands of young men rushed to enlist for the grand adventure of defending freedom overseas, Menzies proved his mettle by immediately resigning his commission. Rather than enlisting, he stayed home to complete his studies and look after his parents and not get shot. He was also active in student politics and journalism, where he spoke out strongly in favour of the war and of conscription, like a man who lacks the courage to jump off a bridge and so begs the government to give him a push.

Later he would be accused of a lack of patriotism for his cowardly desire to stay alive, although when the achievements of his life are weighed up, it is clear that he was always deeply and passionately committed to England. There are also rumours that he was reasonably fond of Australia, which is what you want in a prime minister.

After university, Menzies became a lawyer due to a chronic lack of originality, but in 1928 quit the law to enter the Victorian Legislative Council, representing the Nationalist Party of Australia, a party about which I don't know much, but they sound pretty racist, don't they?

167 There's something very terrifying about universities having their own armies, don't you think?

The next year he founded the Young Nationalists, which sounds even *more* racist – you wonder if he maybe declared war on the wrong side in World War Two.

After serving in the Victorian Parliament for six years, two of them as deputy premier, in which role he fulfilled all the conventional requirements of the deputy premiership by doing nothing at all, Menzies switched to the federal scene, believing himself destined for greatness. He represented the United Australia Party – an *incredibly* racist name – as member for Kooyong.

Menzies was appointed attorney-general in the Lyons government and quickly moved to quash any allegations that the United Party Australia was racist by working as hard as he could to keep a foreigner out of the country.

A Kisch Before Dying

Egon Kisch was an Austrian-Czech writer who opposed and had been arrested by the Nazi regime in Germany, and since then he had travelled the world to speak against fascism. So naturally he was exactly the sort of undesirable whom Australia did not want hanging about the place. After all, we had it on good authority from Adolf Hitler that he was a shady character, and Hitler had never steered us wrong before.

Fortunately, the government already had a mechanism in place to keep bounders like Kisch out of the country: the *Immigration Restriction Act*, which was the cornerstone of the White Australia Policy that Alfred Deakin had worked his beard to the bone in support of. The Act specified that anyone attempting to enter Australia had to pass a dictation test to prove their language skills. Which was only logical – how could anyone get by in Australia if they couldn't speak English, right?

Ha-ha, you idiots! The dictation test wasn't for testing people's ability to speak *English*: it was a test to be administered in *any European language*. So if a Chinese professor or an Indian surgeon rocked up Down Under, swelling with pride about the way they'd thoroughly grounded themselves in the language and culture of their new home, 'Oops! No deal! Here's a test in the Tosk dialect of southern Albania for you. Oh, you don't speak Tosk? Then you are *HARDLY* the kind of person we want here in *AUSTRALIA*, are you?'

The beauty of the *Immigration Restriction Act* was that even by the standards of hard-bitten, inveterate racist maniacs, it made absolutely no sense. Its underlying premise could be dismantled in a matter of seconds by even the dullest-witted of kindergarten students or a reasonably well-educated lizard. And yet, the actual Australian government, made up of technically intelligent adults, was quite happy to keep enforcing it and giving anyone who came from the wrong country the moronic tests, because Australia had decided to be racist and would go to any and all lengths possible to stay that way.[168] It was all fantastically, insanely watertight, and it provides a salutary lesson to the youth of today: become a politician and you can do anything you like no matter how stupid it is.

So Egon Kisch toddled down to Australia and was refused entry on the basis of his unsavoury past as an opponent of the worst people on earth. After trying to find a loophole by jumping off his ship and breaking his leg,[169] Kisch pursued legal means to gain entry to the country, but Attorney-General Menzies was determined not to deviate one inch from his terrible principles. 'We will determine who comes

168 *Plus ça change.*

169 It's a common misconception that anyone with a broken leg gets to enter Australia.

to this country and the lunatic racist methods by which we determine whether they come,' Menzies thundered.

The courts had ordered that Kisch be allowed in, so the government put its nutjob dictation test strategy into action. After Kisch showed that he could, in fact, speak a number of European languages – thus proving that he wasn't only a dangerous subversive, but also one of them fancypants college boys – he was given the test in Scottish Gaelic. Without a good grasp of Scottish Gaelic, how could any man hope to assimilate harmoniously with Australian society?

Kisch responded to the request to prove his fluency in Gaelic by telling the government where they could shove it. 'Gotcha!' Menzies cried, but sadly for young Robert, the High Court made a historic ruling that forcing someone to write the Lord's Prayer in Scottish Gaelic in order for them to enter the country was the brainchild of a Dadaist serial killer, and Kisch was allowed to stay. It was a bitter pill for Menzies, who for the first time in his career felt the sharp sting of basic decency.

Bob Bounces Back

Robert Menzies wasn't one to let a little setback get him down, and he rebounded from the disappointment of the Kisch affair, showing himself to be one of the Western world's great statesmen in 1938 by travelling to Germany and reporting back on what a super guy Hitler was.[170] 'That'll show those idiots who said I was racist,' he told himself.

Soon Menzies' ambition, while elevating him ever higher in the halls of power, also created tension and conflict when he clashed with Earle Christmas Grafton Page, who filled in as acting prime minister

170 To be fair this was quite a common belief at the time: researchers only discovered that genocide was bad later on.

while Joe Lyons was sick. This was under an obscure section of the Constitution, which states that when a prime minister is indisposed his place must be temporarily filled by whichever Cabinet member has the funniest name.

Page and Menzies became bitter enemies. Menzies' foes accused him of having designs on the prime ministership and nicknamed him 'Pig Iron Bob' in reference to his notoriously wrinkled shirts. In 1939, Lyons died – probably neither Menzies nor Page killed him – and the United Australia Party elected Menzies its new leader, causing Page to have a big sook, take his bat and ball and Country Party and go home.

The period from 1939 to 1941 is known as 'the first Menzies prime ministership', or alternatively 'the mediocre Menzies prime ministership', and is notable mainly for two things: Menzies declaring war on Germany, severely hurting the feelings of his old pen pal Hitler, and Menzies being generally hated by everyone in the whole country. Some analysts have suggested that his overwhelming unpopularity may have been a factor in his removal as prime minister.

Also during his first term in charge, Menzies made a trip to England, where several prominent Britons suggested that he should stay on and replace Winston Churchill as British PM. 'How would that work?' Menzies asked, to which his supporters looked at their watches and remembered that they had to give the babysitter a lift home.

The idea of the Australian prime minister replacing the British prime minister, even in wartime, may seem incredibly stupid today, but it's important to remember that in 1941, people *were* incredibly stupid. And it's true that Menzies had his quarrels with Churchill, arguing in Britain for the better equipping of Allied troops in Greece. 'To fight the Germans, Mr Churchill, they will need our utmost support.'

'They got guns,' Churchill shot back. 'Guns are good for shooting!

Bang! They go like that. That'll be good enough for Greece.'

'Mr Churchill, with respect, you are far too dictatorial with respect to your Cabinet and the war effort,' Menzies told him politely.

'I may be dictatorial with respect to my Cabinet and the war effort, but you're prime minister of Australia, and in the morning I'll vomit.' Churchill concluded the meeting by attempting to punch Menzies and then collapsing, sobbing, in his arms.

Menzies went home, disillusioned, to find that people in Australia hated him more than ever. His own party was divided on the subject of Robert Menzies: some considered him overbearing and tyrannical, while others believed he was incompetent and unpleasant. Debate raged over which side was right, until Menzies, after ringing his father and agreeing that 'Who needs this shit?', announced his resignation, leading to the brief administration of Arthur Fadden and then to the prime ministership of John Curtin, a period popularly known as 'Better Than the First Menzies Years'. Curtin went on to win World War Two, something that Menzies, even in his later years, never managed to do.

Apply Liberally to Affected Area

After losing the prime ministership, Menzies suffered something of an existential crisis. What, he asked himself sadly, is Robert Menzies *for*? Seeking to regain his former confidence and vigour, he began a series of weekly radio broadcasts – working title 'Pig Iron Bob in the Mornings, Featuring Wazza and The Keg Man' – in which he expounded on his political theories and pledged his allegiance to the 'Forgotten People'. These were those Australians, Menzies believed, who had been overlooked in public discourse for too long, because they weren't rich or powerful or organised or fashionable or educated or intelligent or attractive or hygienic or living in houses or demonstrating rudimentary tool-making skills. Menzies appealed to the Forgotten People, promising them that he hadn't forgotten them and that if they helped him return to his rightful place sitting atop Canberra's greasy pole, he would continue not forgetting them forever and ever. To this proposition, the Forgotten People grunted their enthusiastic assent.

Menzies had established himself as the Kyle Sandilands of the 1940s, but he remained unsatisfied. At the age of 50, he had already been prime minister, declared war, triggered a schism in a government coalition and fought publicly for the triumph of bigotry over sense, and yet he felt there was so much more for him to achieve. 'All my life,' he confided to a close friend, 'I have yearned to create the Liberal Party, and I believe perhaps finally my time has come.' And so Robert Menzies, legendary founder of the Liberal Party, ensured that history would remember that as a not-inaccurate description by founding the Liberal Party.

The new party's constitution stated that it aimed to create an Australia 'looking primarily to the encouragement of individual initiative and enterprise as the dynamic course of reconstruction and progress'. The bits about rabid xenophobia and the incurable untrustworthiness of the female sex were formally added later, though always pretty much implied. But mainly the Liberals were to be the party of free enterprise, individual rights and the unfettered operation of business, whenever those were convenient.

Early on, the Liberal Party had little success, thumped in the 1946 election as the people expressed the view that a prime minister who sought to become prime minister again was just being greedy. But the 1949 election was a different story. Menzies had revealed to the nation that the Labor Party was, unbeknownst to most citizens, slightly left-wing,[171] and this left a bitter taste in the mouths of Australians who remembered well how the organisation of labour had led directly to the mass execution of the kulaks.

Labor Prime Minister Ben Chifley compounded the widespread suspicion of his Stalinist leanings by announcing his intention to nationalise the banks. Ordinary Australians, outraged by this totalitarian attempt to deny them their right to be swindled by the wealthy, rebelled, and the Liberals seized their chance: Robert Menzies was returned as prime minister on 10 December 1949. 'This time,' he boomed ominously in his acceptance speech, 'I am going to stay here, like, literally forever.' It was no idle threat.

The official record indicates that Menzies' second term as prime minister lasted from 1949 to 1966, although eyewitnesses have claimed it actually lasted for between four and six hundred years. Suffice to say, it was a hell of a long time, and during his tenure Australian society underwent many momentous changes, which everyone did their best to ignore.

The first order of business for the Menzies administration was to address the growing Communist menace that threatened at any moment to start existing. Old Bob saw it as his duty to protect his beloved nation from malign Soviet forces and was quite amazed to find that it had the unintended consequence of making him extremely popular. 'What luck!' he exclaimed, never having dreamt that his unceasing fight against socialism and gallant warnings of the creeping Red Menace that lurked around every corner, ready to destroy our way of life, might have electoral benefits. It's amazing how often this happens: an altruistic statesman does his civic duty by advising voters of the sinister forces seeking to attack them, and completely by accident the voters become convinced that this

171 A flaw they have since remedied.

statesman is the right man to keep them safe and vote for him in massive numbers. Fortune, as they say, favours the selfless.

I don't mean to suggest that fomenting fear and loathing of an illusory enemy was the only reason for Menzies' longevity as prime minister, which is a shame, since I clearly have been suggesting that, extremely strongly, in the previous paragraph. But there's no doubt that the Red Menace was a major focus of his early years as prime minister (not counting his actual early years as prime minister).

Menzies had visited Europe and seen the terrible effects of the Soviet encroachment on the continent. 'If Russia is willing to flex its muscles in Czechoslovakia,' he reasoned, 'why wouldn't they be just as willing to do so in Australia?' Numerous people gave him thoughtful and well-considered answers to this question, but he shrugged them off in favour of formulating a plan to prevent his country from becoming the Gulag of the South Pacific.[172]

Menzies' first idea was to force every potential visitor to Australia to repudiate Marxism in Scottish Gaelic, but this plan was rejected as too confusing. Next he simply attempted to have the Communist Party banned in Australia, on the reasonable basis that he was prime minister and could do what he wanted. The legislation implementing this ban passed Parliament in 1951, but the High Court, Menzies' old bête noire, stepped in to rule the Bill unconstitutional. Having prevented Menzies from kicking a communist out of the country in the 1930s, and now having prevented him from banning communists altogether in the 1950s, the High Court's true purpose became clear: they were communists.

Later in 1951, Menzies put the question to the people in a referendum, asking them to amend the Constitution to give him

172 A title later awarded to Nauru.

the power to ban communism. Only by voting 'yes', he believed, could Australia maintain its freedom, but the 'no' case also had many supporters. The Communist Party was one, which wasn't much of a surprise – and the Labor Party, which was also unsurprising, as everyone knew they were communists already. Finding out that the Young Liberals were also communists was slightly more unexpected, but they, too, pushed for 'no'.

Facing the triple threat of communists, Laborites (i.e. communists) and Young Liberals (who were communists), Menzies had no chance, and the referendum was defeated. This is probably why, today, Australia is a mostly communist country.

Frustrated by the electorate's inability to see that the price of freedom was eternal granting of unprecedented undemocratic powers to him personally, Menzies played the spy card. In the lead-up to the 1954 election, he announced the defection of Soviet diplomat Vladimir Petrov and his wife, Evdokia, and revealed that the Petrovs had extremely disturbing information about Russian spies operating in Australia. The people were shocked and also a little excited, as this was the first interesting thing to happen in Australia since Bodyline.

Some of the Russian spies, it was alleged, were working in the office of Opposition Leader H.V. 'Initials' Evatt. Evatt, however, asked the Soviet foreign minister whether there were spies in Australia, and the Soviet foreign minister told him that there definitely weren't any, so everyone breathed a big sigh of relief and thanked Evatt for checking so thoroughly.

The 1954 election, fought between the Menzies platform of 'We will kill the reds' and the Evatt platform of 'Our Leader is pretty adorable when he acts all grown-up', resulted in a narrow Liberal victory. Menzies also won the 1955 election, which was popularly known as 'The Election That Seems to Be Far Too Soon After the Last One, Surely'.

Australia seemed to have navigated the tricky waters of Cold War hysteria and sailed happily into the harbour of affluence. Prosperity was fuelled by booming post-war immigration, as folks from all over the world with skin light enough to satisfy the Australian government flocked Down Under to work on projects like the Snowy Mountains Scheme, to be written about in books like *They're a Weird Mob* and to be racially abused by people like everyone. Menzies can take great credit for the influx of foreign workers, all of whom spoke Gaelic beautifully. The housing, manufacturing and agricultural industries were also riding high. All in all, Menzies' Australia was living up to its reputation as 'The Lucky Country', an appellation bestowed on it by writer Donald Horne, who observed that Australia was extremely lucky to be so freaking awesome.

The country's purple patch made it unsurprising that Menzies won another victory in the 1958 election, this one such a colossal thrashing that the entire Australian Labor Party was forced to do a lap of Canberra with its pants down. It seemed as though Menzies would reign forever, but it soon became apparent that yes he would.

In the 1961 election, Menzies was given an almighty scare as the ALP unexpectedly showed signs of being alive. New Opposition Leader Arthur Calwell, who had already carved out a stellar career during and following the war as a talented Cabinet minister and skilful bigot, brought new energy and vigour to the Herculean task of knocking off Menzies. Calwell was a devoted Labor man, but no communist – he hated reds almost as much as he hated Asians – and his moderate-yet-nasty leadership style was almost enough to cut the endless Menzies years short. In the end, Labor lost the election by just two seats, their campaign cruelled by the separatists of the Democratic Labor Party, who had split from the ALP in the 1950s in protest at the party's refusal to increase its quotient of arm-flailing religious madmen.

As the 1963 election loomed, Menzies was contemplating his future. He was now, according to best estimates, 3000 years old and had been prime minister since the Diet of Worms, and he was reaching that point in a prime minister's life when his eyebrows begin to think about turning the same colour as his hair. Perhaps it was time for a new generation to step up to the task of government, given that three or four new generations had already grown old and died since he was first elected.

In the 1963 election, Menzies won again easily, any chance that Calwell may have had destroyed by revelations that the Labor Party was being run by 'faceless men'. Who were these men? What hideous experiments had Labor apparatchiks performed on them to allow them to live without faces? Why were experienced politicians entrusting their futures to these hellish, smooth-headed sins against nature? The fear of having their lives controlled by mutants led voters to reject Calwell and his army of unseeing monsters. Menzies was yet again the king of the castle, and Labor and all its sympathisers were, indubitably, the dirty rascals.

Menzies spent the last three years of his reign revelling in the fruits of his labours. As he reclined in the Lodge, enjoying the cool breeze from the palm leaves being waved over him, gratefully gulping the grapes being dropped into his open mouth by his attendants, he looked upon what he had made, and he saw that it was good. There were just a few matters to be cleared up.

In 1963, Menzies was granted the honour of being appointed a

Knight of the Order of the Thistle, an ancient and exclusive order open only to venerable public servants with lisps. He occupies a special place in chivalric history, being the only Australian prime minister to become a Thistle and only the second to be knighted while still in office, after Edmund Barton – who, as you'll recall, doesn't really count.

In 1965, Menzies committed troops to Vietnam and reintroduced conscription, figuring he was going to be gone in a year, so why not get freaky? Both of these actions would cause trouble for his successors down the track but, as always, Menzies' motto was, 'Screw those guys.'

On Australia Day 1966, Menzies, by now weary, bored and bearing the scars of many Balrog-fights, resigned. It was probably the most significant Australia Day since the first in 1788, when Menzies was only in his early thirties.

After politics, he went on to serve as chancellor of the University of Melbourne and Lord Warden of the Cinque Ports, a prestigious and imaginary position granted by the Queen only to the most reliable unemployed old men. This meant that he was also Constable of Dover Castle, but he failed to make any arrests. In 1978 he died, proving against accepted scientific consensus that he could.

Menzies cast a long shadow over both Australian history and his own eyes. He oversaw an unprecedented period of economic growth and prosperity, which is impressive if you like that sort of thing, and that can be largely attributed to Menzies' firm policy of not actively buggering things up too much, a policy quite radical in comparison to many. He was an advocate of reasoned and civil public debate, but could be ruthless when circumstances demanded and made his fair share of enemies: the epithets 'Pig Iron Bob' and 'Ming the Merciless' – the latter a reminder of the unfortunate incident in 1953 when he attempted to destroy the earth – are testament to the fact he was probably kind of a bastard.

Menzies' uncompromising opposition to creeping socialism in all its forms can be largely credited with saving Australia from the Soviet agents who never threatened it in any way, as well as flushing out the secret Trotskyites of the Young Liberals.

Menzies will, of course, always be remembered as a staunch monarchist and lover of Mother England. He described himself as 'British to his bootstraps', which technically made him ineligible to be prime minister at all, but nobody thought to check the 'Bootstrap Clause of the Constitution' at the time. He was an unashamed admirer of Queen Elizabeth II, declaring at a function attended by Her Majesty in 1963, 'I did but see her passing by, and yet I love her till I die.' Few prime ministers have so publicly declared their creepy, stalkerish feelings towards their head of state, and Elizabeth reportedly described the tribute as 'incredibly romantic' in her restraining order application.

Most of all, Menzies will be remembered as a paragon of stability. When he was in charge, Australians felt safe, and warm, and cosy, and slightly aroused, and kind of drunk. As a prime minister he was something like a cross between a kindly grandfather, a watchful mother bear and a large blanket. It's uncertain if any other prime minister has ever generated so powerful a conviction in his people that all is well, and if there's an enduring message of the Menzies years, it is that as long as you believe something enough, it is true.

ESSAY QUESTIONS

1. Translate this entire book into Scottish Gaelic. Did it take long? Do you really think you've earned the right to live in this country?
2. Would you rather have black eyebrows and white hair, or white eyebrows and black hair? Explain thoroughly.

Outplay. Outlast. OutWhitlam.

In which a great Saviour comes to heal the nation but is undone by the fallibility of Man

The post-Menzies years were a confusing blur. First came Prime Minister Harold Holt, who was so skilled at picking winners that he expanded Australia's involvement in Vietnam and eventually found the stresses of office so overwhelming that he decided he'd rather drown than keep being prime minister. That is, unless he was taken by a Chinese submarine or adopted by a friendly tribe of dugongs. Holt's legacy lives on in (real) memorials like the Harold Holt Memorial Swimming Centre, the Naval Communication Station Harold E. Holt and the Harold Holt Fisheries Reserve, making him the PM inadvertently responsible for more sick jokes than any other.

After Holt came John McEwen, known as 'Black Jack' because of his famed ability to count up to 21. McEwen's prime ministership lasted less than a month and ended when officials discovered that he was the leader of something called 'The Country Party', which did not exist.

McEwen was succeeded by John Gorton, who was a popular prime minister despite technically being an orangutan, but lost the confidence of his party room and resigned to pursue a career as a rock formation.

After Gorton came Billy McMahon, who rose to prominence

after proving that he didn't need the magic feather to fly, and sank back out of prominence after proving that he was a loser. Suffering from perceptions that he was weak, indecisive, stupid, ugly, annoying and possibly already dead, he lost the 1972 election, ending 23 years of Liberal rule and ushering in an exciting new era of progress and intellectual stimulation and handsomeness under the dashing and charismatic political buccaneer

Gough the Great and Powerful

Gough Whitlam was a mercurial genius, a comet who streaked across the political firmament illuminating all that he passed over, until inevitably he crashed in flames and wiped out thousands of hectares of prime farming land. Not all of this description is literal, but it is undeniable that in his brief prime ministership, Whitlam brought more incandescent intelligence and irrepressible reforming energy to the nation than Stanley Bruce and Chris Watson combined.[173]

Born in 1916 in suburban Melbourne, Edward Gough Whitlam made waves early in life by achieving fluency in Latin by the age of two months. On his first day of kindergarten, he announced his intention to stand for prime minister and convinced his teachers to sign a petition demanding Billy Hughes's resignation. At the age of 11, Gough's family moved to Canberra, where wise men and shepherds were already gathered to await the boy-child's coming. At the age of 16, he began attending Canberra Grammar School and was awarded a prize on Speech Day by Governor-General Sir Isaac Isaacs, whom Gough immediately tried to sack. After school, he attended the University of Sydney, where he studied law, abandoning his Greek classes after taking

173 You could probably even throw in Arthur Fadden without exceeding his wattage.

a professor's statement that 'Alexander the Great was history's greatest leader' as a personal insult.

When World War Two broke out, Whitlam, despite having urgent business at his Fortress of Solitude, pulled a Reverse Menzies by enlisting in the military. Following Japan's attack on Pearl Harbor, he volunteered for the Royal Australian Air Force, making his mark as the RAAF's first trainee to log more than a hundred flying hours without ever getting into a plane. Despite his unique talents, for the good of morale Whitlam agreed to confine himself to flying Lockheed Ventura bombers. Even while serving in the air force, Flight Lieutenant Whitlam did not give up his political convictions, distributing Labor Party literature, and occasional servings of manna, to his RAAF colleagues.[174]

When Japan surrendered, out of fear of Whitlam's amazing oratory, Gough graduated from university and began to practise law, although he didn't practise for long, as within three weeks he had perfected it. Finding that winning his cases presented too little challenge, he looked further afield and entered the Federal House of Representatives in 1952 as the Labor member for Werriwa, a traditionally safe Labor seat named after the sound made by its early explorer when he was speared to death.

Whitlam quickly gained a reputation for what parliamentary standing orders technically call 'sick burns'. In his maiden speech he responded to an interjection by Black Jack McEwen by stating that 'the time will come when you may interrupt me', a devastating retort that caused the more educated members of the House to marvel at the clever Benjamin Disraeli reference, and the less educated members to comment on how Whitlam was just like Bane talking to Batman.[175]

---

174 Imagine coming back from a hard day being fired on by the Japanese, and getting Labor pamphlets shoved in your face in the locker room. War is hell.

175 Again, not the explorer: the good Batman.

In later memorable speeches, Whitlam referred to MPs Bill Bourke as 'this grizzling Quisling' and Garfield Barwick as a 'bumptious bastard', although after calling Billy McMahon a 'quean', he apologised for his poor spelling.

Unfortunately for him, Whitlam had joined a Labor Party made up mostly of people who were not Whitlam, and he was forced to wait for his chance through the long, depressing Menzies years. It was not until 1967 that he became Leader of the Opposition and quickly reinvigorated the party room with revolutionary new ideas such as 'winning'.

Whitlam reformed the ALP, reducing union influence and embracing the suburban middle class who were sympathetic with many Labor principles but had previously been scared away by lingering fears of purges in the Politburo. The new leader cemented his control of the party by looking it straight in the eye and talking to it in that sexy, mellifluous voice that no caucus could resist. He was determined that Labor should be a modern, aggressive, adaptable party, ready to introduce Australia to the 20th century by no later than 1980.

In the 1969 election, Whitlam scored a major swing against the government but failed to win, a devastating blow to many of the David Williamson characters who had supported him. But his popularity kept on rising, assisted by the internal disputes in the Liberal Party, where ministers were engaged in endless rounds of bickering over which one of them was the most underwhelming.

'It's Time'

In the election of 1972, it was Time. The signs that it was Time were everywhere: on t-shirts, on posters and on clocks, and in a catchy song titled 'It's Time', wherein Little Pattie[176] sang 'It's Time' as a

176 Not to be confused with Big Pattie, which is only $5.95 at Hungry Jack's.

representation of her belief that it was Time.

What was it Time for? Nobody knew, but God it was a wonderful time to be alive. Promising universal health cover, free university tuition, an end to conscription, and the forgiveness of all sins for those who would but humble themselves and believe, Gough Whitlam convinced an entire nation that it was Time to change, Time to grow and Time to give him the keys to the country so that he could take it out back and start doing donuts in it.

Sweeping to victory on 2 December 1972, Whitlam noted that this was the anniversary of the Battle of Austerlitz: at which, he quipped, 'A crushing defeat was administered to a coalition – another ramshackle, reactionary coalition.' 'Ha, ha, ha,' chuckled all the people who pretended to know what he was on about.

But victory was only the beginning for Whitlam. He knew that he had to implement all of his grand plans with the greatest possible speed, as he didn't have much time left before the people tossed him out of office for implementing all of his grand plans with too much speed.

The programmes unfurled by the Whitlam government were many and varied. As well as ending conscription and abolishing uni fees, he established relations with China, supported sanctions against South Africa, eliminated sales tax on the Pill, abolished the death penalty, funded urban renewal, introduced legal aid, made 'Advance Australia Fair' the national anthem, purchased Jackson Pollock's *Blue Poles*, threw the money changers out of the temple, slew a thousand Philistines with the jawbone of an ass and invented the internet.

With such furious activity crammed into just a couple of years, any man would be exhausted and feel himself losing his grip on things. Fortunately, Gough Whitlam was not just any man – in fact, rumours began to circulate that he was a secret gene-splicing experiment meant to demonstrate the viability of human–angel hybrids – and he kept a firm hand on the tiller throughout his prime ministership. He can hardly be blamed if the tiller that he was keeping a firm hand on was made up of an uncontrollable rabble of half-witted human garbage – you have to work with what you've got.

The troubles began with Attorney General Lionel Murphy, who caused controversy by hanging around with police officers when he should have been at work. The troubles continued with the Senate, which frequently refused to do Whitlam's bidding on the basis that he was far too bossy. From the start of Whitlam's term to the beginning of 1974, the Senate voted down 19 government Bills, causing the prime minister to wail, 'Who will rid me of this turbulent house of review?' Sadly, the drunken knights who rushed to Canberra to slaughter the Senate were stopped by the AFP,[177] and Whitlam's troubles continued.

A glimpse of hope for the frustrated Labor Party emerged when DLP Senator Vince Gair indicated that he might be willing to quit the Senate if given a cushy job – this would increase the number of Senate seats open at the 1974 election and give Whitlam a chance of grabbing control of the Upper House. Whitlam promised Gair the post of ambassador to Ireland and rubbed his patrician hands together with glee: absolute power would soon be his.

Alas, the plan was stymied by the unforeseen complication that it was 1974 and the world was ridiculous. With Labor trying to get Gair's written resignation, the Country Party kept him busy at a party where the government couldn't find him until it was too late for his seat to be declared vacant.[178] The affair became known as 'The Night of the Long Prawns', in recognition of the fact that it was stupid. Of course,

177 Tragically the Senate remains alive to this day.

178 This really happened. WTF, Australia?

nowadays, with advances in communications and politicians' 24-hour availability, everyone has to work a lot harder to generate that level of blundering idiocy.

His plot disrupted by the nefarious Opposition, Whitlam yelled, 'To hell with it!' and called a double dissolution, which is a special kind of election wherein you score double points for every correct answer. Labor won, with the Senate now deadlocked and the balance of power held by two independents. The country stood on a knife edge. On one side was a government with a lust for reform that could almost be called reckless. On the other side was an Opposition eager to block the government's plans at every turn. On a weird little third side stood the governor-general, Sir John Kerr, a magical talking bag of wine with strong views on the Constitution and why he found it difficult to make friends.

The Whitlam administration that had started in such a whirlwind of hope and enthusiasm was floundering. The smooth and reassuring affluence of the Menzies era was long gone, and Australia was cringing under the relentless battering of a recession. Inflation, interest rates and unemployment were all rising unsustainably, which is such an odd combination that it took great skill to get them all going the same way at the same time. Whitlam and his team probably deserve a lot more credit than they get for what was really a quite spectacular talent for creating unfeasibly awful economic conditions.

Treasury officials advised a suite of measures to raise more revenue; the Cabinet responded by rolling their eyes and asking the apt question, 'Treasury officials? What would *they* know?' Instead, Treasurer Frank Crean handed down a budget in 1974 that featured a surge in spending, particularly on education, which was logical in a sense: the sooner they got the country's children educated, the sooner one of those children might come up with an idea to fix the mess they were in. Crean said that the Budget Cabinet had become a 'lunatic asylum' – and certainly, if a nurse was distributing powerful pharmaceuticals in there, that would explain a lot.

In November 1974, Whitlam announced more spending and a stack of major tax cuts, following his radical new theory that the best way to fight a bushfire was to burn it down. Pundits began to discuss the possibility that the prime minister literally didn't know what money was. This proved to be untrue: he knew exactly what money was, and he knew the best way to get some – borrow it. With four billion dollars, he reasoned, he could do a whole lot of useful things for the country, and his only problem would be how to repay it, which should be pretty easy if he organised enough celebrity car washes.

Sadly, this brilliant plan collapsed when it became public knowledge that Whitlam and his ministers Jim Cairns and Rex Connor were trying to borrow money from Arabs without approval from the Loans Council. Whitlam had never really seen why a man like himself should need to seek approval for anything he did, and he couldn't see what all the fuss was about, but the media and Opposition got very snarky about the whole thing, and the government continued to suffer from a chronic cash shortage.

At such a time, the last thing Whitlam needed was a refugee row, but that's what he got when Opposition Leader Malcolm Fraser tore into him for not taking in enough South Vietnamese refugees after the war.[179] Whitlam was worried that the refugees, who were fleeing a communist regime presumably very similar to his own, would enter Australia and immediately begin voting Liberal, especially when they

179 This was the start of the Liberal Party's ongoing efforts to make political capital out of the Australian public's desire to let in more refugees.

heard about the Night of the Long Prawns. 'I will not have those fucking yellow Balts,' he ranted, proving that if he had left behind many of the elements of Cocky Calwell's Labor Party, he'd at least retained his predecessor's hearty racism.

Amid all this, Whitlam managed to continue governing Australia despite a considerable body of evidence suggesting that Australia always does best when it's not being governed in any realistic way. He passed the *Family Law Act*, allowing for no-fault divorce and releasing thousands from the unbearable torture of marriage; the *Racial Discrimination Act*, which made it illegal to discriminate against people on the basis of their race unless they were fucking yellow Balts; granted independence to Papua New Guinea and denied it to East Timor; and gave the Gurindji people title deeds to their traditional lands, providing a major boost to Paul Kelly's future career.

Yet despite Whitlam's determination to keep on doing things in the face of the general public's opposition to thing-doing, his government lurched from one disaster to another like Frankenstein's monster in a porcelain kitten shop. Labor was thrashed in the Bass by-election caused by the departure of former Deputy PM Lance Barnard, a week before Whitlam sacked Barnard's successor, Jim Cairns, who had committed the twin sins of misleading Parliament and having sex with a woman.[180] The government was in disarray, and Whitlam was finally learning the hard lesson that being prime minister is more than a matter of simply being an incomparable genius with a natural talent for leadership: you also need the ability to count and a few colleagues with more brains than a steamed lychee.

---

180 Pervert.

Got 'Im, Yes!

The end was nigh when Queensland Premier Joh Bjelke-Petersen, the devious autocrat descended equally from the political traditions of Caligula and Emperor Palpatine, pulled an act of bastardry so low that it almost makes the list of the 500 worst things he ever did. When a Senate seat became vacant due to the death of Queensland ALP Senator Bertie Milliner, the Queensland Parliament blocked the appointment of Labor's nominated replacement, and Bjelke-Petersen filled the vacancy with anti-Whitlamite Albert Field. The government protested as strongly as it could considering it was distracted by all the men arriving to repossess its furniture and the series of spontaneous-combustion incidents affecting various MPs, but the Opposition had got what it wanted – the Senate deadlock was broken.

Fraser's Opposition resolved to block supply, a process by which Parliament denies the government the money it needs to conduct its necessary operations. Opinion is sharply divided on the ethics of this move. Some say it was an act of brute opportunism that held the entire country to ransom for base political motives. Others believe that it was the parliamentary equivalent of refusing to give the guy outside the 7-Eleven two dollars for a train fare because he'll only spend it on drugs. And while it's true that the Whitlam government was to some extent addicted to spending, it's also true that they really needed to catch that train.

By blocking supply, the Opposition ensured that on 30 November, the government would literally run out of money. No problem, you might think: they're the government, they can print some more. Well, you'd think so, but there are a lot of very boring reasons why they can't do that. For one thing, you have to pay the printers to turn the printing presses on, and you can't do that if you have no money. This is where the phrase 'You have to spend money to make money' comes from.

Several attempts were made to reach a compromise, but Fraser remained determined to deny supply, and Whitlam continued to refuse to call an election. And so, Governor-General John Kerr, on the advice of the enormous pink bunny who lived in his oven, decided to act.

Kerr would dismiss Whitlam as prime minister. He asked High Court justice and well-known bumptious bastard Garfield Barwick for his expert opinion, and Barwick finally got revenge for the sick burns of the past, advising Kerr that dismissal was, legally speaking, a pretty great idea.

Had Whitlam known that Kerr was going to ask the Queen to sack him, he would've asked the Queen to sack Kerr, but Kerr made his plans in secret, missing a golden opportunity to invent *The Amazing Race* several decades early. It would have featured both men trying to get to Buckingham Palace before the other. Would Australian history be better off if Whitlam and Kerr had ridden jetskis across the Indian Ocean, been forced to herd goats in Zambia and bungee-jumped off a Slovenian waterfall before a climactic hurtle along the cobbled streets of London in hansom cabs, bowling over beefeaters and holding on to their top hats, in a frantic final rush to beg favour with Elizabeth? Yes, Australia would be. But there's no use crying over spilt milk. As it was, Kerr drafted the letter of dismissal, Whitlam was finished, and we had to wait 30 years for the invention of the Fast Forward.

At 2.34pm on 11 November, the anniversary of Ned Kelly's own dismissal,[181] Malcolm Fraser rose in the House, pausing first to make sure he'd remembered to put his pants on, and announced he was prime minister. Whitlam objected, insisting that *he* was prime minister and that this fact should be fairly obvious from his noble bearing and

181 Which looked pretty clean and civilised by comparison.

nimble way with words. Fraser gave him the royal finger and advised Gough not to let the door hit him on the way out.

That afternoon, Kerr's Official Secretary David Smith stood on the steps of Parliament House and brought the news of the Dismissal to a huge crowd that had gathered there for the live *Norman Gunston Show*. At the end of his announcement, he squeaked, 'God save the Queen', as if that had anything to do with anything. It was a tactical blunder: Smith had given Whitlam the opening to make a memorable and pithy retort that would condemn the official secretary forever to a legacy as the weird-looking little guy in front of Gough when he delivered his greatest sick burn of all. 'Well may they say, "God save the Queen"', E.G. Whitlam declaimed, 'because nothing will save the governor-general!'

What did he mean by this? Was he threatening to kill Sir John Kerr? Was he expressing a sincere hope that an interventionist god could step in to prevent Elizabeth II from succumbing to the alcoholism that plagued his old friend the GG? Was he saying that Elizabeth shouldn't stand too close to John in case of lightning strike?

In the end, we can't be sure what Whitlam was talking about on that day, or on any day – and the fact is, it doesn't matter. What matters is that he said it, and we remembered it, and we were inspired: for that day, a nation was roused to action by Whitlam's noble stance in the face of unspeakable betrayal. So enraged were the people by Kerr and Fraser's stoop to rank political intrigue that they rose up at the election a month later and voted the Coalition in with the largest majority in history. Australia had watched the shocking drama of the Dismissal, and responded with a firm message for posterity: bastardry works *really* well.

Whitlam stayed on as Opposition leader until the next election, but his credibility was damaged by the revelation that he had tried to raise election funds from the Iraqi government[182] – and, in any case, he was tainted in the memory of many by the fact that he had been part of the notorious Whitlam government. Fraser won again in the 1977 election, and Whitlam was supplanted by Bill Hayden, who would go on to become one of Australia's least interesting political figures.

In his post-politics life, Whitlam stayed active, spending most of his time being adulated and occasionally taking time off to be revered. Late in life, he finally achieved his lifelong dream of appearing in a TV commercial for pasta sauce. In 2014 he died, shortly after assuring us all that we would dine with him that night in paradise. He left behind no physical body, simply a burial shroud eerily imprinted with his likeness.

The legacy of Gough Whitlam is remarkable for a man who was prime minister for only three years and spent most of those clinging to a cliff while various people stamped on his fingers. His introduction of free education and medical care for all revolutionised Australia and firmly established the Australian tradition, still observed today, of Liberals trying to take free education and medical care away. He brought a new style to the business of government, a style that emphasised progressive ideas, equal rights for marginalised groups, greater appreciation for the arts and a steadfast refusal to face reality.

Whitlam is remembered today as a Labor hero, but let's be honest, it's not like they've got much else to choose from. That he was a great man is indisputable, especially if you ever asked him, but his career proved that sometimes being the ultimate synthesis of every possible virtue that a human can possess isn't enough, when you're unlucky enough to be born into a country as fundamentally ungrateful as this one.

---

182 This was in the 'sticking pins in the atlas' stage of the budget crisis.

ESSAY QUESTIONS

1. How many people could Gough Whitlam feed with five loaves and two fishes?
2. Do you think that anything could save the governor-general? What about AA?

Labor's Love Lost

In which history's greatest love story comes to a bittersweet end

The '80s were a turbulent time for Australia, and while it's true that this could probably be said about every decade in history, it is almost as true of the '80s as it is of several others. The country experienced great prosperity in the '80s, but also great friction, as the modern globalised economy rubbed uncomfortably up against the insular Australian psyche like the sweaty thighs of a deeply conflicted jogger. The Fraser years, during which the entire country had slowly transformed into a 55-year-old tax clerk, were best summed up by the prime minister's famous assertion that 'Life wasn't meant to be easy.' This blatant lie brought an unremitting gloom to the nation, and lifting the gloom would take a Herculean effort from a couple of extraordinary men: men whose zeal for reform, political acumen and deadly combination of crying and verbal abuse would win over the masses and transform the country, but whose clash of personalities and restless ambition would threaten to tear it apart. In this extract from the incendiary biography Bob and Paul: A Deregulated Romance, the tale of these amazing statesmen is summed up.

Paul stared across the table at Bob, tears in his eyes. 'You promised,' he sobbed hoarsely.

'Don't make this harder than it has to be, Paul,' said Bob, combing his unutterably beautiful hair casually. 'You knew what this was.'

'But you said ...' Paul sputtered. 'You said I could be prime minister, if only I could be patient. We agreed. You *said*.'

'Things change, Paul,' replied Bob, applying a generous amount of tanning butter to his chest. 'When I promised you I would stand down if I won the election, I had no way of knowing that I would win the election.'

Paul stared at his old friend, scarcely believing it had come to this. It had all been so different back in the old days. When he and Bob rode together like the twin heads of a glorious radiation-affected lion, lords of all they surveyed. When they had joined forces in 1983 to cut the legs out from under Bill Hayden, and then repeated the dose on Malcolm Fraser, the future had seemed sweet and fragrant, and filled with promise and progressive yet rational economic policies.

For a while it had worked. Paul had been the greatest treasurer the world had ever seen. Oh, he'd hidden behind a veil of false modesty, self-effacingly describing himself as 'the Placido Domingo of Australian politics' when he knew full well that he was the Enrico Caruso but that the opera-loving Australian public would never accept such arrogance. Inside, he knew how great he was, and he was sure Bob knew as well.

Were they not the perfect team? Paul, with his immaculate suits, impeccable taste in music, astounding grasp of macroeconomics; Bob, with his everyman charm, phenomenal hair, easy way with people. Paul had never got the knack of that last one: where Bob seemed to think nothing of entering a room, shaking every hand, sharing a laugh and making everyone feel that he was their best friend, Paul couldn't ever get more than three minutes into any social function before he'd make some terrible faux pas, like mocking his host's taste in clocks or accusing the ambassador's wife of guzzling from the trough of neo-populist retro-Spinozan anarcho-swill. The worst part was that the people he insulted never even seemed to realise how clever the insults were.

It wasn't his fault that his brilliance wasn't always easy to understand, but he was happy to stand on his results. While Bob pressed the flesh, Paul transformed the Australian economy into something sleek, gleaming and mouth-wateringly agile. Unpopular decisions were all part of that, but Bob had always managed to smooth things over with a merry quip or a friendly tug of the ear or a crowd-pleasing blow to the face in a cricket match.

And now he'd betrayed Paul. 'Of course you can be prime minister,' he'd cooed back at Kirribilli in '88. 'It's only fair after all the wonderful support you've given me. Now excuse me, I have to go "bang the biographer", if you know what I mean.'

Paul didn't know what he meant – he rarely knew what Bob meant. He remembered once when Bob had told him that he thought AB should enforce the follow-on, and he'd briefly considered calling a doctor to treat him for a stroke. Bob never talked about clocks or suits or Mahler, but they were still friends, weren't they? Those long, hot nights spent slaving over the Prices and Income Accord ... they had meant *some*thing, hadn't they? It wasn't only a meaningless industrial relations fling, was it? It couldn't be.

No, it couldn't be. Paul could believe that a man would devise a new industrial relations system with another man just for kicks, but the tariff reductions? The banking deregulations? The privatisation of Qantas? A man doesn't do those things unless he's serious. For God's sake, they'd floated the dollar together – after going through something that intimate, how could Bob toss it all away so callously?

Somewhere they'd drifted apart. He should have known: it takes work to keep a relationship fresh. Back when they were beating John

Howard over the head with the hidden deficit of the Fraser years and twisting Andrew Peacock's arm behind his back until he cried, Paul had foolishly assumed that life would be that blissful and carefree forever. But he should've realised even back then, when Bob went out on the town after the America's Cup, that his prime minister was a free, flighty spirit, susceptible to temptation and prone to preferring a night out celebrating a boat race than an evening in mapping out the restructure of the corporate tax system. With a man like that, Paul thought ruefully, you needed to keep your nose to the grindstone to stop him from flying away.

Paul looked at Bob. The prime minister was leaning back in his chair, sipping iced tea from a yard glass. Even now, Paul felt the awesome force of his charisma. The man was born to be prime minister. As a baby, his first words had been 'capture the middle ground'; Paul's had been 'Armani monetarist'.

'Maybe we should take a break,' he said now, desperately trying to find a way out of this heartache. 'Let's go away for a while, just the two of us. We'll clear our heads, spend some quality time together, experiment with fun new positions on small business tax credits.'

Bob smiled patronisingly. 'Those days are behind us, Paul,' he drawled. 'Time to stop living in the past.'

'*I'm* living in the past?' Paul spat angrily, the tears burning his cheeks. 'You said you'd resign, you said you'd stand aside and let me move the country forward, you said ... you said ...' He dissolved into a puddle of sniffles.

Bob laughed. 'You think you could be prime minister?' he sneered. 'You're a mess, man! You can't even cry properly. I was always the one who cried, remember? I cried for my people, and they loved me for it. If they ever see you cry, they'll run away screaming. Face it, Paul: nobody wants a vampire for a prime minister, no matter how many reserve banks he's got in his pocket.'

Paul exploded. 'That's not true!' he roared. 'The people are ready for a *new* kind of prime minister. They've had enough of prime ministers who have nothing to offer but silver coifs and adultery. They want a fresh approach to leadership, based on solid principles of trade deregulation and verbal abuse. They want *me*, and I'm going to give them what they want!'

Bob laughed again, taking another swig from the yard glass and flicking a brand-new cricket ball idly from hand to hand. 'The people will never embrace you,' he said smugly. 'You don't look like you could seduce an award-winning non-fiction writer if you tried.' He set the yard glass down and leant forward with a malicious grin. 'You wouldn't know where to *start*.'

Paul was flushed with rage, his stomach knotted by indignation and shame, and yet still, when he looked at this great, wrinkly man and his glorious halo of hair, he felt the irresistible pull that had inspired love and devotion in him and the rest of the country for the past eight years. But he knew he must be strong. He had to be his own man.

'You're tearing me apart, Bob,' he said sadly. 'You're tearing the Labor Party apart. The party of Chifley and Curtin, of Whitlam and Scullin and Ros Kelly. Are you willing to do that, just to stay prime minister, which is objectively the worst job in the world?'

Bob didn't answer, but simply flicked the ball from hand to hand again, then put on his America's Cup jacket. Paul got the message: there would have to be blood.

Six months later, Paul stood on the doorstep of the Lodge, nervously jingling the house keys. The die had been cast. The Rubicon had been crossed. The corpse had been buried. The horse had been drowned.

There was now no turning back. The future of the Labor Party was in his hands, and history would judge him severely if he made a Calwell of it.

Who knew, he mused, where this new path would lead him? Perhaps to glory. Perhaps to ignominy. Perhaps he would find himself pursuing an ambitious agenda of social and economic reforms, including furthering the cause of Indigenous reconciliation, forging stronger ties with Asia and introducing a national superannuation scheme that would revolutionise Australians' retirement planning forever, while simultaneously finding himself hamstrung by flagging popularity and internal party ructions. Or perhaps not.

Perhaps he would, desperately trying to salvage his prime ministership, tear mercilessly into an Opposition proposal for a broad-based consumption tax similar to one he himself had proposed while he was treasurer, retaining government only through use of the basest of scare campaigns. Nothing in life was certain, but he had to consider the possibility that he would publicly humiliate the gentle, soft-spoken Opposition leader, the man who had mounted the proposal, with a series of vicious personal insults – Paul might not do this, but what if he did? And what if he caused an unfortunate diplomatic incident by publicly insulting the Malaysian prime minister? What if he was attacked for daring to lay hands on the Queen? What if he easily crushed the challenge of another feeble Opposition leader, only to be crushed himself in a landslide by the man he despised most of all, the lame duck from the '80s whom he had thought he'd thrashed for good?

So many what-ifs, but Paul couldn't let himself become fixated on the hypotheticals. He had a legacy to build – and even if that legacy ended up being one that people thought as being more about eloquent invective and hostile parliamentary combat than constructive hard policy work; even if people remembered the one-liners and the carefully curated hatreds and the time he told everyone 'this is the recession we had to have' more than his groundbreaking fusion of Labor principles with free-market theory to create a truly modern, progressive economy; even if he ended up being seen by some as the embodiment of the degradation of political debate, and by others as one of the purest warriors for the cause to emerge from the Labor movement: those were concerns for another day. He had a country to run.

He turned the key in the lock and entered the grand residence. He sighed with satisfaction. Finally, the job was his. He stepped into the Lodge's rumpus room, and stopped.

There, slouched across the commemorative Francis Forde beanbag, was Bob. His shirt was half-open and, below the waist, he was stripped to his Speedos. Beside him lay an empty yard glass: Paul suspected it hadn't been holding iced tea. 'Came back,' slurred the recumbent ex-PM. 'Came back to my house. Everything gone. Any boss sacks anyone ... mug ... cheated. Hazel ... Tiananmen ... no drover's dog will live in poverty by ... Blanche. Everything gone, everything ... get me AB on the phone, have to organise ticker tape ...'

Paul sighed. Even prime ministers have to do the housekeeping sometimes. He stepped over to the beanbag and gently lifted Bob off Forde's face. 'Come on, old man,' he murmured. 'Let's get you into your favourite ACTU pyjamas.'

'I, sorry,' Bob muttered, crying those shining tears that had won a nation's heart. 'You ...' he said urgently, pawing at Paul's beautifully tailored chest, 'You'll be ... such a great prime minister.'

'Yes, Bob,' Paul soothed. 'That's right. That's right.'

'But Paul, one last time. For old time's sake.'

Paul lay Bob gently on the prime ministerial sofa and stared at him in astonishment. 'Are you sure you want to?' he whispered.

'One last time,' Bob slurred. His hair somehow looked shinier and more perfectly sculpted than ever.

Paul nodded slowly. 'One last time,' he repeated softly. 'Before we ride away.'

He sat next to his old comrade and ran a manicured hand through that gorgeous, angelic mane. The bitter past had been left behind. The future was so uncertain – although there was a chance it would involve a landmark speech in Redfern. But now, just for today, before the roads of Hawke and Keating diverged forever, they would succumb to the divine pleasures, one last time.

Paul pulled out a manila folder. 'Okay, so the key issue is bracket creep,' he said firmly. 'I propose that we adjust the marginal rates to provide relief to the low-income sector that will provide stimulus to ...'

The sun rose over Canberra.

POSTSCRIPT

Paul Keating went on to become one of history's most beloved, or possibly most hated, prime ministers, nothing if not divisive. His ability to find dozens of interesting ways to call people bastards made him revered among Labor true believers, but less revered among non-Labor false doubters. The legacy of his many reforms lives on in Australian society and culture, and when things get really bad, people even wish he'd come back.

Bob Hawke went on to drink a lot and have loads of sex with his biographer. As an elder statesman of the Labor Party, he remained an important voice in debates about the party's future, which does not technically exist. A much-anticipated guest at party conferences, in his later years Hawke's public appearances were invaluable in raising awareness of wind erosion.

Francis Forde was Australia's shortest-serving prime minister ever and died ages ago.

ESSAY QUESTIONS

1. Did you find this chapter a bit weird? Be honest.
2. Have you ever had sex with a biographer? What about a writer of humorous history books?
3. If you had the chance, would you touch the Queen? Do you think you could get to second base?

Elimination Day

In which deckchairs are shuffled while icebergs pay no attention

At the close of the turbulent Hawke–Keating era, Australia was crying out for an end to the constant change and modernisation, and a bit of peace and quiet in which to just sit and do a crossword and think about how pleasant everything was. The Age of Comfortableness had arrived, and it yearned for a hero to lead his people through it. Australia found that hero in the person of John Howard.

John Howard was first brought to life in a garden by a fairy's spell in the 1930s, fulfilling a prophecy that claimed one day a conviction politician would spring forth in the form of a decorative lawn ornament. He grew up in his father's suburban petrol station. Pondering the sweet happiness that his idyllic childhood brought him, he developed a beautiful dream and determined that he would make it come true: one day, he vowed, he would turn the entire country into a suburban petrol station. And he was as good as his word.

As a youth, Howard idolised Prime Minister Robert Menzies, and the combination of his hero worship and his constant exposure to petrol fumes caused him to become convinced that he could become prime minister himself. How he came to achieve this remains a mystery to this day. Did the fumes spread to the entire country? Was that fairy still working? Did he do a deal with Satan whereby the Prince of Darkness guaranteed the existence of the Howard government, in return for which Howard guaranteed to implement the policies of the Howard government? All potentially true theories. But in any event, after years of striving and fighting and working and trimming his eyebrows and slowly learning the inadvisability of comb-overs, Howard did become prime minister, defeating Paul Keating in 1996 on a platform of having never been Paul Keating at any time.[183]

The next 11 years were akin to a warm bath of honey for the country. The economy boomed, society achieved a pleasing balance between nagging fear of and near-comatose indifference to the outside world, and the Australian Test team twice went on world record-winning streaks.[184] God was in His heaven, and all was right with the world. If the odd hiccup popped up, like the mildly contentious introduction of the GST or the occasionally vexing brutalisation of asylum seekers and incitement of racial hatred on a massive scale, it never caused any more real trouble than, say, an illegal invasion of a sovereign country on the basis of phony intelligence might.

All of Australia was agreed: the prime ministership of John Howard was the greatest gift to the cause of relaxed contentment the country had ever seen; and those who weren't agreed were the kind of aggravating malcontents who are just never pleased with anything anyway. You know, Green types and such.

But is it possible that such a long period of stability and tranquillised happiness made the nation complacent? Recall that after the Menzies decades came to an end, the country was thrown into such a panicked kerfuffle that the new prime minister accidentally fell to the bottom of the ocean. Did Howard's tenure have a similar effect, lulling us

183 This is still the main platform of Liberal leaders.

184 Something quite beyond the pathetic PMs we've had since.

into the false sense that 11-year periods of uninterrupted serenity and leisurely low-key bigotry would now be the norm? Because as Howard himself might have said, had he been French or a citizen of the Quebec province of Canada: '*Après* moi, le deluge.'[185] The Howard years were followed by some of the most chaotic, rancorous, treacherous and yet oddly tedious political upheavals seen in this country since Bligh got yanked out from his nest among the dust bunnies.

Truth be told, the upheavals started before Howard even left office. After the 2004 election, when the voters had returned Howard mainly out of a fear that his opponent Mark Latham, if given the reins of power, would literally punch their mothers in the face, the Liberal government's fortunes had declined, and many within the party believed that leadership renewal was desperately needed if Australia was to avoid the greatest calamity that can befall a sovereign nation: Kevin Rudd.

Treasurer Peter Costello, who had made his name with his regular belligerent lettuce attacks on Paul Keating, was urged to challenge Howard for the leadership, but Costello was reluctant to grasp the nettle. If we're honest, Costello was reluctant to grasp anything more troublesome than a warm crumpet – he seemed to believe that the best way to become prime minister was to accidentally trip over a stick and fall down the Lodge's chimney. Certainly the idea of confronting anyone to gain the job was a bridge too far for the man destined to be nicknamed 'Peter Cost-Yellow'.

And so John Howard, mad with power and possessed by apocalyptic visions in which shining angels came to him in the middle of the night and offered him a mighty flaming sword if he would only preside over a massive blowout in middle-class welfare, stayed on, then came to grief

185 Very classy reference, this.

at the 2007 election against Kevin Rudd, a new breed of politician who had been created in a laboratory by combining Howard's own DNA with a Swiss Army Knife. Running on the slogan 'Kevin Rudd: Just Like John Howard but Slightly More Likely to Help You Get Up If You Fall Over in Your Bathroom', Rudd electrified a country that was restless to move into the future and finally ready to be led by a middle-aged white man in glasses. What's more, he spoke Chinese, which seemed sensible.

The youth of Australia rallied behind Rudd, knowing instinctively that an old fuddy-duddy like Howard would never have had the wherewithal to rhyme his name with the name of the year in which he was contesting the election, and Kevin '07 settled into a long and prosperous reign.

The Rudd years began well, with the famous Apology to the Stolen Generations, in which PM Rudd formally apologised for the wrongs that the Australian government had inflicted on the country's Indigenous population over the centuries – and also, by implication, for the wrongs that the Australian government would continue to inflict on the country's Indigenous population over coming centuries. And Rudd's star rose ever higher when the Global Financial Crisis came along.

The GFC[186] occurred when the world's wealthiest and most powerful financial institutions realised that they had been short-changing themselves for years by lending money only to people who could pay it back. 'Lending money to people who can't pay it back, *that's* where the money is,' they said, and passed the orders along before going home to bathe in enormous tubs of liquid gold.

Somehow this plan went wrong, and the world's economy went

186 Not to be confused with the Geelong Football Club, which happened much earlier and has never been recovered from.

into a terrifying tailspin, forcing governments everywhere to take rapid and decisive action to make sure that rich people didn't have to stop getting richer. But it was in Australia that the governmental response attracted most praise from economists: Rudd applied classical Keynesian principles in a way that was quite impressive to anyone who was enough of a geeky shut-in to know what they were, stimulating the economy with major injections of public money, extensive public works programmes and an individual payment of $900 to every taxpayer, most of whom spent it on new TVs or heroin.

And so the Rudd government successfully navigated the country through the financial crisis with hardly a bump, apart from the Home Insulation Rebate Programme, in which Environment minister and former musical seizure sufferer Peter Garrett attempted to jumpstart the insulation installation industry[187] but instead accidentally jumpstarted the end of his career. But apart from that, it was all plain sailing, which made it all the more off when Kevin Rudd suddenly found himself not prime minister anymore.

Rudd's demise was due to several complex factors:

1. His declaration that climate change was 'the greatest moral challenge of our generation', followed by his declaration that climate change was 'a bit of a nuisance, we'll probably get around to it sometime if we have time'.
2. His inability to successfully prosecute the public case for a tax on mining companies' super-profits, after a concerted campaign by the minerals industry warned the public of the dangers of making it less attractive to be a multibillionaire.
3. The arrival of muscular Catholic cage fighter Tony Abbott as

187 I know, I didn't know that was a thing either.

Opposition leader, replacing the urbane but ineffective Malcolm Turnbull, who had himself replaced the not-urbane but ineffective Brendan Nelson. Abbott infused the Liberal Opposition with a new and infectious energy, introducing innovative new campaign tactics such as spandex, disturbing fixed grins and shouting, 'Great big tax!' every five seconds regardless of time or place or subject of conversation.[188]

4. Rudd's own leadership style, which revolved heavily around keeping tight control of all aspects of policy development and political strategy, mostly by screaming obscenities at everyone who worked for him and regularly staying up all night by himself working out ways that he could more effectively ignore his colleagues.

Eventually it all got too much for Rudd's deputy, Julia Gillard, who decided that for the good of the country that she loved and the party she had dedicated her life to, she had to take swift action to advance her own personal ambitions. On 23 June 2010, Gillard perfectly executed a blindside coup on Rudd, thus becoming Australia's first woman prime minister, signalling our transition from a backward-looking, chauvinist society to a backward-looking, chauvinist society that now had a really big target to aim at. She had also begun the exhilarating spin of 21st-century Australia's intoxicating revolving federal door. The next few years would be nothing but colour, movement and incredibly depressing press conferences.

Tony Abbott, who had always suspected that women were out to get him, was relieved to have his suspicions confirmed: a woman was now literally trying to stop him getting the job he wanted. He reacted with ferocious attacks on Gillard, focusing on the supposed illegitimacy

188 He came up with the idea when he shouted it during his wedding vows.

of her prime ministership. Urged on by Abbott, the people turned to the new PM and asked her, just *why* did you have to get rid of Rudd?

'Well, gee, have you *MET* him?' was Gillard's answer, but it was one that did not satisfy the wider public, who had not experienced Rudd's Gordon Ramsay-esque management style firsthand and still regarded Kevin '07 as the kind, helpful, cuddly, wombat-like uncle of the nation who had delivered us from Howard. By contrast, Gillard came across as a cold, insincere careerist, the sort of person who would go around telling stories about vicious misogynistic abuse just because they were true.

The 2010 election went down to the wire. After the votes were counted, neither Gillard nor Abbott could command a majority in the House of Representatives. Formation of government came down to the House's three Independent MPs: Tony 'Straight-Shooter' Windsor, Rob 'Just one more thing' Oakeshott and Bob 'Can only become sexually aroused while shooting crocodiles' Katter.

Katter opted to support Abbott after the Opposition leader promised him a VIP Card for the R.M. Williams Outlet Store. Windsor and Oakeshott took longer to make up their minds, as both leaders made their pitch to them. Abbott promised them great riches for their electorates, taking them to the top of a cliff in the desert and pointing to a glittering city with the words, 'All this shall be yours if you will just kneel down and worship me.' On the other hand, Julia promised a methodical and consultative approach to policy. And so, after a series of elaborately romantic dates with both candidates, Windsor and Oakeshott dramatically presented Gillard with the rose.

Gillard remained prime minister, but she was merely stuck in the revolving door, not out of it. Her reign was spent teetering on the brink of disaster, and the constant proximity of imminent chaos added a certain edge to life in Australia, akin to the adrenaline-flooded feeling of ultra-sensitivity to the very experience of existence that one gets from sharing a sleeping bag with a snow leopard. Gillard proved herself far better at working with her colleagues and subordinates, but proved herself far worse at convincing the general public that she was in any way cuddly or wombat-like. In the end, confronted with the reality that if an election were held tomorrow, Gillard would lose not only to almost any other Australian politician, but also to most of the better-known brands of cheese, the Labor Party had to act. As one might expect, the reasons for Gillard's downfall were complex:

1. Her promise that 'there would be no carbon tax under a government I lead' was seen as contradicting to some extent her introduction of a carbon tax under the government she led. Others protested, insisting that it wasn't a carbon tax, but this too was somewhat contradicted by Gillard's own statement that it was.
2. Her fellow MPs caused her a certain amount of trouble with their antics, including but not restricted to: hiring prostitutes with union funds, musing on vaginas' resemblance to shellfish and being Martin Ferguson.
3. Kevin Rudd also caused a bit of tension by devoting his entire being and essence to the destruction of everything Gillard held dear every day from the moment he lost the prime ministership. Some might call Rudd 'vindictive', but a more charitable view is that he was simply a demonic avenger sent from the legions of Hell itself. Gillard was caught off-guard by Rudd's campaigning, having no idea that a politician, after being betrayed by his own party, might seek revenge, because Gillard had lived in a deep underwater cave with no wifi until the day before she became prime minister.

4. Again, Opposition Leader Abbott's aggressive tactics paid off: he had switched to shouting 'axe the tax', a nice variation, and as time went on added more phrases to his slack-jawed bellowing repertoire, such as 'this criminal government' and 'my name is Tony and I have a bike'.
5. She was, technically, a woman, which had never been the Australian way.

With all these factors contributing to Gillard's plunging popularity, the ALP had to remove her and bring back Kevin Rudd in a desperate attempt to limit the damage of the next election. Rudd gratefully accepted the reward for all his hard work (i.e. crushing defeat), but if being knocked to the mat by Tony Abbott was hardly the most pleasant experience, Rudd at least had the consolation that he had laid waste to the career of Julia Gillard and, as they say, revenge is a dish best served at the expense of good government.

Rudd, as expected, went down to Abbott, who triumphantly announced that 'the adults are in charge', that Australia was 'open for business' and that he was 'going for a bike ride'. Abbott made history as not only the firmest-pectoralled prime minister Australia had ever had, but also as the one most likely at any given time to lick your face.

Early on in the Abbott prime ministership, there was a real air of excitement and hope for the future, but 30 or 40 minutes in, reality began to assert itself. Abbott, who had excelled in the Opposition leader's main role of sowing discord and defeatism among the government, found being in government himself more problematic and developed an awkward leadership style that combined the calm, assertive authority of a baboon on speed with the intelligent, evidence-based policy approach of the mad goblin living in King George III's wig.

Almost from the beginning of the Abbott regime, things started to go sour, as the voting public began to suspect that they had been the victims of an elaborate prank.[189] Abbott was erratic, socially awkward, intolerant and seemingly permanently just seconds away from snapping and headbutting a public servant. His policies were frequently disastrous, as he misread the public's willingness to vote him into office as the expression of a nationwide desire to exterminate the poor: whether medicine, education or helicopters, the Abbott government seemed determined to make everything as unaffordable as possible.

To distract people from his unpopular policies, Abbott adopted a strategy of convincing the entire country that he had been drinking paint. To this end he decided that awarding Prince Philip, the Duke of Edinburgh, a knighthood would be a canny move. This clever gambit, which was insane in so many ways that nobody could decide which one to focus on, momentarily disoriented his enemies, but still there remained some who believed the prime minister to be of sound enough mind to merit a serious examination of his policies.

These people were utterly flummoxed, though, when Abbott went on TV to eat a whole raw, unpeeled onion. This made him the first Australian prime minister to publicly eat a whole onion, but the public found this a dubious achievement at best. There was simply nowhere else to go: Tony Abbott had transcended politics and entered the realm of avant-garde conceptual performance art.

Sadly, he had to go, and in what was now a cherished national tradition, the prime minister was deposed in a leadership spill. Interestingly, the reasons for this were complex:

---

189 And not even *that* elaborate, if we're honest.

1. Abbott's leadership team struggled to stay 'on message' due to numerous distractions, ranging from Bronwyn Bishop's luxurious travel arrangements to Joe Hockey's remedial maths classes.
2. Abbott himself was never able to reassure the public that he would rather be running the country than standing naked in front of a brick wall, punching it until his knuckles bled.
3. He was up against a master tactician in Labor leader Bill Shorten, who possessed the uncanny ability to reduce the government frontbench to a mindless rabble with one check of his notes.
4. God was severely displeased with him.

Abbott made way for Malcolm Turnbull, who wept, for there were no more worlds to conquer.

Having been allowed back into the *Big Brother* house, Turnbull immediately moved to address the problems of Abbott's prime ministership, such as the low standard of parliamentary zingers and even lower numbers of voters fantasising about sex with the PM. His popularity rapidly soared, as Australia expressed its collective relief that finally there was a handsome man lying to them about his plans to drain all hope from their lives, instead of a creepy-looking one who licked his lips too much. As is often the way, his popularity then stopped soaring, but through a combination of cunning strategy, public pronouncements bearing a vague resemblance to achievements, and tricking the Labor Party into spending more time bitching about the Greens than paying any attention to him, he managed to stay on top of things. He also gave birth to the 'Ideas Boom', an exciting new initiative wherein the prime minister suggested that it would be good if everyone had ideas, and then spent millions of dollars to emphasise the point.

Yes, Turnbull had solved all of the Australian government's problems, and if he hadn't solved any of the Australian people's problems, well, you can't have everything. The main thing was, people seemed to like him, which is all you need in a prime minister, if history is any guide.

Naturally, Turnbull's prime ministership had its own issues and challenges, such as the increasingly harsh treatment, abuse and torture of innocent asylum seekers, including children; stagnation of attempts to improve the standard of living in Indigenous communities; rising tides of violence on the streets and in the homes of Australians; increased secrecy and decreased accountability from our leaders in their exploitation of tragedy and crisis to advance their own totalitarian ends; continuous cynical manipulation of social fissures for electoral gain; and rising inequality in society generally. But if we're scrupulously fair, all of that was going on before Turnbull became prime minister, and most of it was pretty popular, so you can't blame him for it. As the saying goes, 'If it ain't broke, don't fix it, and if it is broke, fixing it will probably just annoy people anyway.'

Most of the problems that did beset the Turnbull era weren't even anything to do with Turnbull. Much like Whitlam, or Jesus, he was lumbered with underlings unworthy of his greatness. Most of his Cabinet he inherited from Abbott, so nobody was expecting miracles. Among the most senior ministers were luminaries like Christopher Pyne, the tragic result of leaving a meerkat locked in a room with a syringe full of growth hormone and a copy of *Atlas Shrugged*, and Scott Morrison, who only entered Parliament in the first place after the sewers under the building overflowed.

But even among the well-tailored collection of failed criminals and Disney villains that made up the Liberal Cabinet, one man stood out: Peter Dutton, who entered Parliament in 2001 and within a few short years had gained an impressive reputation for having slightly more blank space on his face than seems appropriate. Dutton, who as Health minister under Abbott saw his plans to reverse Australia's dangerous trend of lengthening lifespans stymied, became Immigration minister under Turnbull, a post in which he somehow managed to live up to his predecessors' reputation for needless cruelty and shameless racism, while also adding his own idiosyncratic flavour of comical incompetence. In Dutton, all the virtues of the modern Liberal Party were brought together in marvellous synergy, and there has possibly never been an Australian frontbencher who has seemed more likely to both waterboard a toddler and accidentally set fire to his own head.

So let's not pretend that Malcolm Turnbull has had an easy time of it as PM. But despite all the obstacles and trials, he has somehow remained indefatigably handsome throughout. Some say that Turnbull's enduring popularity is due in large part to his close friend and ally, Bill Shorten, who as Opposition leader quickly gained a reputation for doing nothing, but as the years passed managed to somehow do less. The sterling support that Shorten gave the Turnbull administration will not be forgotten when the heroes of the Liberal Party are honoured, but the most impressive thing about Shorten has always been his principles, which at times have been almost noticeable.

What Turnbull demonstrated, more than anything, is that the Australian people, more than anything else, desire a firm hand on the tiller, or at the very least a decent distraction from the fact that there isn't one. As Australia moves into an uncertain future, it may be that in Turnbull, we have found the perfect balance of obscene wealth and naked lust for power that makes for an ideal modern leader.

Current estimates suggest that Turnbull will be removed from office in late 2016 or early 2017, and that the reasons for his removal will be complex.

ESSAY QUESTIONS

1. Will you be lectured on misogyny by that man?
2. Explain why you believe that Kevin Rudd wouldn't hesitate even for a second to slide a kitchen knife between your ribs if he thought it'd get him 30 seconds on *Sunrise*.
3. How important is it in politics to have attractive daughters?

The End ...?

Australia has come a long way these past 200-odd years. From its humble beginnings as an obscure case of colonial land-theft, it has become a thriving, wealthy and only moderately evil modern nation. Who would have thought, when the unhappy denizens of the First Fleet were huddled, starving and desperate on the shores of Port Jackson, that one day Australia would grow so powerful and confident on the world stage that it could be abjectly humiliated in a doomed bid to host the World Cup?

Back in 1788, the progenitors of modern Australia knew nothing of globalisation or fracking or Delta Goodrem, but despite their ignorance and offensive smell they had one thing in common with the average Aussie of today: a restless pioneer energy, the pulsing determination to make the world a better place that drove explorers over mountains and across deserts, that pushed soldiers into the midst of enemy fire, that convinced young children of humble origins that they could be prime minister just like their hero Arthur Fadden.

There are those who will say there is no point in looking towards the past, that the important thing is to look to the future. But I ask, how can one know where one is going, if one doesn't know where one has been? The answer: Google Maps. But in a less literal and more pretentious sense, hope for the future must always be based on respect for the past, and in recapping the history of Australia, we hope passionately that we may learn something about ourselves. Usually we don't, but still, it's a great way to pass the time.

What will the next 200 years bring for Australia? More fun wars and exciting political power struggles? Human cloning? Laser guns? All these wonderful possibilities and more are out there. Or it's possible that we'll all die of radiation poisoning, or that the rising seas will swallow us.

Whatever happens to Australia the country, we can be sure of one thing: Australia's history, rich and colourful and filled with heroism and drama, will live on into infinity. And for that we can thank the hard-working historical recappers who work themselves into the ground to keep the flame of history alive for future generations. In other words, we can thank me.

You're welcome.

ACKNOWLEDGEMENTS

In creating this book, I have cause to give many thanks to many people. Big ups to Martin Hughes and Keiran Rogers from Affirm Press, who supported my ideas and backed me to the hilt through every weird and ridiculous gag I tapped out. And also to Affirm's Kate Goldsworthy, who understood all my jokes and helped me make them better.

Thanks and enthusiastic high-fives also due to my astounding family: to my sensational wife, Bec, who patiently tolerates the absurd lifestyle of a writer; to my kids, Jonah, Kaia and Layla, who are the coolest and funniest gang I've ever belonged to; to my mum and dad, who raised me to know that putting words together and making people laugh is a noble calling; and to my sisters, Rebecca, Emily and Alice, three geniuses who each inspire me daily.

Speaking of inspiration, thanks to the muses, friends and allies who have given aid, encouragement and moral support throughout the radiant madness that is writing a book: a huge shout-out and fist-bump to Cam Smith, Wendy Harmer, Roz Hammond, Noni Hazlehurst, Julie Goodwin, Peter FitzSimons, Valdene Pallen, Sean M. Whelan, Sean Bedlam, Dan Hall and Maddie Palmer. Also to Aja Styles and Jenna Clarke at Fairfax, who have always recklessly encouraged my recapping habit.

I don't want to neglect to bend the knee respectfully to Shaun Micallef, Dave Barry, Richard Armour, W.C. Sellar, R.J. Yeatman and

Peter Cook, those who came before me and without whom this book would not exist.

Finally, but by no means leastly, a warmly grateful embrace to all the men, women, children and animals who stitched together the strange and beautiful tapestry that is Australian history, in all its grandeur, magnificence and glorious stupidity. We salute you, every one.